# NOTHING MUCH TO LOSE

The Story
of
2nd Battalion Royal Marines
and
43 Commando Royal Marines

❖

| | | |
|---|---|---|
| Text | Michael McConville | 43 CDO |
| Maps | Ralph Bazeley | 43 CDO |

❖

**Front Cover
Marines of 43 Commando
Advancing—Northern Italy
April 1945**

The Naval & Military Press Ltd

# *NOTHING MUCH TO LOSE*

The Story
of
2nd Battalion Royal Marines
and
43 Commando Royal Marines

Michael McConville—43 CDO
Ralph Bazeley—43 CDO
Brice Somers—2 RM

Publisher 43rd Royal Marines Commando Reunion
(Hon Sec—Norris Peak)

Published by
**The Naval & Military Press Ltd**
Unit 10 Ridgewood Industrial Park,
Uckfield, East Sussex,
TN22 5QE England
Tel: +44 (0) 1825 749494
Fax: +44 (0) 1825 765701
www.naval-military-press.com
www.military-genealogy.com

*In reprinting in facsimile from the original, any imperfections are inevitably reproduced and the quality may fall short of modern type and cartographic standards.*

'NOTHING MUCH TO LOSE'

Foreword

by

<u>Lieutenant General Sir Henry Beverley KCB OBE</u>

<u>Commandant General Royal Marines</u>

It is a great privilege to be invited to write the foreword to this wartime history of the 2nd Battalion Royal Marines and its successor, 43rd Royal Marines Commando.

At a time when we are acknowledging the 50th anniversary of many of the great happenings of the Second World War, it is a stimulating contrast to be provided with a history, which deals with a Royal Marines unit's part in some of those events. The book's particular quality is that it is very much a soldier's story, dealing with troop and unit level actions with realism, humour, humility; and certainly not accorded any unwarranted generosity through the passing of the years- when things went wrong, as they always will in war, they are graphically portrayed in the text. This makes the whole book an honest, revealing, yet proud, record of the endeavours of a significantly Hostilities-Only unit through Iceland to Dakar, Italy and Yugoslavia - the latter being particularly poignant at this time.

43rd Royal Marines Commando Re-Union is fortunate to have an author of international repute amongst their number. Michael McConville, a troop commander in the unit, has woven the reminiscences of individuals into the actions of the time, whilst setting all the events in their proper historical and geographical context. It makes for a fascinating read and demonstrates clearly the singular and fundamentally important philosophy of the Royal Marines Commando: that it is the traditional Royal Marines virtues of high personal standards of bearing, discipline and esprit, blended with the Commando qualities of fitness, determination, initiative and hard training, which brings success in battle.

I commend to you this history which, although conceived, written and published by 43rd Royal Marines Commando Re-Union as a very personal record, fully merits a much wider readership.

*Henry Beverley*

## DEDICATION

We dedicate this History of the 2nd Battalion Royal Marines and 43 Commando Royal Marines to the honoured memory of all colleagues who fought and died in the service of their country, and we seek God's blessing on their relatives who survive them, and on them and us peace on earth and life everlasting hereafter.

J D Wakeling 2 RM
Bishop of Southwell 1970 - 1985

## THE OLD NAVAL CEMETERY

During the Napoleonic War, a small British naval force, under the command of Captain W Hoste R.N. was based on the Island of Vis and engaged in vigorous operations in the Adriatic. Their dead were buried in the Naval Cemetery.

130 years later, another British contingent, including 43 Commando Royal Marines was based on Vis. Their dead were also buried in the same cemetery.

---

## INSPIRATION

The wording of the Memorial Plaque
erected in the old Naval Cemetery 1944

*HERE DEAD LIE WE BECAUSE WE DID NOT CHOOSE*
*TO LIVE AND SHAME THE LAND FROM WHICH WE SPRUNG*
*LIFE TO BE SURE IS **NOTHING MUCH TO LOSE***
*BUT YOUNG MEN THINK IT IS AND WE WERE YOUNG*

# ACKNOWLEDGMENTS

It is difficult in a book of this type to acknowledge fully and in detail one's indebtedness for all the information - written, verbal, maps and photographs - plus friendly help from MEMBERS OF THE RE-UNION and expert advice from other persons and institutions who have all given freely many hours.

The Royal Marine Museum (Linda Coote and Ed Bartholomew) for guidance and permission to publish photographs.

The Imperial War Museum and Walter Jones ex RSR, an old VIS friend, for permission to publish photographs.

Harper/Collins have given permission to reproduce the map on the back cover.

Simon Woodcock for technical advice on printing matters. Major A J Donald RM the recently retired Corps Historian for checking the Awards to Royal Marines and supplying information.

Desmond Clark principal organiser and Miss Amanda Mintz of Gateacre, Liverpool for typing the script.

James Wakeling and Bill Jenkins are thanked for their work on reading and making suggestions to the draft text.

Finally the main contributors - all members of THE RE-UNION.

Brice Somers for the very effective and striking artistic design of the covers.

Ralph Bazeley for his detailed maps and patience in revising the maps to illuminate the text.

Michael McConville, our author of international note, for his many hours of labour writing **NOTHING MUCH TO LOSE.**

                              **J C D HUDSPITH**
                         Chairman - Book Committee
                            43rd ROYAL MARINES
                            COMMANDO RE-UNION

*Also by Michael McConville:*

## NON FICTION

**Ascendancy to Oblivion**: The story of the Anglo-Irish
(Quartet, 1986)

**A Small War in the Balkans**: British Military Involvement in
Wartime Yugoslavia, 1941 - 1945
(MacMillan, 1986)

## NOVELS (As Anthony McCandless)

**Leap in the Dark** (Collins, 1980)
**The Burke Foundation** (MacMillan, 1985)

## COLLECTED SHORT STORIES (As Miles Noonan)

**Tales From the Mess** (Hutchinson, 1983)
**More Tales From the Mess** (Century, 1985)

# CONTENTS

**FOREWORD**
Commandant General Royal Marines ............................... iii
Dedication, Inspiration ....................................... iv
Prologue ...................................................... viii

**PART ONE**   2 R.M.: Midnight Sun and Anopheles Mosquitoes
Chapter 1     Ancestry, Birth and Iceland ............................. 1
Chapter 2     False Starts, Home Defence and a Trip to Africa ........ 10
Chapter 3     Sweat, Frustration and Conversion ...................... 19

**PART TWO**   43 Commando: Central Mediterranean, Italy
Chapter 4     Seaborne Advance to Contact ........................... 24
Chapter 5     Anzio and Ornito ...................................... 27

**PART THREE**   A Year with the South Slavs
Chapter 6     The Yugoslav Kaleidoscope ............................. 34
Chapter 7     Solta, Hvar and Shennanigans at Sea ................... 39
Chapter 8     Life on Vis and Routine Activities .................... 48
Chapter 9     Mljet ................................................. 51
Chapter 10    Brac: Preliminaries ................................... 55
Chapter 11    Hvar 2, Brac 2, Solta ................................. 69

**PART FOUR**   Land of the South Slavs II: Montenegro
Chapter 12    Finneyforce at Risan .................................. 77
Chapter 13    Floydforce : Niksic, Cetinje, Podgorica ................ 87

**PART FIVE**   Italy II: The Line, Comacchio, Argenta
Chapter 14    Refurbishment and Preparation ......................... 97
Chapter 15    Comacchio: Day One ................................... 105
Chapter 16    Comacchio: Day Two ................................... 112
Chapter 17    Argenta .............................................. 116
Chapter 18    Diaspora ............................................. 124
               Comacchio Group - Royal Marines ...................... 126

Photographs and Maps ........................... Between 54 and 55
Awards ....................................................... 127
Sources ...................................................... 130
Index ........................................................ 132

# PROLOGUE

From the earliest days of the long, deplorable and repetitive history of various groupings of the human race settling their differences with other groupings by violence, fighting men have travelled by sea to get at one another's throats and at one another's property. For many centuries these expeditions were fairly primitive improvisations. In maritime European countries they became more formalised during the waves of world wide exploration, colonial expansionism, trade rivalry and plunder of the fifteenth, sixteenth and seventeenth centuries. Sailors when necessary still supplemented their seafaring duties by fighting ashore. But the advantages to warships of carrying a permanent nucleus of seaborne soldiers slowly became apparent.

The British acknowledged the need in 1664 by the establishment of the Admiral's Regiment. The Admiral's Regiment did not have a monopoly of sea soldiering. A number of infantry regiments were also from time to time embarked for long periods for service in ships of the Royal Navy. But the Admiral's Regiment was the direct ancestor of the present day Royal Marines. In the three centuries that have followed their initial embodiment, the Marines - they were made Royal in 1802 by King George III - have taken part in more battles and in more diverse circumstances, than have any other branch of the British Armed Forces. Their most prominent evolved characteristics have been an inherited belief, buttressed by generations of experience, that a firm discipline, an insistence upon a high standard of personal turn-out and excellence at ceremonial drill are essential prerequisites of a reliable performance in battle. They also believed in hard training to meet all foreseeable eventualities. They kept to an advanced standard of physical fitness. They maintain a flexibility of organisation that allows them to put together fighting entities of differing sorts to suit particular and shifting requirements.

One of these entities was the 2nd Battalion Royal Marines. It assembled for the first time in April 1940. From it in 1943, was formed No 43 Royal Marines Commando. The Battalion and Commando between them helped to safeguard the Atlantic sea routes by a brisk and bloodless seizure of Iceland in May 1940; were frustrated participants in a Free French fiasco at Dakar in Senegal later in the same year; fought in some major successful actions in Italy in 1944 and 1945; and in between the Italian ventures passed the best part of a year in active operations alongside Marshal Tito's Partisans in Yugoslavia. Corporal Tom Hunter of 43 Commando was in Italy awarded the only Royal Marine Victoria Cross of the Second World War. The award was posthumous.

This book is an account of the activities of the men of these two related units, parent and offspring, during the years of the Second World War.

# PART ONE

## 2RM: MIDNIGHT SUN AND ANOPHELES MOSQUITOES

# CHAPTER ONE

# ANCESTRY, BIRTH AND ICELAND

As the nineteenth century moved into the early years of the twentieth, British strategic thinking and practice had been dominated by the needs of a small offshore Atlantic island with a huge empire to safeguard itself and its possessions by seapower. A by-product of this doctrine was until the First World War the majority of marines served afloat in ship's detachments. A modification came in August 1914. A Royal Marine Brigade of four Battalions was formed. With a succession of expansions and mutations it fought at Ostend, Antwerp, Gallipoli and in the last years of the war on the Western Front. The reputation of these shore-based battalions was of consistent steadiness and reliability in defence and of dogged persistence in attack. Casualties were high. After two days fighting on the Somme in November 1916, the 2nd Battalion of the Royal Marine Light Infantry came out with two officers and about one hundred and fifty NCOs and Marines still on their feet out of a committed strength of close to eight hundred.

In April, 1918, an amphibious operation against the Belgian coast, more in keeping with the outlook and traditions of the Corps than was the attrition of the blood and mud of a Flander's winter was mounted. German U-boats based upon Bruges had for some time been attacking allied shipping in and around the Straits of Dover. Bruges was some miles inland. The way out to the North Sea for the U-boats was along the Bruges canal. It entered the North Sea at Zeebrugge. If the Zeebrugge exit could be blocked the U-boats would be bottled in. The task was given to a Naval force that was to scuttle three obsolete cruisers in the canal entrance. The harbour was protected by a heavily defended long Mole.

The 4th Battalion, Royal Marines, supplemented by one hundred and thirty marine volunteers from the Grand Fleet, was to storm the Mole and secure it for long enough to provide a diversion that would distract the Mole's defenders from interfering with the scuttling parties in the three cruisers. The raid went in on the night of 22nd April. The blockship operation was only partially successful. The 4th Battalion's attack on the Mole was pressed home remorselessly. When the Recall was sounded by siren, wounded were carried back under fire to the cruiser *Vindictive*, moored alongside the Mole. Slightly more than half the marines who had landed a few hours before were re-embarked alive and brought back to Britain.

The 4th Battalion were awarded two Victoria Crosses. In tribute to the Battalion's gallantry at Zeebrugge it was ruled that there should never again be a 4th Battalion in the Corps. Thus it was that when, after the interval between the two World Wars, another Royal Marine Brigade was formed its battalions were designated the 1st, 2nd, 3rd and 5th. The Zeebrugge operation, its example and some of its survivors left a deep, if not often openly expressed, impression upon its successors who fought in the Corps by land in the Second World War.

Between the wars there were no shore-based Royal Marine fighting formations. Sea service was once again in fashion. In 1924 a committee chaired by Admiral Madden looked into the matter. It recommended that a three-thousand strong brigade should be formed. There was no money to pay for it. The proposal stayed in abeyance.

It came to life again as war with a sabre-rattling Nazi Germany became at first increasingly likely and then inevitable. Conscription in Britain was introduced in April 1939. Treasury funds for expansion of the Corps became available. Orders were at last given for the formation of a Royal Marine Brigade. Reservists were recalled to the Colours. In October 1939, a month after war broke out, the first "Hostilities Only" men were called up. A mixture of volunteers and conscripts were sent for training. The basic training lasted from October 1939 until the early spring of 1940. It was an interlude that allowed for the allocation of regular officers and senior NCOs to the embryo battalions and for all the necessary and complicated preparations that would be required to bring them to life. The differing ingredients of the 2nd Battalion assembled for the first time in a tented camp on the rifle ranges at Bisley on 1st April 1940.

Old-timers from those early days of the 2nd Battalion - in the contemporary shorthand vernacular 2RM - still bless their luck and also the good sense of whoever appointed him, in having as their first Commanding Officer Lieutenant-Colonel A N Williams. "Nick" Williams merged the qualities of a conventional stickler for discipline with those of an idiosyncratic intellectual. As a young Officer in the First World War he had been with the Royal Marine foray to Antwerp in 1914, had served in 2nd Battalion RMLI and been through the bloody fighting at Gallipoli, took part in the suppression of the Irish Republican Easter Rising in Dublin in 1916 and had put in a year at sea on Atlantic convoys as Captain of Marines on *HMS Lion*. He was a qualified balloon pilot. In the middle 1920s he served as Adjutant at the Royal Marine Barracks at Eastney, where in the words of his obituary "he set and demanded standards of discipline and turn-out which......had not previously been experienced." He was a graduate of the Naval Staff Course.

As a battalion commander he exuded common sense and professionalism. An ingrained quirk of his was to be blisteringly offensive to any junior officer he met before about 10 o'clock in the morning; but this indelicacy soon came to be regarded as a rather endearing eccentricity, particularly because for the rest of the day he was charmingly constructive with everybody he came in contact with. The troops loved him. "A highly respected Commanding Officer" one of them later recorded.

Colonel Nick Williams had some good material to work upon. His Company Commanders were disciplined individualists of long service. His junior officers were an amalgam of young regulars and a carefully selected intake of Hostilities Only 2nd Lieutenants. These last were all volunteers who had been undergoing intensive training since October 1939. One of them was 2nd Lieutenant "Jimmy" Wakeling, a Cambridge hockey blue who had been training for the church. (In later life he became an Anglican Bishop.) Along with Wakeling was a batch of five others, Lawrence Podmore, Michael Gatehouse, John Biggs-Davison, Liam Casey and Gilbert Innes, all of whom had been gathered together at Eastney, Portsmouth, for initial training. In January 1940 they were moved to Deal in Kent where they joined up with other young Officers who had started at the Royal Marine Divisions at Chatham and Plymouth. In the deep snow of the coldest winter for years they lived in holiday camp chalets at Kingsdown. Their training continued relentlessly. After two months the six of them were moved on to the rifle ranges at Bisley in Surrey, where they were accommodated in a number of rifle club houses until the battalion was assembled.

When the troops arrived, Bisley Common blossomed into a small canvas township of neatly aligned Bell tents, interspersed with large marquees. 2nd Lieutenant Wakeling proudly took up his first command, that of No 10 Platoon in 'B' Company. The platoon consisted of about forty men, almost all of whom came from Hull. Most of them had applied to join the Navy and had been rather surprised to find themselves as foot soldiers. Their basic training, like that of every other platoon in the battalion, had been at one or other of the three Royal Marine divisions, Chatham, Plymouth and Portsmouth. These were major administrative and training bases, not operational formations. They were now disciplined, physically hard, skilled at parade ground drill and were trained rifle-men. But it was a time of shortages and the more powerful platoon weapons, the Bren Guns and 2" Mortars had simply not been available. Some, not enough, became so at Bisley. Instruction in their use began at once.

Marine Ted Stokoe, who joined on that same day, with a draft that had completed its preliminary training at Eastney, retains vivid memories of Bisley. All four battalions of the Royal Marine brigade were camped on the common. The Corps flag of blue for being Royal, red for the artillery, green for light infantry, and yellow for the Duke of York and Albany's Maritime Regiment of Foot, which sprang from the Old Trained Bands of London from which some of the earliest recruits to the Corps had come in the 17th century, flew outside the battalion headquarters tent. From dawn to dusk there was constant controlled activity: parades, inspections, route marches, weapon training, tactical training. Bugle calls punctuated each day from Reveille in the morning to the Last Post at night. Although some of the marines were continuous service regulars the majority were Hostilities Only men. Stokoe soon developed a profound respect for the Non-Commissioned Officers, professionals with many years service, who saw to it that the Corps' inherited military virtues were kept up to standard.

There were also some striking and occasionally alarming, personalities for Stokoe to observe. Major Picton-Philips the Commander of 'C' Company, a fiery, red haired descendant of a long line of distinguished Marine Officers, flew his own personal flag, red with a yellow lion rampant and had it carried wherever the company went. Reputedly, the son of Picton-Philips had been baptised with water from a tin helmet to a musical accompaniment played by a highland piper. Others to leave a deep impression upon Stokoe's young mind were the flamboyant Lieutenant George Belbin, soon to become adjutant, who stood at six feet six inches and wore an extravagant moustache that complemented the bushiness of his eyebrows; Major Gerry de Bery, a survivor of the assault upon the mole at Zeebrugge; and the athletic Company Sergeant-Major Jock England who later captained the Navy Rugby XV, won the Distinguished Conduct Medal at Walcheren and after the war became a notable international amateur boxing referee.

A universally admired institution was Froggy French, a sturdy, swarthy practitioner of sweet notes upon his bugle, who was also an elegant tap dancer and later became the unit's Postman.

2RM's energetic preparations to equip themselves for modern warfare came to an abrupt end on 6th May. Each man, bearing his portable belongings in the identically prescribed formula of big pack, small pack, water bottle and ammunition pouches, carrying his personal weapon, fell in with his platoon and marched to Brookwood railway station. The necessary heavier stores had been sent away in advance. The battalion was heading for an undisclosed destination. There was much speculative discussion about where they were going. The smart money was on Norway.

In the three years preceeding the outbreak of the Second World War a resurgent Nazi Germany had already, by a mixture of bullying diplomacy and threatened force, reoccupied the Rhineland, incorporated Austria into the Third Reich and taken over Czechoslovakia. The German invasion of Poland, which precipitated the formal commencement of hostilities, was completed in a few autumn weeks of 1939. The means used were thorough, effective and speedy. The *Luftwaffe* held total domination of the air. The ground attack was led by armour, closely supported by dive bombers and followed by infantry, some lorried, some on foot. The final Polish collapse was precipitated by an intervention from the east by Germany's then partner in international banditry, the Soviet Union.

After the dismemberment and occupation of Poland nothing of much significance happened upon the land mass of continental Europe. A British Expeditionary Force went to France and took up its positions to the north and west of a cynical and far from enthusiastic army of French conscripts. There was some minor patrolling but no moves of any importance were made during the winter along the Franco-German frontier by either side. Belgium, Holland, the Nordic countries and the countries of the Balkans proclaimed, with a wistful lack of realism, their neutrality. The major sustained conflict was at sea. German U-boats and some surface raiders, haunted the Atlantic sea lanes between North America and the United Kingdom. It soon became clear that the old bogey of the First World War, the vulnerablitiy of British transatlantic supplies, was once more a serious threat to the island's survival.

In April 1940 the Germans made their first major move of the campaigning season. They overran Denmark within a few hours and invaded Norway. The Norwegians put up a more protracted resistance than had the Danes but they were soon driven by overwhelming force back to their mountains and forests. Norwegian ports, one after the other, went to the Germans. An ill-organised and badly-managed British force was dispatched to Norway to do what they could to help the Norwegians. Some French troops went also. Both of these contingents fought hard but could do little.

This sporadic fighting in the north of Norway was still in progress when 2RM made their march to Brookwood railway station. There were thus some sensible grounds for the deduction by the battalion's amateur strategic analysts that they too were off to Norway. They were in fact wrong. Where they were going was Iceland.

Iceland lies in the North Atlantic about midway between Greenland and Newfoundland. It is a largely volcanic island with an irregular indented shoreline. Its greatest length from north to south is about 220 miles; from east to west about 335 miles. Its northern part is within the Arctic Circle. Its central *massif* rises to over six thousand feet. There is an abundance of glaciers, fjords, more than two hundred volcanoes and a great many thermal springs. Nothing much grows. One per cent of the land is under cultivation and another one per cent under forest. About one fifth of the land surface is suitable for grazing animals. Otherwise the rest of the island is glaciated or lava desert or peat bog.

The island was first settled in the 9th and 10th centuries by Irish religious hermits. These were later joined by like-minded contemplative Scottish monks and more significantly, by belligerent Norse settlers. Until 1904 Iceland was a Danish colony. In 1918 it became entirely responsible for running its own affairs except that it shared the Danish monarchy and the Danes controlled its foreign affairs.

In 1940 the population was about a quarter of a million. A large proportion of these lived in the capital, Reykjavik, the principal port. Other small fishing harbours were found on all its coasts.

It was the existence of these ports that was the cause of 2RM's journey. The newly acquired German naval bases in Norway added a further menacing element to the Battle of the Atlantic. Further conveniently placed points of departure for U-boats and *Luftwaffe* aircraft on the island could clearly compound the problem of keeping the sea-ways open. Conversely, the establishment of British naval and air bases on the island would ease the provision of cover for British convoys. Iceland, decided the War Cabinet, not wasting undue time over the ethics of violating other peoples' inconvenient neutrality, must be seized.

The task went to Sturgesforce; its commander was Colonel R G Sturges, a notable Corps figure who in the First World War had fought ashore at Gallipoli and at sea at the Battle of Jutland. Sturges had at his disposal a small Force Headquarters, the whole of 2RM, an anti-aircraft battery and a coast defence battery. Sturges moved fast. 2RM's train took them to Gourock on the Firth of Clyde where two cruisers, *HMS Berwick* and *HMS Glasgow*, awaited them. The battalion was split into two "flights". The first, led by Colonel Nick Williams embarked in *Berwick* with 'A' Company, commanded by Major Cutler, and Headquarters Company. On *Berwick* were also Colonel Sturges, Force Headquarters and the anti-aircraft and coast defence gunners. Major Pym, the battalion's 2nd in Command, took the rest of it aboard *Glasgow*. Accommodation in both cruisers was crowded and spartan. But the Navy were hospitable and accepted philosophically the need to share their functional sparse mess decks and accommodation with large numbers of large strangers carrying cumbersome personal equipment and for the most part unused to life at sea.

At 3:45 in the morning of 8th May the two cruisers left the Clyde escorted by two destroyers. The convoy soon worked up to a speed of 22 knots but soon afterwards ran in to a very strong north-west gale and was forced to reduce to 15 knots. A reduction in speed was not the only difficulty generated by the weather. Among the Hostilities Only (HO) marines there was a mass outbreak of seasickness that did nothing for conditions in the mess decks and induced a debilitating fatigue. 2nd Lieutenant Jimmy Wakeling, for example, suddenly promoted for the purpose of the expedition to Acting Captain, celebrated his elevation by a confinement to his bunk and the need to send his Platoon Sergeant as his representative to the many urgent conferences which were being held throughout the ship. These dealt with a host of necessary extemporisations, inevitable in an enterprise that had been mounted at very short notice and with no time for thorough preparation, by a partially trained battalion that had not yet been furnished with all its equipment.

The complement of Bren guns and 2" Mortars had been delivered aboard straight from the factories and was still in packing cases. The cases were broken open, the weapons distributed to companies, NCO instructors explained how to use them and they were fired over the side repeatedly. It was found that there were only three Icelandic maps: one a small map of the whole island: one a slightly larger but still small scale map of the Greater Reykjavik area and one a street plan of Reykjavik itself. This last had been run up from memory by an Icelandic interpreter with the battalion.Understandably it held inaccuracies. But it was serviceable enough and all Platoon Commanders took traced copies of it.

There was no reliable information about the likely attitude of the Icelanders to an invasion of their country by foreign soldiers. Iceland had no army but their Police were known to have access to rifles. There were thought to be about two hundred Germans, some of them armed, on the island. Of these a proportion were assessed as active German agents. The majority were German seamen marooned when their ships were unable to get away. As many as possible of these Germans had clearly to be rounded up. A much more gentle approach was taken towards the Icelanders. The troops would go ashore armed and with a limited amount of ammunition. But they were given strict orders not to open fire except in the extreme circumstances of finding themselves confronted with an armed Icelander who was evidently about to shoot at them. In general there were to be no provocations, the Icelanders were to be treated with respect and friendliness, although it would be necessary to secure a number of strategically placed buildings, airfields and so on, the occupation was to be as peaceful as was possible. The Icelanders were to be encouraged to continue with their daily businesses. The Icelandic Houses of Parliament would be inviolate; no troops were to go to the Parliamentary buildings.

At 5 o'clock in the morning of 10th May the lights of Reykjavik were sighted ahead, a strangely evocative vision to people who had experienced eight months of war-time blacked-out Britain. There was a brief snow storm. The two cruisers dropped anchor fairly close inshore. The destroyer *Fearless* came alongside *Berwick*. Battalion Headquarters and 'A' Company, already fallen-in on *Berwick's* decks, some of the troops still dazed and worn-out by sea sickness, went down narrow slippery gangways to *Fearless*. *Fearless* pulled slowly away and headed for the inner harbour. It was very cold. At this northerly latitude there was plenty of light even in the small hours of the morning.

*Fearless* tied up alongside the jetty. Major Cutler and 'A' Company clambered ashore and were joined by a party of Headquarter signallers under Corporal George Lander. Cutler, Lieutenant Podmore's platoon and Lander's signallers immediately set out for the first objective, the German Consul's house. They moved fast in single file. There had been one solitary Icelandic Policeman on the jetty. He asked no questions. On their way to the Consulate Cutler's party was passed by a large saloon car full of cheerful young revellers presumably on their way home from a party, who if they felt any curiosity about the presence in their peaceable town of a fast-moving body of armed foreign troops travelling in a business-like manner, did not pause to comment.

The Consulate building was a large detached house. Cutler hammered briskly on the front door. His party moved in to the doorway. A tall, gaunt man came down the stairs and ordered them out again. He identified himself as Walter Gerlach, the German Consul. Cutler ignored Gerlach's order to go away and in turn told Gerlach to rouse his wife and family and his staff and tell them to prepare to leave.

Gerlach went upstairs again and misused the period of grace given to him to get dressed and to muster his staff. He deposited a large pile of confidential papers in his bath and set fire to it. The smell of burning drifted down the stairs. Cutler, who had thoughtfully equipped one of his marines with a fire extinguisher, took him at a run up the stairs and into the bathroom. The marine put the fire out. There are various accounts of the bathroom fracas, possibly embellished in the folk memory of 2RM. One version has it that Gerlach drew a pistol on Cutler; another that Frau Gerlach was the principal stoker and that Cutler with an uncharacteristic disregard of the social conventions felled her with a solid punch. Whatever the truth of the details, the consequence was that the German Consulate staff were taken into custody and a large number of useful papers, charred in places, rather damp, were available for the intelligence staff. Corporal Lander was able to set up his wireless in the bedroom of a teenage boy. Cutler reported success to battalion headquarters. The prisoners were taken under escort to the jetty.

As soon as *Fearless* had landed the first flight, she turned back and went alongside *Glasgow*. The remainder of the battalion were ferried ashore by *Fearless*. By this time spectators were beginning to assemble. Some were early-starting workers. A few others had heard unusual noises and were simply inquisitive. A small group were British residents, headed by the British Consul. He shook hands welcomingly with the first 2RM officer to approach him and pointed to a collection of taxis and trucks, lined up behind him. He had engaged them without explaining what they were to be used for. The companies of 2RM formed up and moved rapidly to their various objectives in the town: a number of hotels, the wireless transmitting station, the Post Office, warehouses. These were occupied without fuss. Patrols were sent out to round up suspect Germans. A platoon of 'D' Company went by sea to the north of the island and did some more rounding up.

The battalion's only transport was the three motorcycles of the Signal Section but the Consul's civilian transport pool made good this deficiency. A platoon of 'B' Company was motored to a remote settlement in the interior called Kaldalnes. Throughout the day *Fearless* and *Foxhound* continued to unload stores-rations, ammunition and so on - at the jetty and these were distributed efficiently to the outlying companies. By the evening all objectives were in 2RM's hands and the companies were well settled in.

The exhortations from Colonel Nick Williams that courtesy and sensitivity to Icelandic feelings must prevail at all times were honoured to the full. With the exception of the Chief of Police of Reykjavik ("who seemed to have Nazi sympathies", records 2RM's war diary darkly) all senior Icelandic politicians and officials were found to be relaxed and co-operative. They willingly requisitioned buildings and provided further transport. The ordinary Icelanders were equally cheerful and friendly. They presented only one minor difficulty. The parties of marines moving about were hampered by crowds of sightseers. 2nd Lieutenant, Acting Captain, Jimmy Wakeling still looks back fondly to 2RM's stay in Iceland. His recollections are of beautiful blonde girls, cream cakes in the cafes, classical music from Germany on the radio, dried fish widely sold, transport often by taxi and a high standard of living. He was particularly impressed by the fact that the houses in Reykjavik were heated by hot water from the thermal springs.

Vigilance was necessary in case the Germans attempted a counterstroke landing. They never did. After a week the battalion was ordered to stand by for a return to Britain. An army infantry brigade arrived in two transports, *Lancastria* and *Franconia*. Positions were handed over to the soldiers. Stores were reassembled for loading. Outlying detachments of the battalion were called in. Lieutenant Previte, who had commanded the platoon that had been detached to the far north, came back with one German prisoner, making the battalion's total haul sixty-five. 2RM played an Icelandic team at soccer and won 2-1. Mutual messages of goodwill were exchanged with the Icelanders. With the exception of the predicable rantings of one communist editor, Icelandic newspapers and radio broadcasts paid tribute to the "splendid bearing and behaviour of all ranks." The British Ambassador reported that the people were truly grateful for the way 2RM had treated them. Colonel Nick Williams congratulated the battalion on the fact that not one single incident had occurred to bring discredit to the unit. 2RM embarked in *Lancastria* and *Franconia*, leaving behind them Corporal Lander and some signalers to help in the newly established Royal Naval Headquarters at Reykjavik.

They had an uneventful voyage back to the Clyde. Disembarkation was delayed. The port transport staff wanted the troops off as quickly as possible and undertook to forward the battalion's accumulation of stores later. The wily and experienced Colonel Nick Williams would have none of it. He had in the past suffered from the depredations brought about by this sort of arrangement and he refused to move until his men and his stores were landed in a cohesive block. Obstinacy triumphed. Troops and stores were put ashore unitedly. Eighteen days and twenty one hours after 2RM had left Bisley camp they were back there again.

Iceland had been a bloodless and entirely successful opening operation for the battalion. The island stayed under British and later Canadian and American control, for the remainder of the war and contributed significantly to the hard-fought ultimate success of the Battle of the Atlantic. After the war NATO continued to maintain air bases there.

On the return to Bisley there was news to be pondered. The Germans had attacked in western Europe. They had invaded Holland, Belgium and France. They seemed to be doing rather well.

## CHAPTER TWO

# FALSE STARTS, HOME DEFENCE AND A TRIP TO AFRICA

The German offensive in the west in the early summer of 1940 was brilliantly conceived, skilfully and ruthlessly executed, and seemed to German planners to have been a victory that had ended the war. In a few days Holland and Belgium had surrendered. In a few weeks so had France. The British Expeditionary Force, leaving their serious casualties and their heavy weapons behind them, were evacuated over the beaches of Dunkirk. Train-loads of them, passing through the Southern Railway system through Woking and Brookwood, were looked at with curiosity by 2RM. Britain, supported by the distant dominions and colonies of the then British Empire, was now the only nation in the ring against the triumphant Germans. An enemy invasion of the island seemed to be both inevitable and imminent.

Inspired by the new Prime Minister, Mr Winston Churchill, the country looked to its defences. There was a fresh feeling of urgency everywhere. The Royal Marine Brigade experienced it as much as most. The days of a carefully planned, orderly, progressive development of 2RM into a unit trained with complete thoroughness in a sequence covering every aspect of its responsibilities were for the time being over. Every infantry battalion in the British Expeditionary Force had been depleted of men and weapons during the fighting up to the evacuation from Dunkirk. The Royal Marine Brigade was at full strength and held its full stock of arms and ammunition. It was immediately available for necessary work. If the necessity of the work given it was less evident to its practitioners than it might have been, that was the product of thinking in high places about likely German moves and how best to frustrate them with limited resources. The details of the counter-moves being made were known only to a limited number of senior Officers who needed to put contingency plans into shape. As for the rest, they were well trained and adaptable and could be relied upon to do what they had to do when orders were issued at a moment when the need for secrecy was overtaken by the need to ensure operational efficiency.

The first of these mysterious moves came in June, to Pembroke Dock in south Wales. 2RM, along with the rest of the Royal Marine Brigade, were embarked in Dutch ships tied up there. 2RM drew the *Konigen Emma*, a North Sea ferry that endeared itself to no one. Its main disability was that it was too small. Every inch of space was crammed with men, equipment and stores. Personal movement was difficult. Nobody could be told why they were there, aside from the general statement that they were earmarked for an important possible operation. The important possible operation was cancelled as abruptly as it had been conceived and after two weeks of crammed claustrophobia the battalions were disembarked. Their provisional destination had in fact been the neutral Irish Free State. Given German ways with other European neutrals a German backdoor invasion of Britain by way of Southern Ireland had seemed a possibility.

For the next six weeks 2RM were put on coast defence duties in Devon. It was a beautiful summer, a succession of warm cloudless sunny days now looked back upon affectionately by those who were there. The countryside was as attractive as the weather. The battalion was based in the grounds of Flete Castle, under canvas. Defensive positions were dug in and manned upon miles of coastal land. One lucky platoon found themselves encamped in the grounds of a rich benefactor who daily set up a barrel of beer for the use of his guardians. The idyll lasted until the middle of August. The events leading up to its abandonment stemmed from some of the consequences of the French surrender of two month previously in June.

Under the armistice terms forced upon the French in 1940, the country was divided into two parts. The northern part, which also embraced the whole of the French Atlantic coast, was to be governed directly by the Germans. The southern part "The Unoccupied Zone" was the responsibility of a puppet French government set up under the leadership of the aged Marshal Petain, a heroic figure from the First World War but who was by now close to his dotage. His government soon established itself at Vichy. It retained a precarious control over the powerful French Navy.

Italy, scavenging for crumbs after the German success, entered the war on the German side in late June. The Italians also had a powerful Navy. In the days before the French collapse all planning assumptions rested upon the fact that the combined British and French Mediterranean fleets could between them deal with anything that the Italian Navy had to offer. After the collapse, the British were faced with the prospect that in some circumstances the French Navy might either go over to the Germans or have its ships taken by them, thereby upsetting the entire naval balance of power.

One of the many pressing preoccupations of the Churchill government in the dangerous summer of 1940 was how to neutralise this threat. One obvious way was simply to invite French Naval Commanders to steam out of French ports, both in southern France and French North Africa and to rejoin their old allies in a continuing war against Germany. The French Admirals were not responsive. The British, regretfully, then decided that the issue must be settled by force, preferably a minimum of force. French warships in Alexandria harbour in Egypt and in some British ports were boarded in surprise operations. In some cases they were scuttled by their crews, in others immobilised by the boarding parties. Casualties were minimal.

A major part of the French fleet, moored at Oran in North Africa, was less easily dealt with. The French rejected all blandishments. The British opened fire, sank or set fire to several of the ships and caused a great many French casualties. The bulk of the French Navy was now no longer an operational danger. There was however amongst the French an embittered resentment at this drastic treatment by a former ally and for a time there seemed a real danger that Vichy France would throw in its lot with Nazi Germany to fight the British.

Not every Frenchman subscribed to the defeatist and collaborationist policies of Marshal Petain. One of the dissidents, General Charles de Gaulle, a tall, aloof, outwardly cold, touchy and emotionally patriotic French Officer, escaped to Britain in the wake of the Dunkirk evacuation and set up a Free French movement. He recruited a body of like-minded Frenchmen who had also crossed the English Channel. De Gaulle, influenced by over-rosy intelligence reports, reached the conclusion that if he could take his Free Frenchmen to Dakar, in Senegal in French West Africa, the local French administrators, soldiers, sailors and traders would come over to his banner. That accomplished, he thought, the other French African possessions would follow the Dakar precedent. The restoration of French honour, the throwing over of Marshal Petain and his humiliating subservience to Germany and ultimately the freeing of metropolitan France would fall into place.

This scheme was put to Mr Churchill who liked it. The advantages of a renewed active French participation in the war were clear. So, from the purely British point of view, would be the acquisition of a major port on the Atlantic coast of Africa in which British convoys bound for the Middle East and the Far East could be refuelled and resupplied. By the same token, the securing of Dakar by the Free French would ensure its denial to the Germans as a naval and air base that could cause damage to transatlantic shipping.

The Prime Minister's professional military advisors, the Chiefs of Staff and the Joint Planning Committee, shared his appreciation of the value of the taking of Dakar but were less sanguine about the practicalities of achieving it. There was much discussion, consideration, argument and reconsideration in Whitehall; and from Mr Churchill himself some rather discreditable bullying. De Gaulle's original idea had been that it should be an entirely Free French expedition. But he could muster only about 2,500 troops and he had insufficient French ships. It early became evident in the wrangling about the planning that the Royal Navy would have to provide transport for the French troops and a large escort force and as insurance should things go wrong, there should be a body of British troops who, if necessary, could be landed to help matters along. This last task was given to the Royal Marine Brigade.

A central feature of the enterprise was that it should remain in essence a Free French affair. If De Gaulle's negotiators convinced the Dakar French that a transfer of their allegiance was desirable, well and good. If the Dakar French were intractable, there was no intention of embroiling the British part of the force in a major operation that might risk unacceptable losses of ships and casualties. Because the major part of the effort was provided by the British it would have to be under British command, a ruling that the prickly De Gaulle found objectionable but had to accept.

The wheels were then set in motion for what an irritated British Admiral later described as the worst fiasco in British Naval history. The elements in the fiasco were slipshod security, a prolonged series of unforseen delays that compounded the security risk, a major coincidental piece of ill luck, some inaccurate meteorological forecasting and a political misjudgment by the Free French of the attitudes of the Vichy French who controlled Dakar. 2RM knew nothing of these shortcomings. At Plymouth they were issued with tropical uniforms and sun helmets and left by train for another of their unknown destinations. This time it was Liverpool. There they embarked upon the *Kenya* a converted passenger liner from the peace-time Indian run, complete with a string orchestra, Goanese stewards and for the officers, a wine cellar of distinction. The other battalions in the brigade were similarly accommodated in the *Ettrick, Sobieski* and *Karanja*. Curiosity about where these transports were heading was countered by official silence; which in turn was offset by shouted hearty messages of good will from Liverpool dockers wishing the troops the best of luck at Dakar.

The Free French were primarily responsible for this lack of discretion. Ardent young officers had ended a dinner in a London restaurant by charging their glasses, rising to their feet and toasting sucess at Dakar in the presence of a large number of other customers. General De Gaulle himself had been fitted out showily with a new set of tropical uniforms at a London tailor's in Picadilly. Another or possibly the same group of Free French Officers, had publicly toasted the success of the expedition by raising their glasses to Dakar in the bar of the Adelphi Hotel in Liverpool. When the British Force Headquarters was about to leave by train from Euston Station in London a porter accidentally upset a trolley that had carried bundles of documents wrapped up in brown paper. The brown paper broke. There was a sizeable wind blowing. The brown paper's contents, a collection of leaflets addressed to the citizens of Dakar and exhorting them to co-operate with General De Gaulle, fluttered about the platform. Staff Officers scurried to collect them. But many travellers engaged on other matters supplied an interested readership.

The code name for the undertaking was *Operation Menace*. General De Gaulle personally commanded the French part of it. There were two British joint Force Commanders. The Naval Commander was Admiral John Cunningham; the Military one Major General Irwin. Irwin had a remarkable fighting record from the First World War (he had been awarded four DSO's by the age of 26), had commanded a brigade during the fighting that led to the Dunkirk evacuation and had been pulled at short notice from the command of an infantry division to take over in *Menace*. The planning, under pitiless pressure from the Prime Minister, had been so hurried that neither the planners nor Irwin knew much about the capabilities or the limitations of the Royal Marine Brigade. It was not until they were embarked at Liverpool that commanders became aware that the brigade had no training in, or experience of, landing craft work. It thus became necessary to postpone the date of departure and to send the four brigade transports to Scapa Flow for a crash course in amphibious landings.

There were further hold-ups. The crews of some of the French ships had not been paid for several months and refused to sail until they saw the colour of their money. The job of righting this wrong was put in the hands of a junior British staff officer who travelled to London and achieved the extraordinary feat of rousing the appropriate staff of HM Treasury on a Saturday night and persuading them to disgorge about a hundred thousand pounds in notes. Another French maritime impasse then arose. The Captain of one of the French transports mislaid his mistress, who had customarily solaced him on voyages the world over. Until she was found, he said, he would stay where he was; in Liverpool. The official record says obscurely that the problem was solved. Whether the solution was the recovery of the original mistress or the substitution of a new one is unclear.

The convoy of eight transports, four for the British, four for the Free French, escorted by a large fleet of warships including the aircraft carrier *Ark Royal*, was finally assembled and set course to the Atlantic around the north coast of Ireland. Off the Bloody Foreland there was a U-boat attack that damaged a destroyer which had to return to port. Wireless silence was enforced. All communications between the ships was by visual signal. The convoy made a wide swing out into the Atlantic and then turned eastward for the port of Freetown in the then British colony of Sierra Leone. The weather became progressively steamier and hotter. The troop decks were stifling. Most of the marines in *Kenya* took to sleeping on deck. The warm weather reawakened hordes of cockroaches which emerged from the ship's timbers to hang in clusters under the Mess deck tables, swarmed around the deck-head lights and sometimes posthumously found their way into the bread cooked by the Goanese galley crew.

Whilst the convoy was steaming steadily through tropical waters towards West Africa there was a coincidental event in the Mediterranean that was interpreted at the time, wrongly, as an indication that the Vichy French knew about the purpose of the Dakar expedition and were taking active steps to frustrate it. Three Vichy French cruisers, escorted by three destroyers, left the port of Toulon in the South of France for West Africa. The reason for the despatch of this force was simply to get them as far away as possible from France so that they would be removed from any German temptation to take them over.

Their sailing was followed by an extravagant British muddle. The British Consul General in Tangier had been told by a friendly French informant that the ships were on their way. The Consul General at once reported this by telegram to the Foreign Office. He omitted to mark it with any prefix of urgency. It went to the bottom of the heap in someone's in-tray for decipherment. It came to the top four days later when it was sent to the Admiralty. At much the same time the British Naval Attache in Madrid was told as a matter of routine by his French opposite number that the ships had sailed. He too reported by telegram to the Admiralty in London and his telegram, too, was treated in a routine slow-moving manner. After the British Naval intervention at Oran British policy towards the French was delicately balanced between the need to checkmate the French Navy and the urge not to provoke the French into belligerent action on the side of the Germans. Admiral North, who commanded the Atlantic station from a shore headquarters in Gibraltar, had not been informed that the Dakar operation was afoot. He did have ambiguously worded instructions from the Admiralty that suggested that he should not go out of his way to interfere with the movements of French Naval ships to distant French controlled ports where they would be relatively harmless. He accordingly took no action to interfere with the passage of the French cruisers and destroyers through the Straits.

By the time that a smouldering Mr Winston Churchill and the less excitable Chiefs of Staff had stitched all this information together, the French ships were steaming south along the Atlantic coast of Africa. They were chased by the battleship *Renown* and escorting destroyers from Force H led by Admiral Somerville from Gibraltar. Force H were too late. Somerville thought that the French ships might be at anchor at Casablanca but the harbour was shrouded in mist and a Fleet Air Arm reconnaissance aircraft was shot down trying to establish whether they were there. They were not. When visibility was restored the Casablanca anchorage was empty. Escorting ships from operation *Menace* were then diverted to try to bring about an interception. They were unsuccessful. The Vichy French cruisers and destroyers tied up in Dakar harbour.

This seeming determination by the Vichy French to fight it out led the Prime Minister and his advisers in London to decide to call the whole thing off. The *Menace* Commanders, still at sea, saw the situation in a different light. De Gaulle, Cunningham and Irwin argued that the undertaking was still feasible. As they saw it, the rightness of this assessment was re-inforced on 19th September when most of the Vichy French Naval squadron left Dakar. Its ships were confronted at sea and in most cases were persuaded peacefully to lodge themselves in Casablanca and French-controlled ports elsewhere. The suspicion remained that they had left ashore in Dakar reinforcements of men and material to bolster the Vichy French defences.

The Royal Marine Brigade were unaware of these excursions into higher strategy. 2RM in *Kenya*, accompanied by their proliferating cockroaches, steamed slowly onwards. During a pause at Freetown, where beaming African bum-boat traders came alongside *Kenya* and, whilst selling fruit and coconuts, wished the marines good fortune on their forthcoming visit to Dakar, there was much sorting out of stores. These had been loaded haphazardly at Liverpool as they had arrived at the docks without any record having been kept of where anything was. Nobody from 2RM had been consulted about the stowage. The confusion was never resolved satisfactorily but essential items like mosquito nets were unearthed and distributed. The troops, cramped and under-exercised on the voyage were put to enjoyable work in rowing cutters and swimming from up-river islands. This short interlude soon ended. The Force sailed for Dakar.

Everything then went wrong. The imaginative Churchillian concept that the people of Dakar should awake to find themselves confronted impressively by a benign but powerful array of offshore warships was cancelled out by a thick mist, prevalent at that time of year, not noted by the expedition's meteorological advisors. De Gaulle's emissaries, landed by launch, were rebuffed with scorn and some violence. Shore batteries, twice as powerful as those forecast in the intelligence estimate, engaged the British fleet. So too did the 15-inch guns of the battleship *Richelieu*, seriously damaged in the British Naval assault at Oran, but which had made its way to the safe haven of Dakar. A heavy seasonal swell, predictable but also overlooked by the meteorologists, was severe enough to make it clear that if it came to launching landing craft their journey to the shore would be hazardous. French aircraft and submarines went into action in support of the shore batteries and *Richelieu*. Throughout all this long commotion the four transports carrying the Royal Marine Brigade steamed about forlornly in the midst of a sporadically conducted ship-to-shore naval battle, the marines ignorant about what was happening and why and feeling extensively affronted by the turn that matters had taken.

It became increasingly evident that if Dakar were to be taken it could only be done after fighting of the sort that could lead to the naval losses and casualties that were specified as unacceptable in the Force's instructions. There was the allied danger, contemplated anxiously in London, that a major fight conducted primarily by the British against determined Vichy French defenders might so inflame metropolitan French susceptibilities, already soured by earlier events at Oran, that Marshal Petain might declare war upon Britain. On the third day, 25th September 1940, there was agreement between Whitehall and the Force Commanders. The operation was called off.

This decision did not commend itself to the junior officers of 2RM in *Kenya*. They gathered together under the chairmanship of 2nd Lieutenant John Biggs-Davison and prepared what they saw as a realistic alternative plan for the subjection of Dakar. Instead of all this futile manoeuvring about in front of the city, they argued, the battalion should be landed a few miles up the coast where a railway train would be commandeered. The train would then carry the battalion into the main station in Dakar, the French would be taken by surprise and the whole thing would be over. Biggs-Davidson led a delegation of subalterns to put this fancy scheme to Colonel Nick Williams, who had been pacing the deck irritably. Williams rejected it out of hand. He described its submission as "mutiny". Despite the fierceness of this brush-off, Biggs-Davison and his fellow mutineers reached the conclusion that Nick Williams was feeling pretty mutinous himself.

For some months an anonymous chronicler or possibly a committee of chroniclers, had recorded the various movements of 2RM to the tune of "Hallelujah I'm a Bum", a lugubrious ballad about the misfortunes of American hoboes during the pre-war depression. The wording of the latest entry in this saga was:

"To Dakar we went,
With General De Gaulle,
We steamed round in circles,
And did sweet fuck-aulle."

This sums it all up rather more neatly than the official history does.

The *Menace* Force dispersed. The warships returned to a proper war. The Free

French transports went to Duala in the French Cameroons, from which General De Gaulle was able to take the initial steps in winning over the French African possessions to his side. The Royal Marine Brigade went to Freetown in Sierra Leone and was split in half. 1RM and 5RM returned to the United Kingdom. 2RM and 3RM were left in Freetown to counter any possibility that the Germans might try to establish a U-boat base in the Cape Verde Islands. The Germans did not try.

*Kenya* stayed in the Freetown anchorage with 2RM. An advance party of the battalion, led by Captain Tyndale-Biscoe, set up a tented camp ashore at Willberforce. It was a miserable place. There were no floor boards available for the tents and no beds. Nightly tropical storms washed out the tents, a proportion of which were regularly blown down. The food was indifferent, and nutrition was not helped by the marines' parochial reluctance to eat local vegetables and fruit. A training programme of route marches, musketry, exercises and the rest of it was soon in full swing.

In October 2RM were moved to Lumley camp, which if anything was less attractive than had been Willberforce. Lumley was still under construction. It was sited beside a swamp and an African village. By day two thousand African labourers swarmed about, laying down concrete bases and putting up huts. Their notions of sanitation were deplorable and the camp was filthy. 2RM continued with its training programme.

In November there came the first cases of malaria. Anopheles mosquitoes which down the centuries have done more damage to armies than their armed opposition has ever effected, lived a congenial life in the stagnant swamps of Sierra Leone. Their bite carried the malarial virus. They were ingenious in penetrating mosquito nets and mosquito veils. Mepacrine, which later in the war became a standard malarial preventative, was not yet available. Quinine was issued and the troops took it daily on parade under the supervision of officers. The mosquitos still won. At first their toll ran at five or six malarial cases a day. It soon rose to fifteen. Some mitigation was found by sending one company at a time to *Kenya* moored in the harbour, where mosquitos did not fly.

The figures continued to rise. By January 1941, out of 2RM's total strength of six hundred and five, 34.5% had become malarial casualties. It was a debilitating disease. Lieutenant Brice Somers, the Signals Officer, one of the victims, described its symptoms as an unimaginably splitting headache, sweating out litres of water into the bed and then being unable to even raise an arm to scratch one's nose. There was a sad consequence to the disabling of Somers. Shortly before he went down, the steering on his motor cycle had become dangerously unstable. He had no time to report this before being taken to a hospital ward on the *Oxfordshire*. His Signals Sergeant, "Chippy" Millerchip, a much liked and supremely efficient member of the battalion, rode off on the motor bike. He was killed.

The Freetown stay ended in February 1941. Its seeming pointlessness, the enervating climate, the inroads of the mosquitoes and the squalid living conditions could have demoralised a less resilient and less disciplined unit. 2RM ignored these obstacles by an insistence upon smart turn out, hard training, a devotion to all available forms of sport, domestically organised troop concerts and a sensible programme of permitted leave to the not too enticing charms of Freetown.

Without regret, the battalion embarked in *Kenya* for the journey home. *Kenya*, it was then discovered, was another casualty of tropical ailments. Her hull was encrusted with barnacles, which slowed her down to 8 Knots. She chugged slowly to Gibraltar and put in for careening. 2RM were told that the quicker they chipped off the barnacles the sooner they would go home. They chipped. They were then piqued to be put on border protection duties on the Rock.

The last leg of their journey was in Atlantic storms through which *Kenya*, made top-heavy by having Assault Landing Craft instead of life boats at her davits, rolled spectacularly. Equipment, lifebelts and crockery crashed about from one side of the ship to the other. So did incautious marines who did not clutch something stable. Bren gunners in duffel coats swayed about on the upper deck on anti-aircraft duty, wondering about what sort of German pilot would be idiotic enough to get airborne in this sort of weather. Some consolation for the discomfort was piped over loud hailers from the bridge. The storm would keep U-boats quiet. The weather abated when *Kenya* reached the outer Hebrides. U-boats became active again and escorting destroyers dropped depth charges. There were no losses. *Kenya* and the rest of the convoy moored in the Clyde. 2RM went thankfully on two weeks foreign service leave.

# CHAPTER THREE

# SWEAT, FRUSTRATION AND CONVERSION

For two and a half years, between the return from Dakar until the summer of 1943, 2RM trained. It went by sea to Loch Fyne in the west of Scotland and to Scapa Flow in the Shetlands for practice in the use of landing craft. It marched for miles, sometimes along roads, more often across country. It climbed cliffs. It rehearsed specifically for a planned role in a series of operations that were cancelled one after the other. In one of the earlier exercises, which involved a thirty one mile approach march to put in a mock attack on the railway station at Killin, it became evident that tropical life in West Africa and its attendant diseases had left their mark. Too many men fell out on the march. There was a great shake-up. One of its victims was Colonel Blandford, the successor of Colonel Nick Williams, who was replaced as Commanding Officer by Lieutenant Colonel R W B Simonds.

"Bonzo" Simonds was thirty-six years of age when he took over 2RM. He had joined the corps in 1924, had put in considerable service with the Atlantic Fleet and at the age of twenty-nine had become one of the youngest ever adjutants at the depot at Deal. Early in the war he had been the second-in-command of 3RM. He came to 2RM with a tremendous reputation as a fierce disciplinarian, who spared neither himself nor anyone else. He was particularly severe with junior officers, one of whom years later described the early months of the Simonds regime simply as "bloody hell". He did not generate much personal affection. He did earn a universal respect. He soon had the battalion fully fit and back to standard.

The Royal Marine Brigade had been expanded to become the Royal Marine Division. The Division never fought as such. Most of it became progressively more frustrated and restless at the abandonment of one projected operation after another. In May 1942, Major General Sturges, who as a Colonel had led Sturgesforce in the Iceland expedition, with a skeleton staff from the Royal Marine Division Headquarters took three brigades to seize Diego Suarez in the north of Madagascar. The brigades were found from the army.

Few in the Royal Marine Division knew it at the time but the reason for the Division's continuing inaction lay in an unedifying lingering dispute between the War Office and the Admiralty. The Admirals still held to the by now outdated traditional concept that amphibious operations were for them to control. The Generals argued that with the Germans now in occupation of most of continental Europe and the Japanese in occupation of large areas of the Far East and the Pacific, all ground operations mounted from the island of Britain would in essence be amphibious. If the Royal Marine Division wished to take part in them it should modify its organisation to conform with those of Army Divisions. It would then be fitted for incorporation as part of any expeditionary force that was sent anywhere. The Admirals refused to give way.

The Royal Marine Division lost its operational role. It went on training as hard as ever, without anyone at the top being able to see much prospect of the training's being put to fruitful use. 2RM trained in the Highlands and Lowlands of Scotland, in South Wales, in the Isle of Wight and in Hampshire. Battalion Headquarters was attacked by hit-and-run *Messerschmitts* at Ryde in the Isle of Wight and a marine was killed and several wounded. It was the only act of war, an unsatisfactory one, to come the way of a superbly fit battalion during a long lean period of seeming aimlessness.

In early 1943 matters were put on a more sensible footing. Admiral Lord Louis Mountbatten, the Chief of Combined Operations, wanted more Commandos for his organisation. A ready-made source was at hand in the shape of the Royal Marine Division which, in any case, Mountbatten feared might wither away unless it was soon put to productive use. The First Sea Lord also cherished ambitions for the use of under-employed marines. He needed crews for the large number of landing craft of all sorts that were being manufactured for the cross-channel invasion of Normandy, planned for the middle of 1944. Mountbatten, the First Sea Lord, and General Hunton, the new Adjutant General Royal Marines, reached a compromise. Seven of the battalions in the division would be slimmed down and converted to Commandos. Each battalion was about nine hundred strong. The strength of a Commando was about five hundred. The manpower saved would crew landing craft. The truncated battalions would go in turn through the Commando Basic Training Centre at Achnacarry, in the Scottish Highlands, the ancestral home of Cameron of Lochiel. The training area was bleakly beautiful, midge-ridden, mountainous, rocky, rain-sodden and boggy.

In the Spring of 1943 2RM were in Nissen huts at Hursley Park near Winchester. The battalion's last day of existence was 31st July. On 1st August it became No 43 Royal Marine Commando.

The original wartime commandos had been formed as an improvisation after the Dunkirk evacuation. The first priority of the times was given to the defence of Britain against invasion. At the same time consideration was given to the formation of a force for cross channel raiding operations. The Royal Marine Brigade were the obvious candidates. They were trained, intact and had not lost men and weapons at Dunkirk. They were considered at first to be indispensable for home defence and were then committed to operations elsewhere: one that actually happened, Dakar and ones that were planned, aborted, but tied up the brigade's resources. The task of forming the new force went to the Army.

The Army decided that what was wanted were picked volunteers who would be asked to put their names down for "Special Services of a Hazardous Nature". There were several times as many volunteers as there were vacancies. Colonels chose their own Officers who in turn interviewed and chose their men. Training was rigorously hard, in much the same mould as that of the Royal Marine Brigade. Initially the new raiding units were known as Special Service battalions. The name was soon changed to Commando, with the enthusiastic endorsement of Mr Winston Churchill who had sound personal reasons to recall the hardiness and initiative of the Boer Commandos in the South African war of forty years earlier. Initial high hopes of early action were largely frustrated. There was a shortage of everything from landing craft to tommy guns. There were a few small scale raids on the French coast and on the Channel Islands but none was conspicuously successful.

They were specially chosen men who were physically hardy, accustomed to taking risks and prolific of innovative ideas. They were proud of their volunteer ethos. A volunteer Royal Marine Commando, initially labelled "A", subsequently numbered No 40, was formed in 1942 and took part in August of that year in a calamitous raid on Dieppe, in company with the 2nd Canadian Division and Nos 3 and 4 Army Commandos. 40 Commando lost heavily and its casualties included their Colonel. 3 Commando fared a little better. 4 Commando achieved a brilliant local tactical success.

By 1943 the army commandos had won for themselves a redoubtable reputation. They had suffered the usual vagaries of warfare but had fought with skill and verve in amphibious actions on European coasts, in the Middle East, and in North Africa.

Another Royal Marine Commando, No 41, was formed later in the year. Predictably, when Royal Marine battalions were arbitrarily transmogrified, there was some Army commando scepticism and resentment. The marine stand-point that the Corps had been engaged in amphibious landing operations for two hundred and fifty years before the Army Commandos had ever been heard of and that tradition, discipline, and thorough training would produce efficient fighting men capable of undertaking any imaginable Commando task was advanced with vehemence. In the light of co-operative mutual experience the early friction slowly died down but it was still being sustained by both sides of the argument by some zealots until the war ended.

Since the days of its birth and growth, 2RM had progressed through a period of advancing adolescence. In the early, Nick Williams, days the Commanding Officer and the 2nd in Command, all the Company Commanders, the Regimental Sergeant Major, all the Company Sergeant Majors, and all the Sergeants had been regular long-service Marines. By 1943 Hostilities Only Officers had matured sufficiently to take over the command of the companies. The subalterns were still largely Hostilities Only. The Company Sergeant Majors and some of the Sergeants were regulars but promotion from the ranks to Corporal and Sergeant had become frequent.

Colonel Simonds was faced with the task of choosing who was to stay and who was to go in the conversion of the battalion to the commando. He retained those Officers he wanted, got rid of the ones he didn't and accepted without fuss the applications of the ones who expressed a preference for landing craft over commando soldiering. The former Company Commanders, now Troop Commanders, went through a similar process in converting hundred-man companies to sixty-man troops. They too shed the unsuitable, were sympathetic about accepting the applications of people who wanted to go to landing craft and kept the marines whom they judged to be most fitted for commando soldiering. They were particularly gratified to find that a large number of Yorkshire old timers, from whom 2RM had originally been raised, discussed the matter amongst themselves and decided that they did not want to be separated. They stayed.

The reorganisation was soon completed. The next step was for 43 Commando to go as a body through the rigours of the Achnacarry training. This austere establishment was presided over by Colonel Charles Vaughan, a remarkable soldier who had been a Regimental Sergeant Major in the Buffs, ex-drill sergeant in the Coldstream Guards during the First World War. His outlook and practices appealed to the marines. Early morning parades were formal affairs, with emphasis upon turnout and drill. For the rest of the crowded days and some of the crowded nights, there were speed marches in which troops carrying a full burden of weapons, ammunition, equipment and full water bottles marched seven miles in one hour and twelve miles in two hours. There were assaults using live ammunition upon objectives on mountain-tops and mountain-sides. There were river crossings and lake crossings opposed by simulated defenders who fired continuous bursts of Bren gun fire closely over the heads of the attackers. There was a lot of swinging around on ropes in trees on the Tarzan course. Cliff climbing and abseiling were supervised by a seemingly deranged former steeplejack. A mysterious-looking gypsy, currently a Sergeant, gave nauseating lessons on how to survive by eating rats and mice baked in clay. There was a primitive form of boxing, called Milling in which two teams took it in turns to enter the ring at one minute intervals to try to knock the stuffing out of their opponents.

At the end of it all 43 Commando were as fit as could be. They were awarded their green berets. They moved to Ramsgate in Kent.

# PART TWO

## 43 COMMANDO: CENTRAL MEDITERRANEAN, ITALY

# CHAPTER FOUR

# SEABORNE ADVANCE TO CONTACT

In November, 1943, 43 Commando were still at Ramsgate living in "Civvy Billets". Civvy Billets provided one of the nicer charms of commando soldiering in the United Kingdom. In order to cut down on the diversion of manpower to administrative and maintenance jobs necessary in barracks, a lodging allowance (13 shillings and 4 pence for Officers, 6 shillings and 8 pence for other ranks) was paid to everybody. Volunteer landladies provided bed and board and the kinder ones threw in laundering and occasional weapon cleaning as part of the service. So long as the troops paraded where and when they were required to, their domestic arrangements went unquestioned.

Training was still persistent and the new slimmed-down organisation had become familiar. There were now five fighting troops, each 65 strong, four of them commanded by Captains, one by a Major. Each troop was divided into two sections, each commanded by a subaltern. The sections in turn were divided into subsections, each commanded by a Sergeant. The officers were armed with Colt .45 automatic pistols, the Sergeants with Tommy guns. The subsections had two Rifle Groups and a Bren Group, each commanded by Corporals and Lance Corporals. With Troop Headquarters were the Troop Commander, the Troop Sergeant Major, a signaller, a Royal Army Medical Corps orderly, the 2" mortar group and the PIAT group. The Projector Infantry Anti-Tank was a primitive rocket launcher of unpredictable performance, sometimes given to savaging the handler. Because initiative at all levels was required, there was a high proportion of junior NCOs.

Supporting firepower was provided by the Heavy Weapons Troop, of four 3" Mortars and four Vickers Medium Machine Guns. Direction and specialist service came from Commando Headquarters - the Commanding Officer, Lieutenant-Colonel Simonds; the second-in-command, Major Neil Munro; the Adjutant, the Intelligence Officer, the Signals Officer, the Administrative Officer (the new name for a Quartermaster) the Doctor and his medical section, and the Padre.

The whole organism packed its effects and said goodbye to its landladies on 9 November. They were off to another unknown destination. Only Senior Officers were told where.

## SEABORNE ADVANCE TO CONTACT

They embarked at Liverpool in a comfortable but crowded passenger liner, the *Monarch of Bermuda,* converted for the duration to trooping. They sailed to the Clyde to join an escorted convoy. Their ongoing journey was undisturbed by U-Boats or intrusive German aircraft. On 23 November they passed through the straits of Gibraltar and made accurate guesses about what would come next. Two days later they left the convoy and landed at Algiers.

They passed nearly six weeks in Algeria. It was a time of inferior accommodation, speedmarching, field- firing exercises and defending their possessions from some of the most talented thieves they had yet met. On 2 January, 1944, they embarked in one Landing Ship Tank and two Landing Craft Infantry. Foul weather delayed departure. On 4 January the L.S.T. was able to sail. The L.C.I.s were still shore bound and followed later. On 6 January the L.S.T. steamed into the bay of Naples. That part of the Commando aboard her disembarked. They were met by Brigadier Tom Churchill, Commanding No 2 Special Service Brigade, and Colonel "Pops" Manners of No 40 Commando. Trucks awaited the new arrivals and they were driven to the small village of Vico Equense. The L.C.I. passengers joined them shortly afterwards.

After more than two years of inconclusive fighting in the western desert abutting the African shore of the Mediterranean, the British and Commonwealth troops of 8th Army scored a decisive victory in October 1942 at El Alamein, slightly to the West of the Nile Delta. The follow-up to this success was complemented by the landing in Morocco, Algeria and Tunisia of American and British armies. There was much hard fighting, but by the spring of 1943 the whole of North Africa was in allied hands.

The next move was to continental Europe. Sicily was invaded in July and the last German and Italian soldiers were thrown out of it after six weeks. Landings on the Italian mainland were made at Taranto in the East, without much opposition, and at Salerno, south of Naples. The Salerno lodgement, by American and British troops, was a hard-fought and at times precarious battle that lasted for twelve days. The Germans ultimately withdrew. The Italians had meanwhile surrendered. The Italian campaign, a skilfully conducted German series of withdrawals, punctuated by ferocious defensive actions when the ground was suitable, developed a pattern that was to last for a further eighteen months. Much of the Italian ground suited the Germans very well. The central spine of the Appennines supplied a plethora of naturally defendable positions. Rivers flowing East and West from the mountains provided formidable river obstacles on the coastal plains. By far the most daunting of the German held barriers was the Gustav Line on the southern approaches to Rome. It extended from the West coast to the Abruzzi. Interlinked fortified positions studded the mountains and covered the river crossings. Its pivot was the huge hill block of Monte Cassino, on the summit of which was an ancient and famous Benedictine monastery. The hill and the monastery dominated Highway 6, the road from Naples to Rome.

Unsuccessful attempts to break the German line at Cassino had been made by the Americans. A new option was planned. After a further frontal assault by American, British, New Zealand and Indian troops had developed, two infantry divisions, one British, one American, would be put ashore at the small port of Anzio between

Cassino and Rome and behind the German Gustav Line defences. This landing was timed to take place early in January 1944. An early ingredient in the concept was to have been the landing of an American parachute battalion to seize a wooded hill and its surroundings on the outer perimeter of the landings. The American parachutists became unavailable. The job was given to the commandos of Brigadier Tom Churchill's No 2 Special Service Brigade.

There were four Commandos in the Brigade at the time. Two of them, No 2 and No 9 (Scottish) Commando were Army; two, No 40 and No 43 were Royal Marines. Because of their special training and of their ability to move fast over almost any kind of country, and also because this speediness carried with it the handicap that they lacked most of the support weapons and administrative infrastructure of more conventional infantry battalions, the Commandos in Italy were usually committed piecemeal to individual tasks long distances apart. At the time of Anzio, Brigadier Tom Churchill had at his immediate disposal only half of his brigade, No 9 Commando and 43. No 40 were committed to a programme of deep patrolling beyond the River Garigliano, an outlying component of the German defence complex centred upon Monte Cassino. Advanced elements of No 2 Commando were on their way to the Dalmatian island of Vis, off the Yugoslav coast, where they were to operate in conjunction with Marshal Tito's Partisans.

## CHAPTER FIVE

# ANZIO AND ORNITO

43 Commando's part at Anzio, brief, effective and almost bloodless, was as good an introduction to modern warfare as any unit could have hoped for.

Anzio was then a small fishing port, flanked on either side by extensive sandy beaches. For some distance inland the ground was flat. It then rose erratically to the low outcrops of the Alban hills. 1st British Division was to land on the beaches to the north of the town. 3rd American Division was to go ashore to the south. U.S. Rangers, the American equivalent of the British Commandos and who had in fact done part of their basic training at Achnacarry, were to seize the port itself. The two Commandos were to follow on the heels of 1st British Division, pass through them, march seven miles to the wooded hill that was their objective and defend it until the Beachhead main force caught up with them.

The whole expedition, the ships and craft carrying the troops, the Naval escort, the warships that were to provide artillery support, set out from the Bay of Naples on 20 January. Brigade Headquarters, No 9 and 43 travelled in a Landing Ship Infantry, the *Derbyshire*. At 5 o'clock in the morning of the 22nd they were transferred to Landing Craft Assault and headed in to their selected beach. The L.C.A.'s run in came under sporadic shell fire and 43 suffered its first two casualties, two marines not too seriously wounded. The half-brigade landed while it was still dark, met no opposition, crossed the beach fast and formed up in line of march beyond it. A distant German 88mm gun dropped some shells in the middle of 43 and near to Brigade Headquarters and there were four further casualties between the two. No 9 Commando led the advance. Brigade Headquarters and 43 followed. A few Germans were met on this leg of the journey, rear area people going about their daily chores and seemingly unaware that their accustomed peaceful haven had been transformed into the centre-piece of a major assault landing.

No 9, who by now had passed through a battalion of the Scots Guards manning the initial beach-head perimeter, killed a few of these casual wayfarers and captured a few more. The 2" Mortar Team of 'E' Troop of 43 scored a direct hit on a German armoured car, which passed No 9 Commando smoking heavily. No 9 continued to go straight. 43 were sent off to the right and reached their first objective, a level crossing. Some German movement was sighted on the wooded hill and the two Commandos assaulted it simultaneously from either flank, under cover of supporting fire from their 3" Mortars. 43

had some minor brushes with the enemy between the level crossing and the hill itself and took six prisoners. By 2.45 in the afternoon, the hill was secured and both Commandos took up defensive positions, digging in deeply. They were isolated and well ahead of the forward British troops.

After nightfall patrols were sent out in all directions. On the following morning the American Rangers, who had had a stiff fight in Anzio town, joined up with and then passed through the Commandos. Later in the day the forward British beach-head troops arrived and incorporated the hill in their defences. The job of the two Commandos was done. At 7 o'clock in the evening they were withdrawn to Anzio town where they spent a noisy night under shellfire and aerial bombing. Early on the following morning they embarked in a Landing Ship Tank and arrived back in Naples that same afternoon, 24 January.

Anzio had been a useful educational experience. The lessons learned there were applied elsewhere in the months that lay ahead. Orders to move to the first elsewhere soon came.

A few days after the return from Anzio of the two Commandos to their requisitioned accommodation in villages on the south side of the Bay of Naples, Brigadier Tom Churchill was summoned to meet General McCreery, the Commander of X Corps. X Corps' two divisions, No 46 and No 56, had been in action continuously since the Salerno landings and although the General did not say so specificaly were pretty well exhausted. He wanted, said the General, No 9 and No 43 Commandos to move to 56 Division and place themselves under command in a counter-attack role in hilly country north of the river Garigliano.

The Commandos were motored up in lorries, uncomfortably, along winding narrow mountainous roads on the following day. They arrived at 2.30 in the morning at a rendezvous east of Sessa, where they were to bivouac for the night. There were routine jobs to be done and dawn was imminent before anyone got much sleep. On the next day there was a familiar military happening, a change of plan. The Commandos were now to go to 46 Division, settle themselves temporarily in an area North of Monte Tuga and assault two hill features from which the Germans had been bothering 46 Division. The hills were Monte Ornito, about two thousand feet high and Monte Faito about two thousand five hundred feet. The nearside of Monte Ornito was about three quarters of a mile ahead of 46 Division's forward positions. Faito was behind Ornito. In that steep, up-and-down country, three quarters of a mile on the map was significantly further on the ground.

Tom Churchill, bringing with him Colonel Ronnie Tod of 9 Commando and Colonel Simonds of 43, drove by jeep to 46 Division's Headquarters, housed in a small cluster of caravans on a hill-side olive grove. The Divisional Commander, Major General Hawksworth, was peremptory, rather ill-mannered, and not particulary well-informed about the precise locations of his leading battalions. He wanted Ornito and Faito taken, he said, and showed little further interest in the complicities of the task.

Churchill and the two Commando leaders spent the rest of the day on a visual reconnaissance. They left in their jeeps at about 10 o'clock in the morning, crossed the Garigliano by a pontoon bridge that was under intermittent shell fire, drove on for a mile or so and then started climbing on foot. A guide supplied by the York and Lancaster Regiment led them upwards in a climb that became progressively steeper. At 5 o'clock in the afternoon they reached a crest manned by the forward section of the York and Lancaster Regiment and by an artillery observation post. Immediately ahead lay the ground that was to be crossed in the attack, a valley between the British and German front lines. Beyond the valley loomed Monte Ornito and a crest to its left, marked on the map as Point 714. These were the brigade's first objectives. Two miles behind was the higher summit of Monte Faito. Churchill, Tod and Simonds took a good look at everything relevant and scrambled thoughtfully back to their jeeps.

In the meantime No 9 and 43 had been brought by the brigade staff to within striking distance. The early part of their travels from the bivouac area had been in trucks. But the last bit was a hard march on foot across the Garigliano and up steep, rocky tracks to their assembly area on the top of Monte Tuga. The last of them were in by 4 o'clock in the morning. They had had much exertion and little sleep for two succeeding nights. If they were to be at their best in the assault they needed a day's rest. Tom Churchill telephoned General Hawksworth and asked for a twenty-four hour postponement. It was conceded grudgingly.

The open air on an Italian mountainside in an early February night provided uncomfortably chilly sleeping quarters. Extreme tiredness made this disability of small consequence. Everyone off duty slept deeply in the dark hours before dawn. Captain Jock Hudspith of 'A' Troop slumbered in relative luxury. Marine Boak, Hudspith's M.O.A. (Marine Officer's Attendant, the Royal Marine equivalent of an Army Batman) was a conscientious and kindly man who heated two sizable stones over a fire and produced them to keep his boss's feet comfortable. Hudspith had also by chance found something soft and almost warm, unidentifiable in the dark, on which to rest his head. He awoke at daylight to find that his pillow had been a recently dead horse.

The daylight hours of 1st February were spent by the commanders in adding refinements and adjustments to the outline plan that had already been settled upon. It had been hoped that as many as possible of the attackers would be able to examine the objectives from behind cover but for the first part of the morning a thick mist masked the valley and the mountain beyond. Later in the day the mist cleared sufficiently for the Troop Commanders and some of the Section Commanders, to be able to study what lay ahead of them.

The plan was for a penetration operation, carried out in a long single file. 43 were to lead, scale Ornito up a narrow goat track and seize the summit and Point 714 to the west of it. It would have been quite a climb even if there had been no interfering armed Germans spread about it in scattered positions. Hudspith later described it as like going from the bottom to the top of Ben Nevis.

43 were to start at 6.30pm after darkness had fallen. No 9 Commando were to go one hour later, at first following the route of 43, branching off to the right to head for Monte Faito behind. Because all recent attacks by 46 Division had been preceeded by preliminary artillery shoots, which inevitably alerted the defenders to what was in store for them, the attack was to be a silent one. Every item of equipment that jingled or jangled was either abandoned or strapped down into quietness. The approach route was too

steep and difficult for 'F' Troop to carry up their heavy weapons of 3" mortars and medium machine guns and they were left out of the affair. The entire divisional artillery of 46 Division were on call by the Commandos. Gunner Forward Observation Officers were to move with the attacking troops.

In the original concept the idea had been that 43 would make its way straight down to the valley floor, cross it, and scale Monte Ornito from its immediate front. It later became known from the forward British battalion that a German position, defended by about two platoons, high up on the hill side, had the valley under observation and shelled it vigorously when they saw or heard any British movement. This news generated a final modification to the plan. The valley was a place to be avoided. 43 would begin by swinging round further to the east and then assault up the eastern slopes of Ornito.

It was bright moonlight when they set out. 'D' Troop led. Its commander, Captain John Blake, accomplished some remarkable navigation. He steered the whole long column over rising, broken country that he had not previously seen, with the help only of a map that he consulted at intervals using a shaded torch. There was some German shelling and machine gun fire almost from the beginning. Blake led on with assurance to the foot hills of Ornito and headed steadily for the top. 'C' Troop, Captain Bob Loudoun, were dropped off as a flank guard when about one third of the way up and took up all-round defensive positions on a spur projecting to the east. 'C' Troop were shelled and machine gunned spasmodically and suffered some casualties, including the first marine of 43 to have been killed in action.

'B' Troop, Captain Gerry Schooley, and 'A' Troop, Captain Jock Hudspith, slogged on upwards in the wake of Blake and 'D' Troop. Colonel Simonds was well up with the forward troops. One of the risks attendant upon an arduous climb in unknown country during which sporadic mortar, shell and machine gun fire came down irregularly and unpredictably, was that after a temporary hold-up at some point in the file, a marine might lose contact with the man in front of him. To reduce the chance of a severance, Lieutenant Douglas Gregory had been made a link-man with the job of ensuring that everybody was kept closed up and following on in the right direction. It was an arduous climb for everybody but more so than most for Gregory. He had to move up, then partially down again and up once more. Despite his best efforts one section of 'B' Troop, led by Lieutenant David Leatherbarrow, did in fact go astray, drifted away on its own and was able only to rejoin the Commando on the summit shortly after daybreak.

'D' and 'B' Troops, fighting bitter little fire-fights as they went, reached the summit of Ornito after a five hour ascent. 'A' Troop, which was to have shifted slightly to the left to Point 711, came under heavy fire from a nearby German position to the west. Hudspith sent Lieutenant Desmond Clark's section to dispose of this nuisance which Clark did with dispatch. Hudspith and the rest of his troop reached Point 714 in the teeth of a heavy German artillery barrage but found the Point deserted. Clark's section joined him there shortly afterwards.

All three troops were now where they should be. Digging in on rock was not possible. They built "sangars", surrounds of stones and rocks that provided some protection against small arms, mortar and gun fire; although near misses could add uncomfortably to zinging metal mortar bomb and shell fragments by including sharp fractured bits of rock in the delivery.

Most of the sangar construction was completed by dawn. In the daylight the German mortaring and shelling, much of which during the night had been dropped blind in pre-set defensive fire tasks, could now be directed by observers with a clear view of what was going on. One of the incidental complications to the Commando was that the high, jagged slopes of the mountain-top blocked the sending of wireless signals. Communications brokedown completely. The Gunner Forward Observation Officer, however, had a more powerful set and he was able to report progress back to his own battery, who in turn let Brigadier Tom Churchill, in his brigade headquarters in a pigsty near the start line, know how things were going. Churchill also heard from wireless signals that No 9 Commando on their journey to the right to Monte Faito, had run in to serious trouble. Concentrated German shell fire had wounded Colonel Ronnie Tod, killed his second-in-command, Intelligence Officer and Regimental Sergeant Major, wounded four of his five Troop Commanders and hit about half of the whole force. No 9 Commando were ordered by Churchill to break off their attack and to pull back through 43's position on Ornito.

The first of them reached there at about 7.30am. The 9 Commando wounded, along with the 43 Commando fewer wounded made their way slowly to the rear, down the steep track, some limping, some helping one another along, some on stretchers. About thirty German prisoners taken by 43 Commando were also sent back under escort and provided some of the stretcher bearers for the wounded.

As the day progressed there was more heavy shelling, more mortaring and more machine gunning from German Spandaus. 43 held on dourly. They paid particular attention to a hill lying below them to their front. On this hill, intelligence had reported, was a German reserve company that would clearly provide the nucleus of any German attempt at a counter-attack. This came in the late afternoon. It was driven off by all the 43 Commando weapons that could be brought to bear and by the massed artillery of 46 Division, who laid down a highly spectacular, noisy, prolonged and effective barrage.

After the repulse of the counter-attack German shelling and mortaring continued. 43 were not shifted by anything that the Germans could do but were pleased when the shifting was done on the orders of their own side. By midnight the 5th Battalion The Hampshire Regiment had relieved the Commando on the summit. The marines formed up and retraced their steps down the hill-side and through the valley.

On the way down, still occasionally subjected to random German shelling, there were widespread personal reflections upon the German contribution to the events of the previous day and night and upon some more diverting domestic experiences. Much relished was the moment during the early phase of the advance, still undetected by the enemy although his routine harassing fire was troublesome, when the disciplined silence was suddenly broken by an intriguing noise, like the tap on a kitchen sink abruptly turned to full. The source of this gushing sound was disclosed within a few seconds, in a roared outbreak of foul-mouthed complaint by a marine who had, he explained colourfully, been urinated on by a mule. This hard luck story had induced extensive and tactically unwise laughter and was a great reliever of tension.

The unsanctioned appearance on the summit of Ornito by Doctor Crowther, the unit's Medical Officer, an Australian alcoholic who had been an infantry soldier in the Australian Army during the First World War, was also something to cherish. Crowther's persistent tenderings of out-dated military advice to busy officers who didn't want to take it had added a mild touch of surrealism to the proceedings. So too did the less bellicose contribution of Rear Admiral Sir Walter Cowan, a tiny septuagarian who had been in his prime in the days when Britannia really did rule the waves and who so regretted the passing of that golden era that he was determined to die in action. The Admiral had attached himself to Tom Churchill's Brigade staff, where he was made most welcome. He had followed No 9 Commando towards Mount Faito and he came back with them through 43, dressed in a green beret and carrying a shepherd's crook. Opinion was divided on whether he was a fine old fellow or a silly old fool, but his presence was a reminder that life was what you made of it; whatever, in the Admiral's case, that was.

At the foot of the hill stood another, this one still professionally functioning, senior officer, a tall lone General. Lieutenant Desmond Clark, leading his section of 'A' Troop, called to them to march to attention and saluted the General. It was the X Corps Commander, General McCreery, who had taken the trouble to welcome the troops back and to thank them. General Hawksworth of 46th Division neither thanked them nor left his Divisional Headquarters.

43's part in the initial phase of the Anzio landings had been a gradual introduction to the realities of warfare as conducted against the Germans in Italy. Casualties had been light. Helpful lessons about the identification by noise of incoming German projectiles of all sizes and where they would be likely to land, had been absorbed. It had been not much more than an elaborate Field Firing Exercise with a live enemy. Ornito was different. Out of a committed strength of three hundred the Commando lost six killed, one missing believed killed, two others missing and subsequently found to be killed, and twenty six wounded. It had been a hard test of endurance, determination and skill. The test had been passed on all counts. A small handful who had failed it were immediately removed elsewhere.

The value that the Germans placed on Monte Ornito was demonstrated by its later record. The summit changed hands five times between February and May 1944, until it was finally stormed by Tunisian Goums of the French Army during the breakthrough of the Gustav Line and the clearance of the way to Rome and the north.

By 6th February, 43 were back in their billets at Vico Equense. There was administrative tidying up to be done after the battle. The familiar, relentless, round of training was resumed: amphibious exercises with Landing Craft Infantry; physical training; mountain climbing; speed marches; signals exercises; tactical rehearsals. A variety of captured German weapons had been brought back both from Anzio and Ornito, and an Enemy Weapons Circus toured every troop and gave instruction in their use. At noon on 25th February the Commando left on a train journey, in cattle trucks, for Bari, a port in the south east of Italy. Their destination, undisclosed as usual to all but Senior Officers, was Vis, the westernmost of the Dalmatian islands off the coast of Yugoslavia. The Commando landed on Vis on 28th February.

# PART THREE

**A YEAR WITH THE SOUTH SLAVS**

# CHAPTER SIX

# THE YUGOSLAV KALEIDOSCOPE

The Germans had invaded Yugoslavia on the 6th April 1941. The campaign lasted for twelve days. The Yugoslav General Staff, overwhelmed by the customary German sophisticated interplay between armour, motorised infantry and the total domination of the skies by the *Luftwaffe*, surrendered unconditionally. The young King Peter, some of his ministers and several senior officers of the Yugoslav armed forces were flown from an airfield near Niksic, in Montenegro, to Cairo. They set up a government in exile. Niksic was to become well-known to 43.

For some months following this debacle no news came out of the country aside from that provided by the Axis and Quisling newspapers and wireless. It became clear from these that Yugoslavia, the land of the South Slavs, a country formally united only since 1918, had been dismembered politically. Much of Serbia, parts of Slovenia and the eastern Vojvodina were retained as a direct German responsibility. The Italians, who had assisted the Germans in the invasion, became the rulers of Montenegro, about half of Dalmatia, Kosovo and western Macedonia. They were also given the part of Slovenia not wanted by the Germans. The Bulgarians and Hungarians, German scavengers too, split between them most of Macedonia, the west Vojvodina and a little part of Croatia. Croatia itself extended by the incorporation of Bosnia and much of Dalmatia became, in name at least, an independent state under the leadership of Ante Pavelic, a fascist zealot who set about cleansing his new domain by massacring Serbs, gypsies and anyone else who did not conform to his own notions of what constituted ethnic Croatian purity. All these new arrangements used the minimum of German manpower. The reason for this economy became clear in July when the Germans launched operation Barbarossa, the invasion of the Soviet Union.

The country's history had been long, colourful - mostly blood red - and complicated.* One constant was the recurrent urge of most South Slavs either to rise violently against foreign occupiers of their country or to fight equally fiercely against their domestic neighbours. Special Operations Executive, the British organisation designed to foster guerrilla uprisings in Nazi dominated Europe, was at first ignorant of what was happening in Yugoslavia but was fairly confident that, given the precedents,

---

* *Events in the 1990's illustrate the constancy of the inherited trend.*

resistance to the Axis occupiers would soon be under way. This belief was confirmed in August 1941. The Royal Navy radio monitoring station at Portishead on the Bristol Channel intercepted the first of a sporadic series of weak signals from a set transmitting in the Balkans. The sender's claim, soon authenticated, that they were guerrillas operating under the command of Colonel Draza Mihailovic, who had been Chief of the Operations Division of the Yugoslav General Staff at the time of the invasion, led to the first post-invasion British intervention in war-time Yugoslavia.

It was on a small scale. Captain D T Hudson, a mining engineer who had worked in Serbia and who was fluent in Serbo-Croat, landed by submarine in the Gulf of Kotor on 20th September 1941. With him were two Royal Yugoslavia Air Force officers and a radio operator. Hudson's brief was exploratory. He was to contact, investigate and report on all resistance elements, regardless of their nationality, religion or political belief. His daily life was arduous, his communications tenuous but he passed back to S.O.E. Cairo some unexpected information. Mihailovic, a regular officer in the Royal Yugoslav army, was loyal to his king and to the general ethos of the old kingdom of Yugoslavia. But his was not the only guerrilla force in the field. A major influence in the Yugoslav resistance was provided by the previously clandestine Communist Party, now highly active under the leadership of a man whose *nom de guerre* was Tito, real name Josip Broz. The enthusiasm of both these resistance groups to get to grips with the Germans, Italians and the rest of them, was to a large extent offset by their bloodthirsty detestation of one another. A civil war between Mihailovic's Chetniks and Tito's Partisans was soon in full swing. It continued throughout the rest of the war years. To this internal conflict between the Chetniks and the Partisans was added their shared abhorrence of the excesses of Pavelic's Ustachi in Croatia and the ferocity with which they countered it. Further bloodletting was generated by extensive opportunist banditry and by exploitation of the chaos to settle old hereditary scores. For neither the first nor the last time the South Slavs were in a condition of internal lethal volatility.

The initial British interest in these murderous shenanigans had been an attempt to find out what was happening in the largest country in the Balkans, with a view to determining who was resisting the occupiers effectively and how the resistance could be nourished. A series of British missions were parachuted in by S.O.E. Cairo. In the early days these went exclusively to the Chetniks. The mission reports were discouraging. Mihailovic, they said, was less concerned with fighting Germans and Italians than he was in disposing of his mortal enemies, the Partisans. Mihailovic's Chetniks, presumably acting in accord with the ancient devious Balkan practice of lulling one's foe into complacency and then striking at the right moment, were openly collaborating with the Germans and the Italians. It was also evident, through intercepted Ultra German wireless signals, that in parts of Yugoslavia outside of Mihailovic's control, notably in Croatia and Bosnia, the Partisans were fighting hard against large numbers of German troops.

In 1943 S.O.E. parachuted in a mission led by Captain Bill Deakin to the Partisans. It landed in a major battle in Montenegro and made the first contact with Tito in the two years since Hudson had first met him. Deakin's reports confirmed to S.O.E. Cairo that the Partisans were an impressively organised fighting body, who, their diversions against the Chetniks aside, were staunchly committed to the destruction of all things German. The British reaction to these findings was to parachute weapons, ammunition and medical supplies, along with further British liaison teams to identifiable Partisan formations. The Chetniks were similarly provided by enhanced drops to them. But it became clear that the convoluted Balkan politics of the thing were eroding any serious attempt by Mihailovic's people to fight the Germans. The period of joint supply to both Partisans and Chetniks came to an end. The Chetniks were abandoned in early 1944. All British support thereafter went to the Partisans.

In September, 1943, the Italians changed sides. Italian troops had since the time of the invasion in 1941, been in control of the Dalmatian coast. They were now bewildered by the officially ordained shift in their loyalties. They did their best to fight off the Germans who came in to dispossess them. The German reaction to the Italian surrender was predictably swift, hard and efficient. They cleaned up the Italians. But one measure they had to postpone was the clearing of the Dalmatian islands in the Adriatic.

The islands are the residual-limestone peaks of a mountain range inundated by the sea through some bygone geological disturbance. They have all the characteristics of their origin: steep hillsides, lots of rocks, sparse tillage and pasture. They provided a living for a hardy breed of fishermen and hill farmers, who harvested fish, vegetables, sheep, goats, grapes and olives. By nature and inheritance the islanders did not take kindly to aggressive interference by strangers. They were, in late 1943, almost solid in their adherence to the Partisans. Communism may have appealed to some of them. Ferocious independence of spirit inspired most. When the Germans set about the takeover of the islands, the islanders put up a fierce resistance, seemingly doomed in the long term to failure.

They were not the first European people who found themselves unable to withstand the pressures of German military muscle supported by air power. By the end of 1943, the Germans had taken all the islands but one: the westernmost one, Vis. On Vis were assembled two weak brigades of Partisans, armed, clothed, and equipped with loot from enemies they had killed. As things stood, these Partisans were in no position to resist for any length of time a determined German attempt to take the island.

Things did not stand. They were transformed by the consequence of the foresight of Brigadier Fitzroy Maclean, the Commander of the British Military Mission to Marshal Tito's headquarters. In the previous September the British 8th Army had landed on the mainland of Italy and had advanced northwards up the Italian east coast. The Dalmatian islands were now in easy reach of vessels of the Royal Navy and of aircraft of the Royal Air Force. Maclean's view was that the Partisans would be helped immeasurably if an offshore base could be secured and held by a joint Partisan and British garrison. What he wanted was an island which would be stoutly defended, would be a stronghold from which amphibious raiding parties could harry the coast and the German held islands, would be a rallying point for the Island Partisans and would be a distributing centre for their supply. Ideally it would have a defensible harbour for the use of R.N. coastal forces who could then more easily get in among German coastal shipping. And, as a unlikely bonus it would accommodate an airstrip from which RAF fighters would be able to penetrate more deeply and for longer periods, over the mainland in support of Partisan operations.

Maclean had visited Vis in the autumn and had found that it met all these desiderata. It had two small fishing ports: Komiza on its west coast and Vis town on the north east. An area of flat land, at the time under olives and vines, lay in the centre of the island. An RAF officer, who accompanied Maclean to Vis on a later visit, was satisfied that this small plain had the makings of an airfield.

Maclean then set about the difficult job of persuading senior commanders in Italy and cabinet ministers in London, that an infantry brigade should be furnished to provide the island garrison. He had little luck. All infantry brigades were already bespoke for continuing operations in Italy, from which several British divisions had been withdrawn to the United Kingdom for planned use in the forthcoming invasion of Normandy. As the situation in the islands deteriorated Maclean became more concerned than ever about his hopes of getting British troops committed to Vis.

It was a chance social contact that allowed his ambition to be fulfilled. A personal friend of his was Major Randolph Churchill, the Prime Minister's son, who had been with the Commandos at the Salerno landings. Maclean, while in Italy, met Randolph Churchill who took him to a New Year's Eve party given by the Commando Brigade headquarters in Molfetta. Maclean, in the course of this party, explained his preoccupations to Brigadier Tom Churchill. Maps were studied and minds made up. Tom Churchill said that he thought island operations met ideally the outlook and training of his commandos and that he would be delighted to commit as many as he could so long as Maclean's proposal was approved by the Theatre Commander, Field-Marshal Alexander.

Maclean went one further. The Field Marshal endorsed his recommendations and took him to Marakeesh in Morocco where the Prime Minister was recuperating from an attack of pneumonia. The Prime Minister also gave his endorsement. In early January 1944, within ten days of the New Year's Eve party, Lieutenant Colonel Jack Churchill with two hundred men of No 2 Commando landed on Vis. With them were about one hundred men from the United States Special Operations Group, men of Yugoslav and Greek extraction who worked directly to the Office of Strategic Services in Washington.

No 2 Commando had lost heavily at Salerno and the replacements were still undergoing intensive training in Italy. Once they were up to standard they too went to Vis and brought the unit up to full strength. 43's arrival at the end of February doubled the island's garrison. Brigadier Tom Churchill and his advanced brigade headquarters soon assumed command of all British troops on the island. These now numbered No 2 and 43 Commandos, a battery of Bofors light anti-aircraft guns and a troop of the Raiding Support Regiment, equipped with Browning heavy machine guns. The R.S.R. had been formed in the Middle East by parachute-trained volunteers and was designed to supply heavy weapon support to Balkan Guerrilla operations. From that time onwards there was no real threat to the safety of the island of Vis. Its main function became as a base for aggressive raiding operations.

It is unlikely that anyone in 43 had ever heard of Vis before they were actually told that that was where they were going. The island had, in fact, a small but honourable place in British naval history. During the Napoleonic wars a squadron of British ships, with the standard complement of marines aboard, was based on Vis from which it harried the naval and land forces of the French and their associates in and off Dalmatia. Some relics of the stay of Captain William Hoste and his men still existed in 1944. Two forts protecting Vis harbour were still known as Fort George and Fort William. There was a little, overgrown British Naval cemetery also in Vis town in which lay the graves of those of Hoste's force who were not buried at sea. After an interval of more than 130 years the cemetery was once more to be used for British Military and Naval fatal casualties.

# CHAPTER SEVEN

# SOLTA, HVAR AND SHENNANIGANS AT SEA

In the late February days, 43 found Vis to be physically bleak and climatically inhospitable. Temperatures were low. Winds were high. There were two of them. The *Bura* blew from the North, the *Jugo* from the South. They brought with them torrential rain, and churned up the surrounding seas into a creamy, frothy, maelstrom. The island itself was about eighteen miles long and eight miles wide. Its limestone hills rose craggily to its highest point, Mount Hum (1926 feet). The few roads were narrow, stony, and winding. The indigenous inhabitants were simple, tough, hospitable people who fished the surrounding waters from schooners, cultivated olives and vines and fruit trees, made wine, and distilled *Rakija*, a plum brandy of sinister powerfulness. The nearest thing on the island to an industrial enterprise was the Komiza anchovy canning factory. Upon these isolated people, who for generations had experienced not much more than the natural cycle of procreation, birth and death was suddenly superimposed a military and politically active Partisan presence which proclaimed an ardent communism and a large number of British troops with a cynical view of politics but an urge to get on with the war. The islanders rose to the occasion magnificently.

Simonds deployed 43 Commando with care. Its primary role, like that of all the other troops in the island, was defensive. Troop positions were sited, singly or in pairs, where they could best counter any German seaborne or airborne attack. Existing accommodation in these localities was non-existent. The marines lived in tents or in improvised shelters. The years of training in 2RM and in the early days of 43 Commando had polished their adaptability, and they were skilled in making themselves comfortable in unpromising circumstances. They did so.

If the terrain and the late winter weather were uncompromisingly harsh, the welcome provided by both the islanders and the two Partisan brigades was not. They liked the idea of evidently well-intentioned, well-trained, and well-equipped foreigners coming to their assistance at a time when their ability to run their own affairs was being violently hamstrung. Communist rhetoric from the Partisan leadership was accordingly muted. Suspicious Marxist dogmatism, later on in the campaign to become a severe irritant, was not in the early days an issue.

The Partisan leadership were eager to co-operate and did all in their power to help and encourage the raiding activities of the British force. Whether they were technically qualified to provide a genuinely effective co-operation had still to be tested. There were the handicaps of differing military doctrines and a shortage of interpreters to frame the views of one side in a manner clearly intelligible to the other. But making allowances for these inevitable disabilities, there was no reason to believe that relations between the two allies would not prosper.

The rank and file of the Partisans were objects of mixed marine admiration and censoriousness. In their miscellany of captured weapons, and clothing of mixed German military, Italian military, and civilian provenance they were at first appearance a ragged crew. But they were hardy in the extreme, marched hard, fast, and long, sang beautifully harmonious Slav songs, and were generous with what few resources they had. The censoriousness was directed at their easy-going ways in the use of fire arms and at their treatment of prisoners. The customary challenge of *Stoj* from a Partisan sentry was as often as not accompanied by the instantaneous firing of his gun or was sometimes preceeded by it. With prisoners they were ruthless. Large numbers were butchered, and the point was soon reached at which Brigadier Tom Churchill recommended to Allied Forces Headquarters at Caserta in Italy that unless the Partisan High Command introduced measures approximating to those that conformed to the Geneva Conventions, he should be authorised to abandon any attempt at joint Partisan-Commando operations.

Everyday life on Vis for the marines was frugal. There was a shortage of most sorts of food. The rations brought in from Italy were on a scale that was less nutritious than was sensible. Wine was plentiful. Sex was more or less unobtainable. The necessarily puritanical Partisan code, enforced mercilessly because in mixed units of men and women physical or emotional attachments could only prejudice the safety of the whole, ruled that sexual relations were in abeyance for the duration. The military crime of pregnancy was a capital offence. Few Marines were prepared to put potential partners at risk.

The first components of 43 Commando to see action in the Dalmatian islands was the Vickers Machine Gun Section of 'F' troop, the Heavy Weapons Troop. They accompanied Colonel Jack Churchill and No 2 Commando on the first large scale excursion in the campaign, to the island of Solta. Jack Churchill had with him the whole of 2 Commando, 17 officers and 138 other ranks of the United States Combat Group, three captured Italian 47-mm guns, two of them manned by a Light Anti-Aircraft regiment, Royal Artillery, and one by No 2 Commando. The Churchill command group included the 75 year old retired Rear Admiral Sir Walter Cowan still as on Ornito with his green beret and shepherd's crook, quietly enjoying the possibility of imminent death in battle.

In practice the 43 Commando machine guns took no part in the fight. They were not needed. A combination of bluff, intimidatory broadcasting over a loud hailer by Jack Churchill, and the intervention of 36 Kittyhawk fighter bombers of the RAF brought about a rapid collapse in the morale of the German garrison of the town of Grohote. They, the entire German strength on the island, surrendered. They had had a few killed but one captive German officer, 97 captive German rank and file and 6 captive Croat policemen were duly brought back to Vis on 18th March.

## SOLTA, HVAR AND SHENNANIGANS AT SEA

A little time after the Solta operation the whole of 43 Commando became embroiled in a complicated series of events upon Hvar, chosen by Tom Churchill and his planners as the next objective for a major attack. The top planners appointed were Colonel Bonzo Simonds of 43 Commando and Major Ted Fynn, the second-in-command of No 2 Commando. When concentrating upon planning, a full-time job which involved the making of detailed arrangements and the co-ordination of timings with Commander Morgan Giles's naval headquarters and with Partisan commanders, Simonds handed over 43 Commando to his second-in-command, Major Neil Munro, a young South African. Similar arrangements were made on operations when the force landed was accompanied by a large number of Partisan allies and British supporting arms. Simonds acted as Force Commander. Munro ran the Commando.

Hvar is a long, thin island with its length running from east to west, and its thinness from north to south. It has a slightly bulbous western end, where the coast breaks up into a series of creeks, bays and inlets. The ground is hilly and rocky. On the north shore, about one-third of the way from the western tip of the island, is the small port of Jelsa. It held a German garrison of a size about which there were conflicting Partisan estimates. The highest figure on offer was 450, the lowest 120. As matters turned out, the best guess seemed to be about 200. The orders to 43 Commando were to destroy the German garrison of Jelsa.

An unusually large reconnaissance party left Vis harbour aboard a Partisan schooner at dusk on 12 March. Neil Munro, who was to command in the assault, took with him a total of five officers, one from each of the fighting troops, Colour-Sergeant McCartney of the Heavy Weapons Troop, Lieutenant Roberts, a naval officer whose job was to assess the merits for landing purposes of two alternative beaches, two Partisan interpreters and two Partisan guides. The journey was made on a calm sea in brilliant moonlight. The schooner reached its destination and anchored offshore. The party was ferried in in dinghies, made a rock landing and climbed, leaving Roberts in the schooner to go off to inspect his two beaches.

After a night at Partisan headquarters in a very large cave, Munro's team split into groups and went to look at the Germans. The viewers were protected by a screen of Partisan lookouts, to give warning of any attempted German interference. This co-operative Partisan contribution was to some extent cancelled out by the insouciance with which the Partisan commander led the entire party over a skyline, exposing them to the gaze of anyone in Jelsa who chanced to be looking in their direction. At least one alert German was.

An investigative German patrol fell in. A head count by the visitors put it at sixty-six men. In mid-afternoon the patrol set out towards the mountains where Munro's people were. There had, however, been ample time for everyone to make a thorough study of what he was looking for. There was a clear view of German defensive positions, billets and administrative buildings in Jelsa, and of about 200 German soldiers, who could be heard as well as seen 'strutting about the town'.* Approach

---

\* Whether they really strutted, or just walked about like anyone else, is, in the light of hindsight, open to question. In the mythology of the times, German soldiers moved themselves on foot by strutting.

routes for the attack were noted. All work completed, the tourists, less Captain John Blake and Colour-Sergeant McCartney, who went for one last look at something of particular interest to them, moved down to Blue beach, the second of the two under examination by Roberts. There the Partisans supplied them with an excellent meal, washed down with *vino*. The German patrol closed in on the hills overlooking the beach. The Partisan sentries stood to. There was concern about what had happened to the absent Blake and McCartney. Shortly before midnight the schooner reappeared and put in to the beach. Blake and McCartney were already aboard. The German patrol had still done nothing offensive but the Partisans wasted no time. The party were hustled into the schooner and were back in Vis by 3 a.m.

Afterwards, Neil Munro considered that he had taken too many people with him. With a few exceptions, future 43 Commando reconnaissance parties were restricted to two or three men. One of these small patrols, of Lieutenant Gregory, a wireless operator and two marines, embarked at Vis in a schooner bound for Hvar on the night of 20th March. Fellow passengers in the schooner were Lieutenant Odendaal and a sub-section of a dozen NCOs and marines. Their destination was a tiny island to the south of Hvar named Scedro, upon which, it was thought, there might be a German observation post with a radio. If so, Odendaal was to dispose of it.

Gregory was dropped off on Hvar, where he was met by Partisans. Odendaal landed on Scedro, searched it, found no hostile wireless station, and was hospitably received by the inhabitants (total population, twenty-eight). Some of the Scedro men visited Hvar twice daily, and brought back interesting reports to Odendaal, who wirelessed them to Vis. Gregory, similarly well served with information on Hvar, was also reporting to Vis. If the information were true, and both Odendaal and Gregory were getting identical accounts, the Germans had removed all their Hvar garrisons with the exception of the one at Jelsa, which they intended to evacuate in turn on the night of 22nd March.

Lieutenant Frost, 43's Intelligence Officer, was sent urgently to Hvar from Vis in 'a very small craft' to get more elaboration of this news than Gregory could send in coded wireless messages. Frost brought with him an American radio and its crew from the US Operations Group, whose sets were infinitely better than anything the British had yet produced. After a fifteen-minute, very informative briefing by Gregory, Frost headed back to Vis at 2.15 a.m. on the 22nd. A high sea had risen, visibility deteriorated, and the very small craft missed Vis altogether. But at 6.15 a.m. Vis was found again, along with two German Messerschmitt 109 fighters that flew close overhead but made no passes. Frost landed in Vis harbour soon after eight o'clock.

Tom Churchill called a conference at ten. The objective of the Hvar operation was changed from the destruction of the garrison of Jelsa *in situ*, to the destruction of the garrison of Jelsa before it could leave the island of Hvar. The job was to be done by 43 Commando, 280 strong, working in collaboration with 400 Partisans of two battalions of 1st Dalmatian Brigade. A bombing attack on Jelsa by RAF aircraft based on the Italian mainland was part of the plan. Simonds was overall commander of the force.

Munro led the Commando. Captain Bogdan, a well-liked figure with a fierce moustache, commanded the two battalions of Partisans. It was the first large-scale joint British/Partisan operation.

The troops embarked in Vis harbour in the early afternoon, the Commando in LCI 260, the Partisans in five schooners. The navy provided an MTB escort and motor mine-sweepers, who picked up at least one mine in the Korcula Channel, south of Scedro. The marines were landed dryshod at an excellent beach at Coromin Dolac, earlier checked by Roberts, on the south coast of the island. The five Partisan schooners arrived at 8 p.m., two-and-a-half hours after the LCI.

Gregory and Odendaal were waiting on the beach when the LCI touched down. Odendaal had brought his subsection over from Scedro in four rowing boats, rowed by the helpful islanders. The latest word about Jelsa was that the Germans planned to move out at 10 p.m. The RAF bombing raid had gone in during the afternoon, and by all accounts had done no good to German morale. Simonds ordered the Commando to press on with all speed to surround the town and to prevent German embarkation. The Heavy Weapons Troop were to occupy a spur overlooking the harbour. The Partisans were to go to a position in the hills commanding the town, there to stay in reserve until matters became clearer at dawn.

The force marched across the spine of the island, 1500 feet high, tramping amid the rocks, weapons at the point of balance on shoulders, ammunition, food and water in pouches and water bottles slung from waist belts, spare kit and mess tins in packs on their backs. They were in their positions surrounding Jelsa by 10 p.m. Nothing much seemed to be happening in the town or harbour. Things started to happen on the hill tracks outside the town about half an hour later: the Germans were trying, not to evacuate by sea, but to break out by land.

About 150 of them, accompanied by a mule train, blundered in the dark into Commando Headquarters and 'A' Troop, commanded by Captain Jock Hudspith. There was a short, noisy, confused melee. When it eased the German column had split into two groups, one clattering away to the south-east, the other to the south-west. They left with Hudspith five dead, four prisoners and the mule train. The train was loaded with wireless equipment, ammunition, and personal baggage.

The German south-east party, about a hundred of them, next ran into the Partisans on the high ground at Juraj. There was another melee, at the end of which ten more Germans were dead and thirty more had been captured. The Partisans lost four killed and had fifteen wounded in this fight. The remaining Germans made back towards Jelsa again, and once more found themselves among Hudspith and 'A' Troop, who killed a further six and took two more prisoner. Two marines were wounded in this second clash. The Germans, in small groups, broke north. The rest of the night was passed in the reshuffling of the various troops of the Commando to block tracks on likely German escape routes. The 3-inch mortars, on their spur above the harbour, banged away at German movement seen in the town near the church. Three more dead Germans were found there the next day.

By morning the contest had become something of a hunt. One of the Partisan battalions was sent to sweep the western end of the island. One was told to stay in reserve. Meanwhile 43 Commando searched eastwards and made contact several times with dispersed bands of opponents who further split themselves up and went into hiding in the woods. The mortars caught one larger than average group in the open on a track near the north coast. A concentrated shoot killed fifteen of them. Ten others surrendered to the Commando, and another twenty, chased by the Commando, surrendered to the Partisans. At four o'clock in the afternoon the hunt was called off. The Commando reassembled at the beach. The Partisans stayed on Hvar. After a six-hour passage with a high sea running, 43 disembarked at Vis harbour at five o'clock on a bleak, wild morning.

Simonds added up the balance sheet. No. 43 Commando had three wounded and two missing. The Partisans had four killed and fourteen wounded. The bodies of fifty German dead had been counted, and there might have been some uncounted ones. Eighty German prisoners had been taken. So had seventeen Italians, who were not included in the count because 'they did not fight'. Simonds, like every other British soldier who had seen it at first had, was full of praise for Partisan fighting spirit. Partisan assaults during the night action had been determined. A woman Partisan had been killed in one of these attacks, an event still sufficiently strange and impressive to British troops to be recorded in Simonds's official report.

On the mechanics of co-ordinating operations between British and Partisan forces he was cautiously sceptical: 'They (the Partisans) were a little difficult to control. After landing, they were with difficulty stopped from going down into the Jelsa-Stari Grad area, where they would have got involved in a shooting match with the Commando. As it was, there was a certain amount of firing on their part against British troops. The Partisans were too ready to believe information received from civilian sources....In one case, a Commando Troop was reported as German.' The cost to the Germans of the Solta and Hvar raids had been high. The British and American forces on Vis, already formidable, were to become stronger still.

During the autumn of 1943, while the Germans were forcing their way down the Peljesac peninsula, and were making their first tentative attempts on the islands, the Royal Navy's contribution to future operations in the eastern Adriatic was being shaped in the south-eastern Italian port of Brindisi. Two flotillas of mixed motor torpedo boats and motor gun boats were allocated the task of helping the Partisans by landing arms and ammunition in the Dalmatian islands, of patrolling the channels between the islands by night to break up German attempts at landings, and to disrupt German inter-island sea traffic. Lieutenant-Commander Morgan Giles was in overall command of the naval force. It was fast and manoeuvrable, bore a formidable armament and was led and manned by men of spirit.

The MTBs and the MGBs were of similar basic design, seventy feet from stem to stern, powered by three engines; the MGBs of twenty-one knots. Each boat was crewed by three officers and twenty-seven ratings. The MGBs, were fitted with quick-firing pom-pom guns forrard, a 6-pounder aft, and twin Vickers machine-guns on either side of the bridge. The Vickers were backed by 20-mm Oerlikons. Depth charges were carried aft.

In their earlier trips to the islands the commanding officers of these craft quickly identified two ways of enhancing their operations. The first was to take a plentiful supply of spare fuel, carried in forty-gallon drums. The second was to make use of simply designed camouflage netting. Coastal Forces interceptions were almost invariably undertaken by night. By day, as was found by experiment and investigation, conditions were perfect for the mooring of the craft in concealment at any one of a large range of suitable places among a large choice of islands. The Mediterranean is tideless. There were innumerable small creeks with rocky steep-to shores. A craft moored close to the rocks, its outlines disguised by the spread of a cloth-mesh net, painted to match the greys and browns of the rocks and fastened asymmetrically to bamboo outriggers, was indistinguishable from its background at 500 yards in broad daylight. From these lying-up berthings, observers could disembark, climb convenient hills and, if in luck, note German sea movements for attention after nightfall.

Many of these night patrols were uneventful and routine, with no contact made. Their cumulative effect was the establishment of British Naval superiority approaching dominance in Dalmatian waters. The Yugoslav Navy museum in Split lists the tally of RN Coastal Forces successes for 1943-4 as one German destroyer, *Neouwa*, and eighty-four other miscellaneous craft sunk, twenty-four captured and thirteen damaged. The capturing of boats required boarding parties. The navy had earlier provided their own, but in action every man on an MTB or an MGB had essential functions to perform, and it would clearly be helpful if the boats could carry boarding parties additional to their crews. With the warm endorsement of Lieutenant-Commander Morgan Giles, the Senior Naval Officer, Vis, the job was taken on by the Commandos, almost from the moment of No 2 Commando's arrival. 43, when it arrived, did its own share of licensed piracy.

An essential component of the boarding pattern was the depth of the Adriatic close in to the shore of the islands and to that of the rocky capes and bays of the mainland. It was possible for MGBs and MTBs to lie silent and in concealment a few yards offshore. The most productive tactic was to approach selected prey suddenly and at speed from astern, and then board.

MTB 651 (Lieutenant Horlock, RNVR) and MGB 647 (Lieutenant Mountstephens) slipped from Komiza on the night of 2 April. The Senior Officer, Lieutenant-Commander T G Fuller, one of several Canadians who were outstanding in Coastal Forces actions in Dalmatia, was embarked in Horlock's MTB. After some fruitless prowling along the shore of Mljet, they sighted a small schooner. She was boarded, captured and taken in tow within fourteen minutes. Booty taken included explosives, land mines, a jack hammer drill, cigarettes, cigars and eight bags of delayed Christmas mail for the German garrison of Korcula. There were four German prisoners.

On the next night the same two craft took two more schooners, and their crews and cargo, near Prsnjak island. One carried a deck cargo of 20-mm cannons. Each had a defensive armament, captured unused, of four machine guns and boxes of stick grenades.

Two nights later MTB 651, this time in company with MGB 661 (Lieutenant Cole, RNVR) towed home a schooner laden with wheat, boarded, again without resistance, off Murter island. Fuller was out again with MGBs 661 and 647 on the night of 6/7 April. This time he had with him a Partisan interpreter and a ten-man Commando party. After some of the customary conversation with fishing boats - one fisherman who had previously run a fish shop in Los Angeles was given a present of a tin of soya link sausages - a 400-ton schooner came into view. Both boats closed fast to within 150 yards and trained their guns on it. The Partisan made sinister threats over the loud-hailer about instant torpedoing and throat-cutting unless her crew surrendered. Cole brought his MGB alongside, using as a fender the schooner's dinghy in its davits at the rail. The Commando boarding party swarmed over the rail in the manner of the old-time Spanish Main. The schooner's crew made no attempt to use their 20-mm Bredas or their light machine-gun. The schooner was towed back to Komiza by MGB 647, carefully negotiating a minefield on the way. The rations of the garrison of Vis, Partisan and British, were supplemented by 125 tons of butter, flour, barrels of sauerkraut, and goulash.

On the 11th, Fuller, in MGB 647, accompanied by MGB 661, and with Commando boarding parties again embarked in both, lay twenty yards offshore in Kosivina Cove, Murter island. At 11pm the moon rose and gave a visibility of fifteen miles. There was no phosphorescence. It was an ideal night for a cutting-out action. This began shortly after two o'clock in the morning, when a north-bound convoy of three German I-lighters, an Italian assault craft, two small schooners and a motor launch came slowly into view. The most heavily armed of the I-lighters was towing the assault craft and one of the schooners. The two MGBs closed in at speed, blaring threats in Italian over their loud-hailers of immediate mass sinkings if there were any resistance.

The threats were ignored. The centre I-lighter opened a heavy fire when the MGBs were thirty yards away. A violent few minutes followed. An I-lighter hit by 6-pounder fire from each of the MGBs, rammed the Italian assault craft. The schooner which had been on tow was attached to the assault craft's bows, and caught the concentrated fire power of an MGB firing at about ten yards' range. The MGBs cut the German line, swung hard-a-port and circled the tail-end of the convoy. The convoy ceased fire. Two of the I-lighters had already sunk. MGB 661 went alongside the third, prior to boarding, but the Commando boarding party commanded by Lieutenant Desmond Clark, had been deafened by the gunfire, and did not hear the order to board and were positioned on the wrong side of the MGB. The first lieutenant of 661 found himself alone on the I-lighter, whose commander tried to shear off. The first lieutenant shot him. Then 661 put another short burst into the I-lighter, and its surviving crew surrendered. It sank a few minutes later. 43's boarding party boarded and took control of the schooners.

The MGBs returned to Komiza with the motor launch and the two schooners in tow, all heavily shot about, and with thirty-five prisoners, assorted tool kits, several crates of German and British uniforms, and personal possessions packed for travel.

The Germans among the prisoners all spoke excellent English. They were from a sabotage unit and had been on their way home on leave.

MGB 661, with Fuller again aboard, and in company with MGB 646 (Lieutenant Knight-Lacklan, RNVR), returned to Murter island three nights later. Their first task was to land a Commando reconnaissance party. These were put ashore without incident, and the two boats lay close inshore, awaiting passing German traffic. A tug towing a tanker, which in turn was towing a lighter, appeared shortly before midnight. The tug was very close to the tanker, and their unified silhouette seemed to be that of an elderly destroyer. Fuller took no chances. He left out the loud-hailer announcements, and opened fire from both boats when the convoy was within range. Nothing came back at him, and he realised that he had been mistaken. He stopped after two minutes. All three enemy vessels were boarded, in the hope of a further delivery of prizes to Komiza.

The hope was largely frustrated. The tug was by now incapable of manoeuvre, and the tanker was holed so badly that she was on the verge of sinking. MGB 646 towed the lighter and its cargo of hay back to Vis. MGB 661 stayed behind to sink the other two. The tug went down without difficulty. The tanker remained afloat after it had been further riddled by repetitive shelling and a boarding party had tried to blow a hole in her bottom with a depth charge. So 661 fired the last of her ammunition into the hulk, assumed that it would not last, and hastened back to Komiza, bearing the tug's guns and everything else of use that had been stripped from its deck.

An Admiralty assessment of the time had this to say: 'It would be difficult to find in any theatre an area better adapted to Coastal Forces than the Dalmatian coast, and the successes of the Flotillas which have operated there show that no opportunity of action is missed.' 43 could reasonably nod modestly towards its share in the earning of this accolade.

# CHAPTER EIGHT

# LIFE ON VIS AND ROUTINE ACTIVITIES

Forty-Three's arrival on Vis had doubled the strength of the British garrison. A precariously held island outpost had been transfigured into an advanced springboard for aggressive action. Shortly afterwards, Allied staffs in Italy examined the implications for the Italian campaign of diversionary Partisan operations in Yugoslavia, recognised them as beneficial, and decided that an enhanced allocation of resources would make a sound military investment. One of the main beneficiaries was Vis.

An infantry battalion, initially the Queens, later the Highland Light Infantry, was sent to take over responsibility for island defence. No 111 Field Regiment, Royal Artillery, with twenty-four 25 pounder guns, arrived also for island defence, soon to provide artillery support on major raids. There were further anti-aircraft guns, RAF fighters for the airstrip, the strengthening of the Raiding Support Regiment, sappers, an Ordnance Corps detachment. The Partisans were equipped with British uniforms and British weapons. Landing craft of most types were freely available. During the early spring months of 1944 the Vis potential changed out of recognition.

Nightfall and spring arrive abruptly in the Mediterranean. With spring came beauty, never entirely obscured by the winter, but now abundant and more evident to the eye. The rain diminished. The wild wind abated. Wild flowers - cyclamen, gentians, purple orchids blossomed lavishly on grey-white hillsides. The hills rose craggily to their highest point, Mount Hum. From almost anywhere on the island there were vistas of twinkling blue-green sea, framed in the irregularities of limestone cliff. To the east could be seen a lovely panorama, the sunlit sea studded by the other islands, Hvar, Solta and the looming heights of Brac, white when the light was at its brightest, but after dawn and before dusk a pattern of shifting mauves and blues and ochres. Behind them all on the mainland, stood the towering backdrop of the Dinaric Alps, gleaming with snow in winter and early spring, still gleaming in summer because the reflections from the jagged white limestone mountains gave the illusion of snow. Spring and summer skies were almost unfailingly blue. The air was pure, scented as the days grew hotter by wild thyme.

Against this background of beauty 43 operated for six months. The Partisans' official island grapevine information collections provided an excellent intelligence service. It was supplemented by the constant dispatch, usually by 'Jugboat', Partisan schooners, of reconnaissance patrols of German-occupied islands. The chief purpose of these little expeditions was, of course, the close observation of German dispositions, but all sorts of ancillary information that might be of future use was logged in too: the suitability of coves for the beaching of LCIs; the state of tracks; the location of wells; the nature of civilian sympathies. Support on the islands for the Partisans was extensive, but not unanimous. Some islands were solidly pro-Partisan. On others there was a variable number with loyalties to the Ustashi or to the Chetniks, or who wished a plague upon all householders. The intricacies of internal Yugoslav strife were beyond the understanding or interest of most British soldiers. The prevalent simplification was that if you were allied to the Partisans then it followed that the Partisans' enemies were yours too. This left out some convoluted ideological intervening levels but it made practical sense. A pro-British Chetnik backer, say, might not want to betray a British recce party to the Germans, but if he could he would certainly tell all about Partisan visitors, with whom the British were inextricably mixed. The potential consequences were the same for both Partisan and British.

These extracts from the patrol reports of spring 1944 give the flavour of what life was like on enemy held islands and of the type of information that was sought. Captain R G Schooley and Lieutenant Abbott, travelled to Hvar: 13th April: 2300 hrs. Arrived beach below Zarac. Met by Americans.....The Germans have mortars at Borovik with Observation Post on the NE slopes of Hum. There is constant patrolling on this line. The bulk of the German forces....is about 800....14 April: On our return to Sveta Vedelia we learned that a German patrol had passed through our OP at about 1100 hrs, and proceeded by the track to Vrishir, and had confiscated furniture and livestock there.....15 April:....we were able to observe a long stretch of the road Selca-Brusje. At 1500 hrs we heard the sound of MT (motor transport), and a few moments later a 3-ton open truck came round the corner and stopped....About 10 Germans jumped off the truck carrying a light machine gun, and deployed on the high ground left of the road. Fire was opened at us from a range of 200-250 yards....we succeeded in moving to another position about 500 yards SE of Grablje....On our return to Zarac we learned that the Germans had entered Grablje on foot, and were drinking heavily and confiscating fowl. *Remarks:* We noticed that the Germans were very slow in getting in to action, and appeared erratic and indiscriminate with their fire.

On 27 April Captain J P Blake and Lieutenant D B Clark arrived on Uljan (an island far to the north, well beyond the normal operational radius of the Vis force):

Enemy positions: Town of Preko; Germans, 3 officers and fifty men. Ustashi, 1 officer and thirty men. Weapons: 6 machine guns, no mortars. Positions: They had bunkers with two single strand wire fences around their whole position. The nearest fence was approximately 50 yards from the German bunkers. Mines between the fences. Main exits from the German occupied parts of the town had wire barricades, which were drawn across at night, or during alarms....Some nights 14 men patrols either went to Kali or Lukoran....Hill Post 942992 (the figures are a grid map reference): All German. 1 officer and 50 men. 4 machine guns. 4x81 mm mortars.

2x2 inch mortars. Bunkers with single strand wire fence with 'S' mines. Had cleared field of fire on top of hill...

Just as there had been on the outward voyage, there was much hitch-hiking between islands on the way home. Blake and Clark finally reached Vis on 3rd May, in a Partisan ship bringing back wounded from central Bosnia.

If a major operation was planned, gunners might join the reconnaisance team, in search of gunlines for their own artillery, but most expeditions were smaller, concentrating on German gun positions, wire entanglements and minefields. There were many of these schooner trips, but only a very small proportion of them led to raids.

# CHAPTER NINE

# MLJET

The strength of the forces by now gathered on Vis was displayed on 22nd May 1944 on the island of Mljet. This was the scene of Operation Foothound, by common consent of those who took part in it the most exhausting test of endurance of all the British Commando operations mounted in wartime Yugoslavia. 'It was probably the most concentrated fatigue ever experienced by the Commando,' wrote Major Neil Munro in his report.

The essence of the difficulty was that too much was attempted over too hard country in too short a time. Brigadier Tom Churchill, who led it, described the Mljet operation as, simply, a failure. The lie of the land aside, there was an unusual defect in the quality of the Partisan guides provided. On the other islands they had seldom fallen below the level of the superb. They knew every track, mapped and unmapped, every short cut, every obstacle, every inch. On Mljet they got lost.

The force that embarked in six LCIs in the Vis ports on 21st May was the largest British and American expedition that had yet set out from the island for battle. Tom Churchill brought with him his Brigade Headquarters, the whole of No 43 Commando, the whole of No 2 Commando, a troop of the newly arrived No 40 Royal Marine Commando, a company of the Highland Light Infantry, nominally island garrison troops but with a flexible and co-operative colonel, the whole of the United States Special Operations Group, and the four 75-mm pack howitzers of No 11 Troop of the Raiding Support Regiment. The six LCIs had a naval escort of motor gun boats. Support from Spitfires, carrying bombs, was on call. The object of the raid was to destroy the German garrison, estimated to number between 200 and 250 men, distributed among four wired and mined strongpoints on hilltops, two of which were about 1500 feet high, and two about 1200 feet. The plan was to land shortly after midnight. No 2 Commando would head east for the two higher hills, No 43 for the two lower. The 40 Commando troop and the Highland Light Infantry company would move to the east coast of Mljet to put a Stop above Sovra Bay, to cut off any German attempt at escape by sea. The hilltop objectives would be softened up by Spitfire bombing before the two Commandos attacked, and the assaults would be shot in by the RSR pack howitzers. The entire job was to be completed, with the troops re-embarked, by the late afternoon of the day of landing.

The convoy mustered at sea off Komiza, made course for Mljet and arrived in front of the selected beach half an hour before midnight. A beach party from the US Operations Group were the first ashore. They confirmed that it was the right beach, and that it was clear of enemies. The beach, about seventy-five yards wide, was of shingle, in a cove surrounded by high wooded hills, with only one narrow footpath as an exit. Next to land were 43 Commando, who found it to be harder than was customary. One of the ramps on LCI 281 was out of order. The other nearly broke off, and had to be held manually in position by two seamen. LCI 308, carrying the other half of the Commando, put in alongside 281 and was also found to be suffering from ramp trouble. One was totally jammed, the other partially so. The second one was coerced down after a twenty-minute delay. 'Disembarkation was extremely slow'. The single narrow path from the cove up the hillside further slowed the initial progress of the column. In addition to his normal full complement of equipment and ammunition, each man carried a 3-inch mortar bomb, weight ten pounds, in his pack. The heavy weapons, mortars and medium machine-guns, were broken down into loads carried on the backs of their teams. It would have been hard work for everybody in the best of circumstances.

The circumstances became steadily worse. The gradients of the hills of Mljet are possibly the steepest in the whole Dalmatian group of islands. The paths were rough and indistinct, sometimes petering out altogether. The advice from the Partisan guide at the head of the column was that if the Commando continued along the track, or what there was of it, the whole long snake would at sun-up be in clear view of the highest of the German positions, thus both forfeiting surprise and offering an invitation for the calling down of artillery fire from German gun emplacements on the mainland. The advice, later found to be wrong, was taken. Also accepted was an offer by the guide to lead the procession along another track that followed the north shore of Mljet. There was no track. The column had to hack its way for two miles through dense, tangled scrub.

Wireless silence, an important adjunct to surprise, was the rule of the day. It did nothing for co-ordination. Simonds, back at 43 Commando Headquarters, and with nothing to suggest to him that the planned timetable was by now an illusion, reported to Brigadier Tom Churchill that his Commando was where it should have been at the time. 43 was in two separate groups, Neilforce led by Major Neil Munro, and Blakeforce led by Captain John Blake. They should have been on two separate start lines, on the lower slopes of two separate hills, at the top of which were two separate German positions, both forces ready to go in shortly after dawn. Tom Churchill called for his air support. Twelve Spitfires roared in at 6.15am and bombed spectacularly. At this time Neilforce and Blakeforce were miles away, still chopping a path blasphemously through the resistant thickets of the north-coast route.

The undergrowth was at last penetrated. The steep paths continued as sharp and as ill-defined as before. Munro reached his start line at 11am, five hours late. Blake reached his at 1.30pm, seven-and-a-half hours late. From shortly after the dawn airstrike there had been a certain amount of desultory two-way, long-range shooting, by the heavy weapons of both sides, the British ones positioned on a hill well behind the bush-whacking assault troops. The four German-held hills were mortared, machine-gunned and shelled. The Germans reciprocated both from their local resources and by calling down shoots from the mainland guns. Remarkably little damage was done to the British side. Probably much the same applied at the German end of the exchanges. The Germans were well protected in rock and log shelters. Some of the zeal with which 43's mortar and machine-gun crews discharged their weapons was not attributable to a devoted enthusiasm to engaging the enemy. They were moved by the reflection that the more ammunition they fired, the less of the bloody stuff there would be to carry back over those bloody hills again.

By 2.30pm, 'C' Troop of 43, led by Captain Bob Loudoun, and part of Neilforce, was on top of the first objective. The Germans, it seemed, had abandoned the hill some time previously. No 2 Commando had also taken the first of their two assigned hilltops. For the remainder of the afternoon there were further fire-fights with the two outstanding strongpoints, more oath-ridden manoeuvring up and down rock faces, and fairly persistent but totally ineffectual German mortaring. It all lasted much longer than it should have. The naval force commander, Morgan Giles, had earlier in the afternoon told Tom Churchill that for naval reasons he wanted the time of re-embarkation of the troops to be brought forward. Churchill called the operation off. Both Commandos were ordered to disengage at 4.30pm, march back to the beach, and get aboard the LCIs by 6pm.

Wireless conditions were bad. Blakeforce got the signal through its chance interception on a short-range 38 set, and tramped off over the mountains again on the first leg of their journey home. Neilforce, whose 18 set was out of order, missed the message altogether. Munro continued to struggle on the heights among intermittent mortaring and shelling for a while longer, until the withdrawal signal at last reached him. By then one of his troops, 'E' commanded by Captain Lee, was enmeshed in a local small-arms battle with two Spandaus, and Munro had some difficulty in extricating it.

Most troops were embarked by 8pm. Two LCIs sailed for Vis at once. Another waited for Neilforce, the advanced element of which reached the beach at 1 am. 'C' Troop, who acted as rearguard and who were encumbered by a wounded marine who had to be carried all the way, did not get in until 2.30am. Four marines had fainted from exhaustion on this march.

Almost everyone on the Mljet operation found himself involved in a lot of toilsome clambering upwards, carrying something heavy on his back and shoulders. Newly issued felt-soled boots were stripped to ribbons on the sharp volcanic rocks of the tracks and hillsides. Denim trousers had suffered similarly from the spiky bushes. Neilforce were a ragged-looking company when they formed up on the jetty at Vis after disembarkation at nine o'clock on the following morning. Their drill movements were as polished as ever, but the condition of their clothing would not have escaped notice on the parade ground of the Royal Marine depot at Deal. They had marched a total of eighteen miles across the most unpleasant country that any of them had ever encountered, had climbed, and descended from, several mountains of over 1000 feet, and had been shot at spasmodically.

The casualties to the raiding force in Operation Foothound were one killed, one wounded and seven missing. Of the missing, it was later discovered, a small party with Colour-Sergeant Stevens had been caught in a minefield. One man was killed. The others, with Stevens, became prisoners-of-war. A few days after the disembarkation at Vis, Captain Bob Loudoun and a small support party went back to Mljet in a motor launch. They recovered two brigade signallers who had fallen out on the march, and also Marine Reg Skinner of Loudoun's troop. Skinner had mislaid himself during a halt. He had subsequently had a lively time, dodging German search parties. His account of his sojourn at the bottom of a well, in which he sat while his searchers chattered away at the top of it, provided much entertainment in the months ahead.

# NOTHING MUCH TO LOSE

**Photograph and Map
Section**

## PHOTOGRAPHS

### ICELAND 1940

Lt. Col. A. N. Williams, C.O. 2nd Bn. R.M. on jetty at Reykjavik.

Major S. G. Cutler, 'A' Coy. studying documents at German Consulate, Reykjavik.

Corporal T. P. Hunter, V.C.—The only Marine to be awarded the V.C. in World War II.

Lieut. W. G. Jenkins, D.S.O.—The youngest Marine Officer to be awarded the D.S.O. in World War II.

Royal Marine Commando Memorial, Lympstone
Night fighting patrol armed with Thompson Sub-Machine Guns.

VIS, 1944, Lieut. T. A. S. Taylor and members of 'D' Troop, Long Distance Recce Patrol.

Jug Boats—Multi Purpose/Multi Functional—Being unloaded by British troops at an Adriatic Island.

Partisans embarking at VIS to carry out a raid.

Postcard sent by Cpl. Tom Hunter, V.C. to his Mother. Nazi flag captured on Yugoslavia mainland.

Panoramic view of the town of VIS.

43 CDO Royal Marines—Brew-up before attack on Comacchio.

3 inch Mortar Team in action at Comacchio.

'A' Troop 43 CDO R.M. advancing at Comacchio.

"Fantails" loaded with Commandos.

River Reno—Part of 43 CDO R.M. moving up in the last minutes of daylight.

River Reno—Assault boats carrying Mortar team across the river.

River Reno—Assault boat bringing back the wounded.

### "OUR SUCCESSORS"

C.O. and detachment from Comacchio Group, Royal Marines on the unveiling of the Memorial to Cpl T. P. Hunter, V.C. at Porto Garibaldi, Italy in April 1992.

## MAPS

2 RM's Overseas Postings in 1940.

Mediterranean Theatre of War 1944 to 1945.

Attack on Monte Ornito—River Garigliano.

Dalmatian Islands and Mainland Yugoslavia.

Our Base Camp for many months.

June 1944—Battle to relieve pressure on Tito

Solta and Brac—Scene of many raids

The Mainland—Around Dubrovnik and South of Sarajevo.

Commando Brigade Attack at Comacchio.

Argenta—The Final Break Through.

## ICELAND 1940

*Lt. Col. A. N. Williams, C.O. 2nd Bn. R.M. on jetty at Reykjavik.*

*Major S. G. Cutler, 'A' Coy. studying documents at German Consulate, Reykjavik.*

*Corporal T. P. Hunter, V.C.—The only Marine to be awarded the V.C. in World War II.*

*Lieut. W. G. Jenkins, D.S.O.—The youngest Marine Officer to be awarded the D.S.O. in World War II.*

**Royal Marine Commando Memorial, Lympstone**
*Night fighting patrol armed with Thompson Sub-Machine Guns.*

*VIS, 1944, Lieut. T. A. S. Taylor and members of 'D' Troop, Long Distance Recce Patrol.*

## JUG BOATS—MULTI PURPOSE/MULTI FUNCTIONAL

*Being unloaded by British troops at an Adriatic Island.*

*Partisans embarking at VIS to carry out a raid.*

*Postcard sent by Cpl. Tom Hunter, V.C. to his Mother. Nazi flag captured on Yugoslavia mainland.*

*Panoramic view of the town of VIS.*

*43 CDO Royal Marines—Brew-up before attack on Comacchio.*

*3 inch Mortar Team in action at Comacchio.*

*'A' Troop 43 CDO R.M. advancing at Comacchio.*

*River Reno—Part of 43 CDO R.M. moving up in the last minutes of daylight.*

*River Reno—Assault boats carrying Mortar team across the river.*

*River Reno—Assault boat bringing back the wounded.*

**"OUR SUCCESSORS".**
C.O. and detachment from Comacchio Group, Royal Marines on the unveiling of the Memorial to Cpl T. P. Hunter, V.C. at Porto Garibaldi, Italy in April 1992.

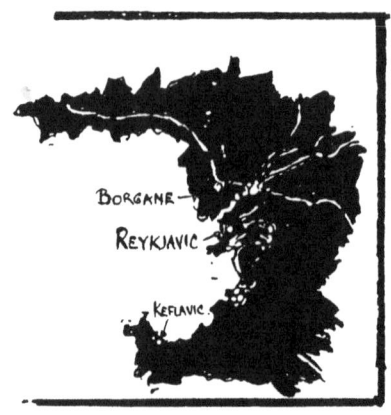

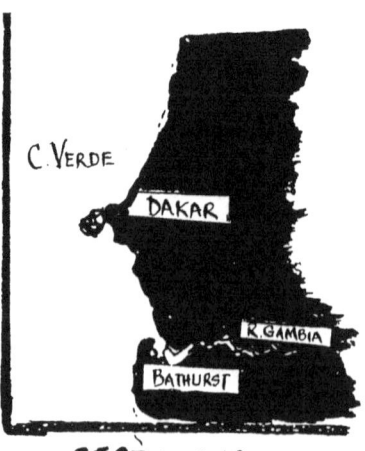

2 RM's Overseas Postings in 1940.

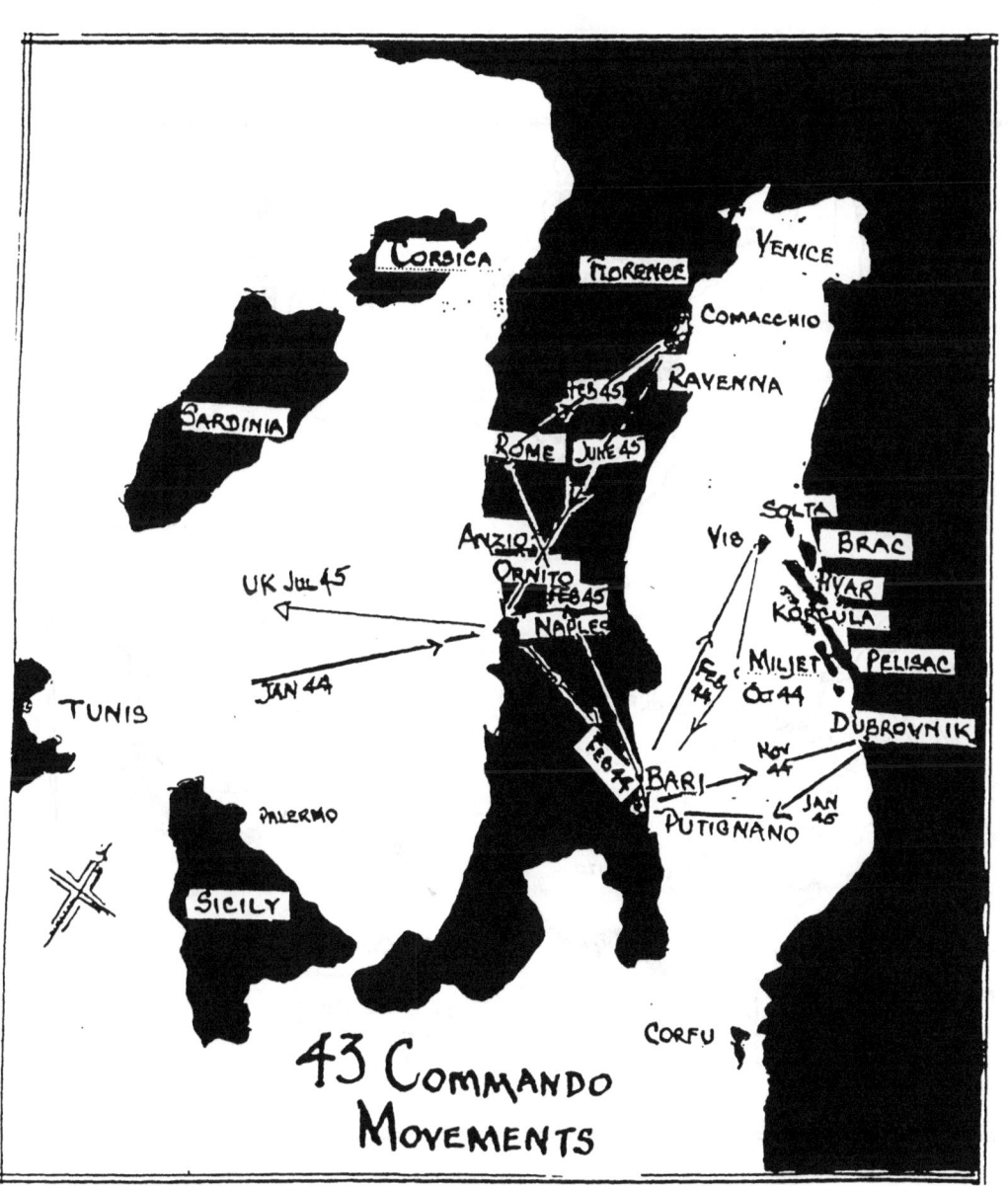

*Mediterranean Theatre of War 1944 to 1945.*

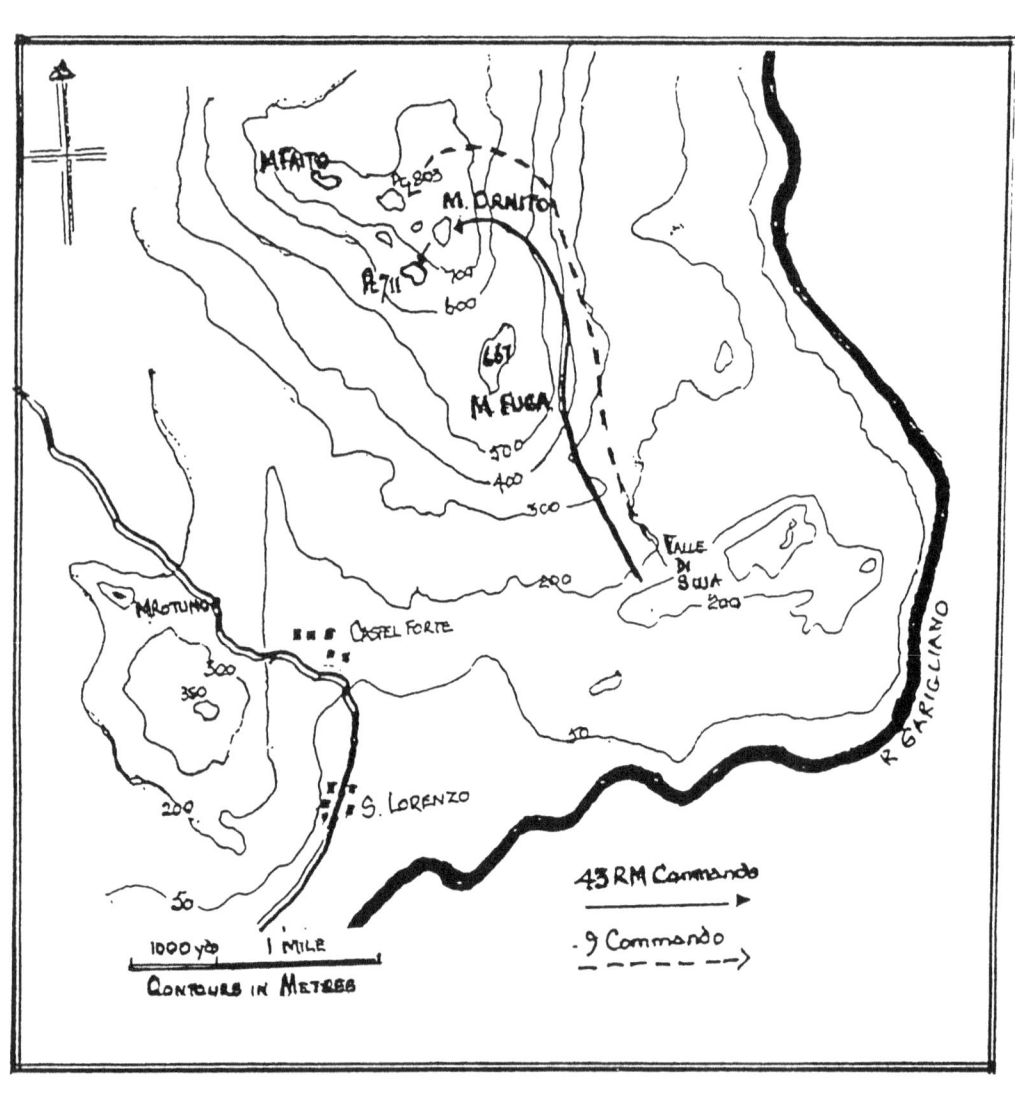

*Attack on Monte Ornito—River Garigliano.*

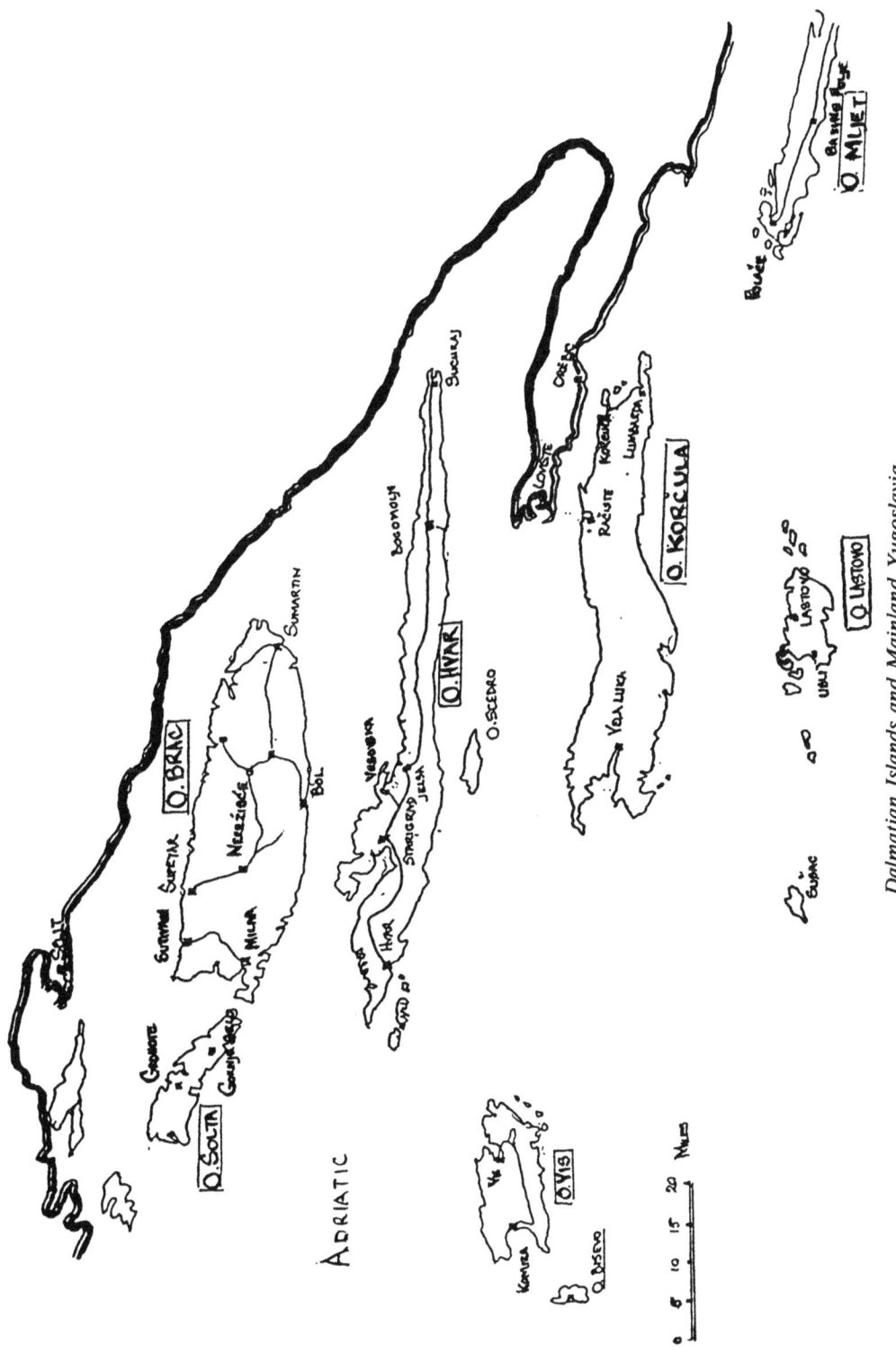

Dalmatian Islands and Mainland Yugoslavia.

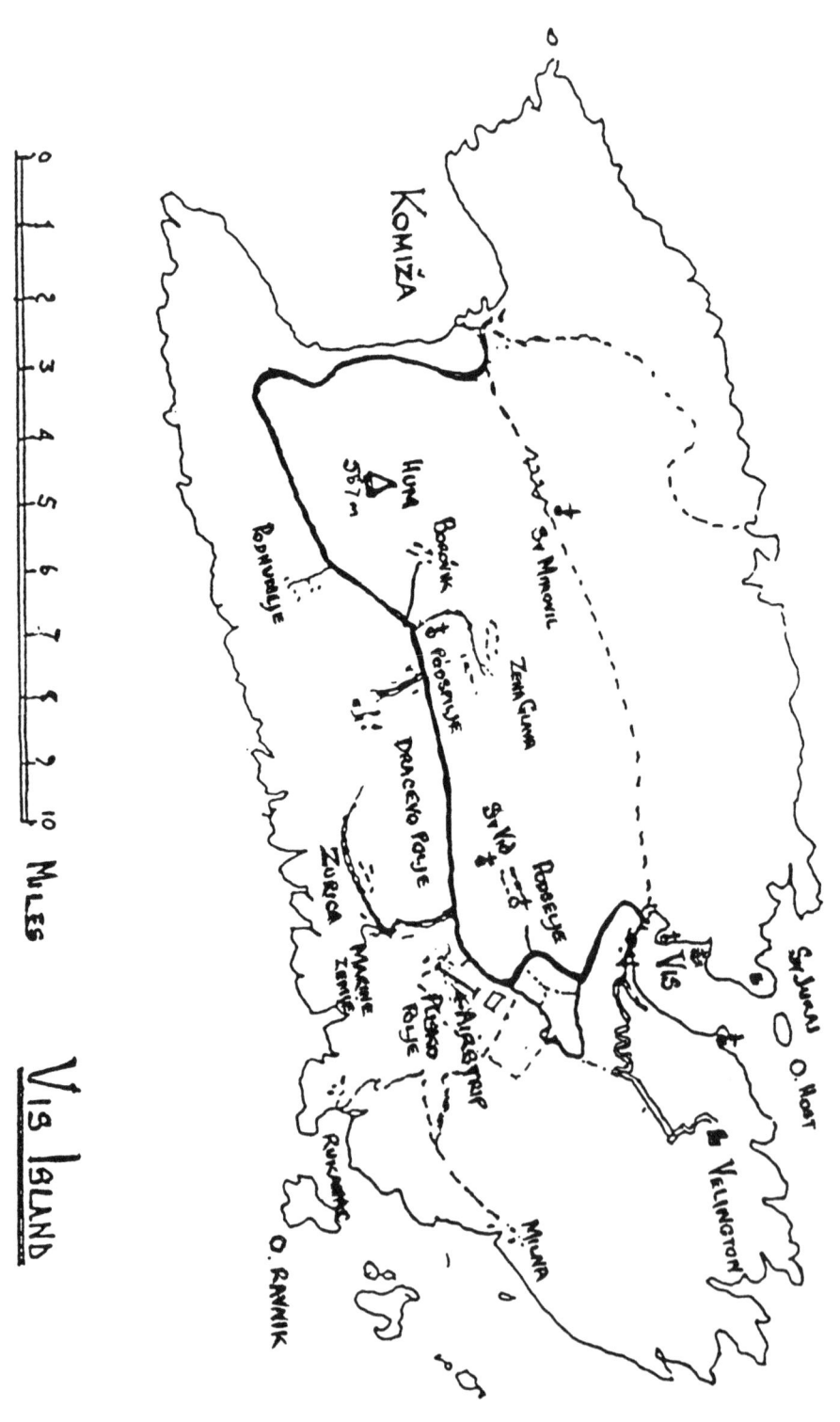

*Our Base Camp for many months.*

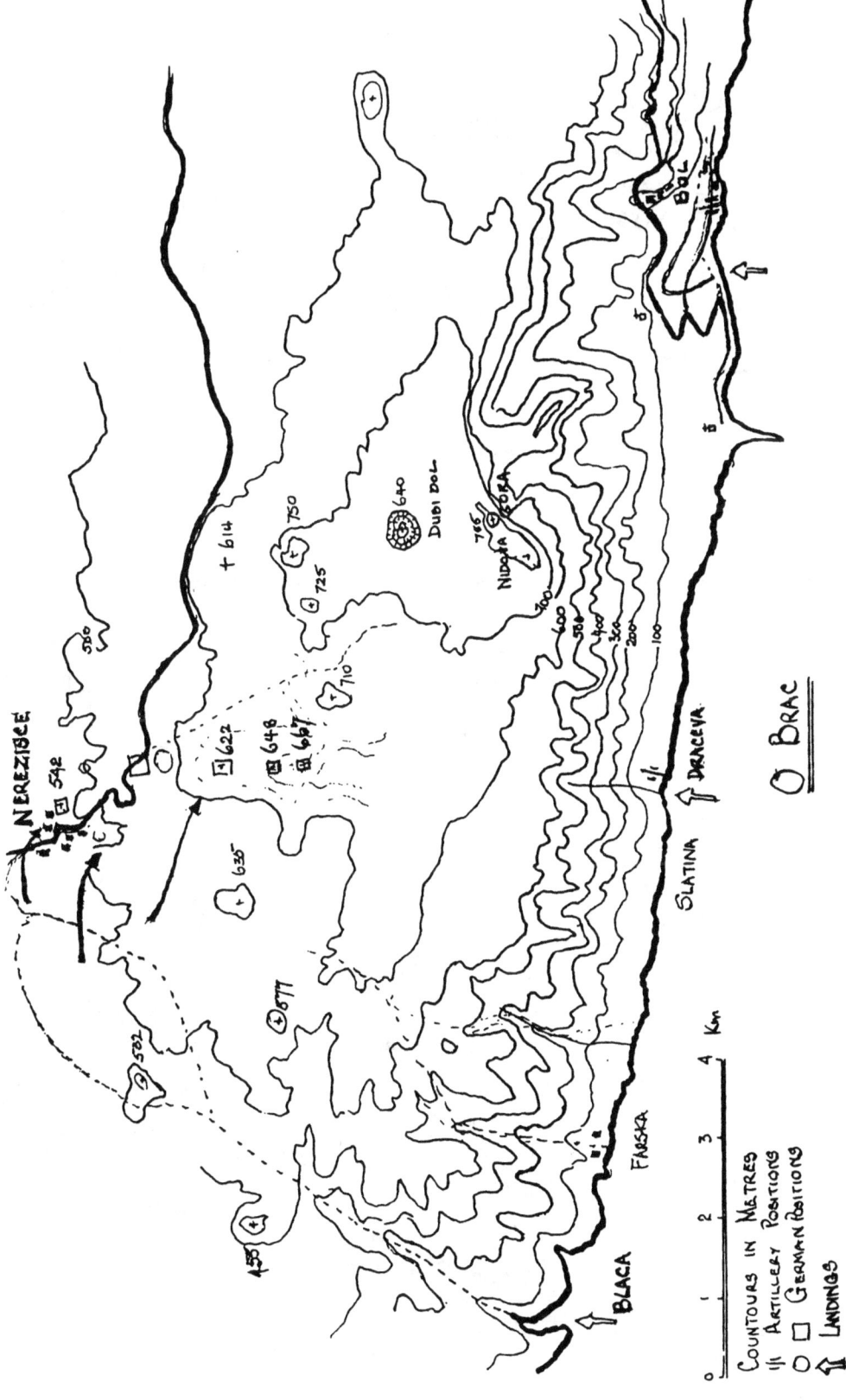

June 1944—Battle to relieve pressure on Tito

*Solta and Brac—Scene of many raids*

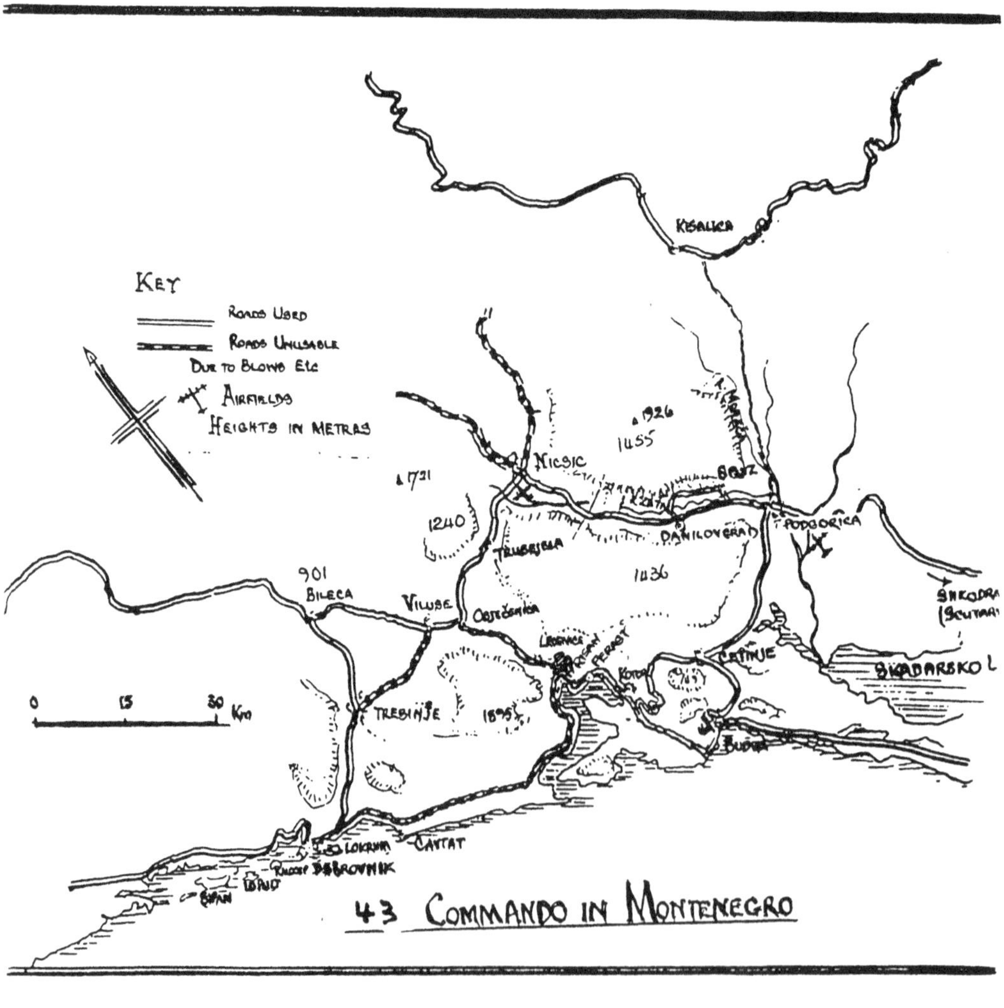

*The Mainland—Around Dubrovnik and South of Sarajevo.*

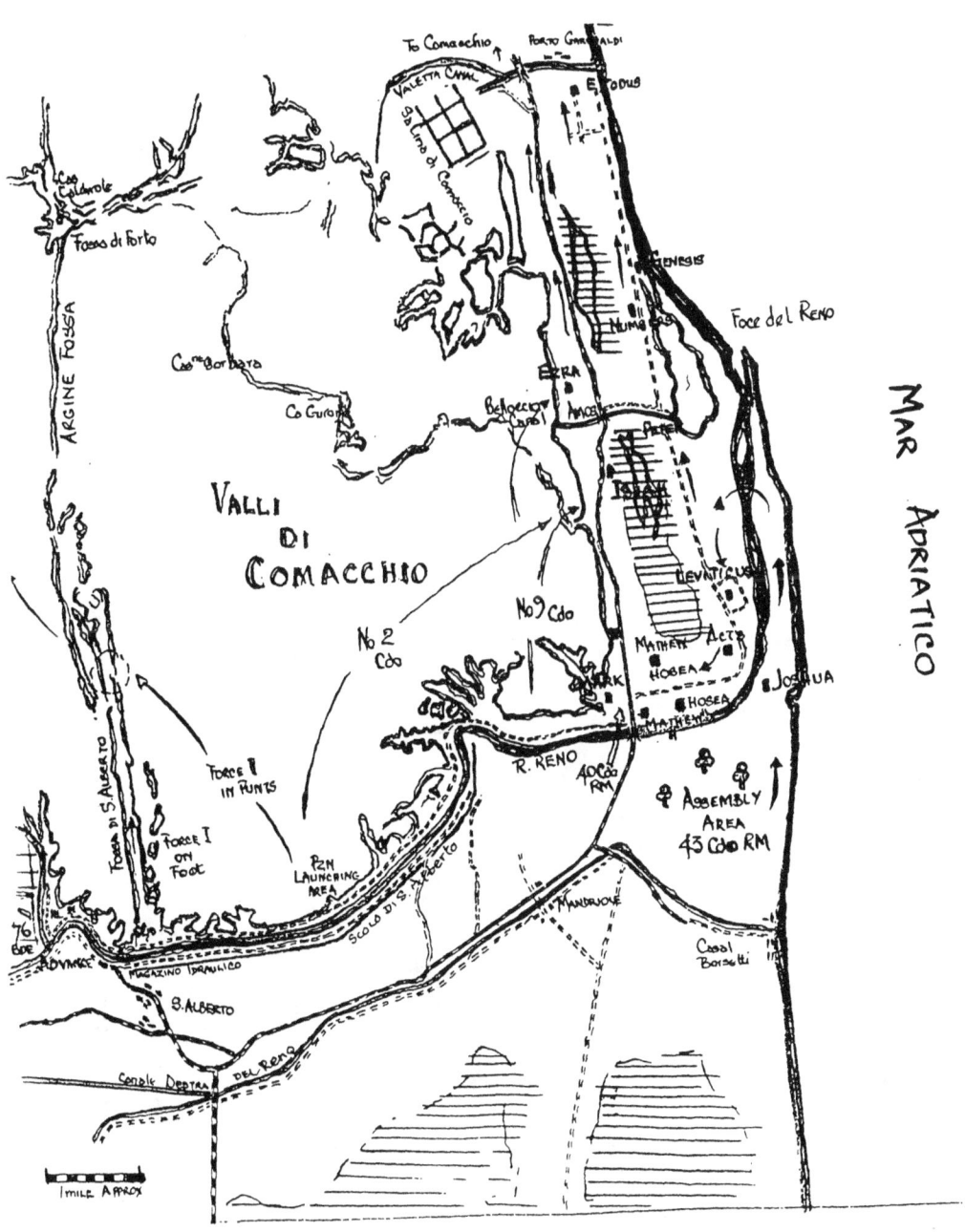

*Commando Brigade Attack at Comacchio.*

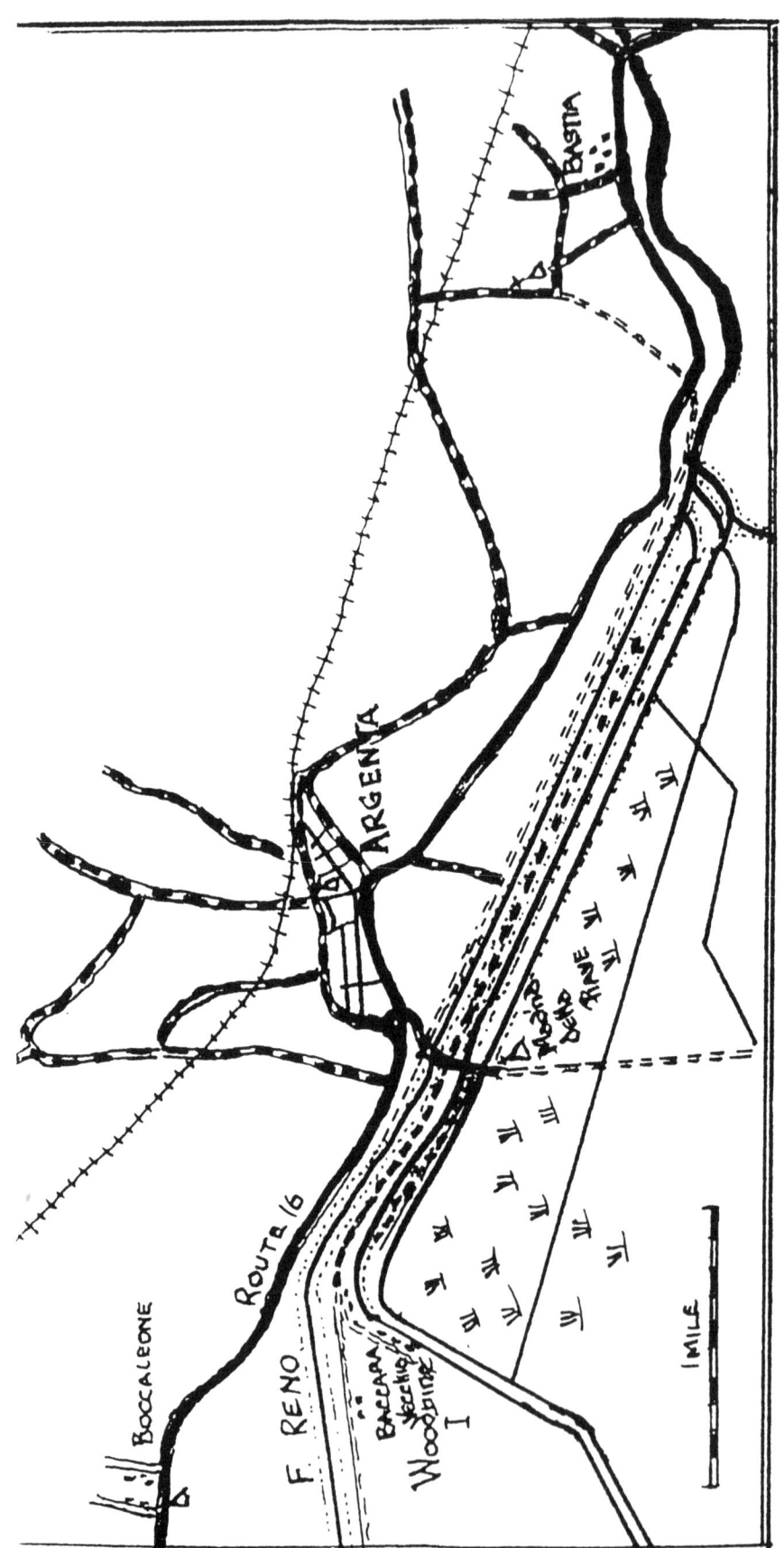

*Argenta—The Final Break Through.*

# CHAPTER TEN

# BRAC PRELIMINARIES

For some weeks Combined Operations Headquarters in London had been urging Brigadier Tom Churchill to come home for personal discussions, always more fruitful than exchanges of views by letter and signal. He was to leave as soon as a convenient opportunity presented itself. One seemed to do so, shortly after the abortive rigours of the Mljet foray. No other immediate island operations were on the drawing board. Churchill left for London on 26th May, prepared to answer questions about the relatively new Royal Marine Commandos and about Commando lessons learnt in the Mediterranean that might usefully be applied elsewhere. Before his departure he handed over command of the Vis British force to his brother Jack.

Later on the same day the first reports began to come in of an elaborately mounted German airborne attack on Tito's headquarters at Drvar in Bosnia. Fighting was fierce. Partisan casualties were heavy. Tito, most of his main staff, and the British Military Mission with them broke free.

But the Drvar assault had been only the centre-piece of a much wider plot for the elimination of the Partisan leadership. There were integrated German interventions from many directions. Tito, his staff, his bodyguard and the Allied missions were kept constantly on the move, wriggling and feinting their way through one enemy threat after another. Effective co-ordination of Partisan activity was, in the circumstances, impossible. Tito ordered that all Partisan formations and units, everywhere, should take early positive action to divert German attentions from himself and from his immediate companions, between them the brain and nerve-centres of the entire Yugoslav liberation movement.

The Partisan response to this instruction was of necessity *ad hoc*, but it was on the whole widespread, violent and effective. The British, to whom it was an appeal rather than a directive, also reacted promptly. In the seven days after the Drvar assault, the Royal Air Force flew one thousand or so sorties in attacks on targets in Yugoslavia with the aim of interfering with the German hunt. There were, too, some brisk arrangements for a major involvement in an amphibious operation of the British troops on the island of Vis. The preliminary order, of which a badly blurred copy is preserved in the Public Record Office at Kew, was wirelessed by Brigadier Miles, who commanded Force 266 from his headquarters in Bari, to Colonel Jack Churchill. This signal was to instigate an operation that in terms of British manpower was the largest undertaken in Yugoslavia during the

Second World War, and that in terms of blood and talent lost was the most expensive. It reads in full:

> TO JACK FROM BONZO. TITO HAS ORDERED PARTISANS TO CARRY OUT DIVERSION BY ATTACKING HVAR, BRAC, PODGORA, TO EASE HIS SITUATION AND ASK OUR SUPPORT. CONSIDER THAT NOT MORE THAN 2,000 PARTISANS SHOULD BE USED. WE MUST BE PREPARED UP TO ONE COMMANDO, ONE TWENTY FIVE POUNDER BATTERY, ONE TROOP 75 MM, RSR, ONE HEAVY WEAPON TROOP, COMMANDOS. MY SUGGESTED PLAN, 500 PARTISANS HVAR, OBJECTIVE JELSA: 1,500 PARTISANS PLUS COMMANDO AND SUPPORTING ARMS, BRAC, TO LAND SOUTH WEST ISLAND AND ADVANCE ON NEREZISCE. FOTALI PREPARED TO PRODUCE FIVE (5) LCI'S. PROBABLE DATE OPERATION NIGHT 30/31st. OR 31st/1st. PEARSON ARRIVING BY AIR 29th MAY TO DISCUSS PLAN YOU AND CERNEY. WILL ARRANGE RAF AND RN SUPPORT ON RETURN TO TARANTO, PM 29th MAY. WILL PROCEED VIS WITH SASO, COS FOTALI 30th MAY IF NECESSARY.

The RSR were the Raiding Support Regiment. FOTALI was not, as it sounds, an Italian fishing port, but was short for Flag Officer Taranto and Liaison Italy, the full title of Admiral Morgan of the Royal Navy. SASO was the Senior Air Staff Officer. COS FOTALI was Admiral Morgan's Chief of Staff. Cerney was the Partisan commander on Vis.

Although Miles described his scheme as a 'suggested plan', and although some later modifications were made to the original concept, no senior Commando officer seems to have queried, or pressed for an alternative to, its central element, the advance upon Nerezisce of whatever Commando was chosen. Nerezisce was an upland village, once routinely occupied by Germans in sequestrated billets. The raids by 2 Commando on Solta and 43 Commando on Hvar had persuaded the Germans of the unwisdom of taking their opponents too lightly on the islands. There had been a radical reshuffling of German dispositions.

German soldiers were no longer lodged in relative comfort, and with relative vulnerability, in requisitioned school buildings and the larger houses. They had been withdrawn to the heights of commanding hills, upon which they had blasted prepared defensive positions of stone and concrete linked by trenches and surrounded by belts of mines protected by barbed wire. From each of these fastnesses there was only one way out, a narrow track. The stronghold of the former Nerezisce garrison, reinforced, was on a hilltop, Point 622. The position's physical approaches and its artificial defences combined to make it formidable. Miles's signal had mentioned no more than an advance towards it. It was inevitable, if a satisfactory diversion were to be made to ease Tito's difficulties, that an assault would have to be made upon it.

The Commando chosen for the job was 43.

Colonel Pearson, the General Staff Officer 1 (G1 for short) of Force 266, flew to Vis from Bari for the planning conference on the morning of 29th May. The conference, attended by all the commanders of the troops who would take part in the raid, was first briefed by the Brigade Intelligence Officer on what was known of German strengths and locations on Brac. Pearson then gave the outline plan. Commander Cerney and the commander of the Partisan XXVI Division joined the discussion. No 2 Special Service Brigade's report on Operation Flounced, the code-name for the undertaking, records:

The discussion was long and many proposals and counter-proposals were made. It is never easy to plan in conjunction with the Partisan authorities, not only because of the language difficulty, but more particularly because their whole system of planning and their ideas on military tactics, whilst very successful when conducted by them alone, are so different from ours that it is difficult to arrange a properly co-ordinated detailed plan of attack.

Forty-one years later Tom Churchill, was more succinct: 'this conference was a most woolly affair, with the commandos asking stupid questions and making promises which they couldn't carry out.' The conference finally came up with firm conclusions. Pearson flew back to Italy during the evening with an agreed provisional plan and with specific requests for the kind of support that the ground force needed from the other two services. Colonel Jack Churchill, the appointed Force Commander, was insistent upon elaborate air backing.

In Taranto there were consultations at a rung or two higher up in the hierarchy. Admiral Morgan (FOTALI), the Air Officer Commanding 242 Group and Brigadier Miles of Force 266 agreed the contributions to be made by their respective commands. Miles, on behalf of all three, signalled an outline of the plan to Allied Forces Headquarters at Caserta. The date of the landing was put back until the night of 1/2 June so that detailed planning could be further refined and to allow time for the assembly of all the necessary naval craft. Some last-minute adjustments were made to the plan. Operation Flounced was on.

Viewed from the air, or on the map, Brac is rather a plump-looking island, much more so than its skinny neighbours, an attenuated oval with its edges fuzzed by coves, bays and headlands. The longer sides of the oval curve gently, approximately from east to west. The shorter ends, both irregular, run roughly from north to south. The island's maximum width is about twenty miles. Its maximum depth is about ten. A quarter of the way along the coast from the western end of the northern shore is the small port of Supetar. At the southern tip of the eastern end is another small port, Sumartin. Almost exactly in the centre of the south coast is an even smaller fishing port, Bol.

The interior of Brac is hilly and stony. In the nineteenth century Brac stone was famous and Dalmatian sea captains carried it to the United States - St Patrick's Cathedral in New York is built from it. Among the limestone rocks are vineyards, vegetable gardens and scattered patches of grazing for mountain sheep. There are stunted trees and much scrubby undergrowth. Movement on foot through the intricate hills and valleys of this pile of stone is hard work, particularly when the movers are encumbered by up to sixty pounds of weapons, equipment, food, water and ammunition.

There were several independently conducted but inter-related components of the plan.

The main task of the Partisans, 2500 in all, was to seal off the German garrisons in the northern port of Supetar and in the eastern port of Sumartin. The eastern Partisan force, which was supported by a troop of mountain guns of the Raiding Support Regiment would have to start by dealing with an outlying German position at Humac, a village about ten miles to the west of Sumartin, and then drive the Germans progressively eastward. No 43 Commando, whose objective was the German strongpoint system on the heights of Point 622, south-east of Nerezisce, was given additional fire support in the shape of the Heavy Weapons Troop of 40 Commando and extra help for shifting stores and ammunition from a rifle troop of 40 Commando acting as porters. The Commandos were to land at Blaca Cove, on the south-west coast of the island. Jack Churchill, the British ground force commander, was to go with them, accompanied by a skeleton staff from 2 Special Service Brigade Headquarters. To inhibit German reinforcement of Brac from the mainland, the RAF had agreed to undertake an intensive bombing programme of the mainland harbours of Split, Omis and Makarska. Artillery support for the Commando assault upon the Nerezisce position would be provided by a battery of 25-pounders, eight guns, later supplemented by two more, of 111 Field Regiment, Royal Artillery. The chosen gun position was at Bol, in the centre of the south coast. The Battery Commander was Major Pat Turner.

Before all this could be put properly into motion there was a potentially threatening obstacle to be disposed of. Some two miles to the north-west of Bol is the highest peak on the island Vidova Gora, approximately 2400 feet high. From its summit there was a clear view of most of Brac, including the approaches to the Commando objective above Nerezisce. Vidova Gora was known to be manned by a German artillery observation post. Unless the post, thought to be guarded by about thirty soldiers with two machine-guns, could be taken out right at the start of the operation, it would be able to direct accurate shell and mortar fire from German emplacements upon the island and the nearby mainland on to both Commandos and Partisans, on the march or forming up for their various attacks. The job of eliminating the Vidova Gora post was given to 'B' Company of the 2nd Battalion, the Highland Light Infantry. The company was led by Major R.S.H. Brotherhood.

The Jocks left Vis in Partisan Schooners. They were landed at the wrong beach, made an exhausting cross-country approach march, and assaulted Vidova Gora by night. The observation post was more strongly defended than Partisan intelligence had suggested. Nearly all the HLI officers and senior NCOs became casualties, and the post was not taken. But the impact of the assault was sufficient to neutralise it, until it was captured by Partisans on the following day.

An indication of the haste with which the operation was mounted, or possibly a product of the length, and what Tom Churchill called the woolliness, of the planning conference held on Vis on 29th May, was that the 'Object' defined by Colonel Bonzo Simonds in his orders to his subordinate commanders was different from that laid down by Force 266, accepted by Colonel Jack Churchill and transmitted to the leaders of every element in the force.

The 'Object' of 2 Special Service Brigade Headquarters, as recorded in their report on the operation, began with a preamble about the German attack on Tito's headquarters at Drvar, and quoted his orders to the Partisans to initiate diversions. The Partisans on Vis were to carry out one of these 'in order to prevent the enemy from moving further formations from the coast against his (Tito's) HQ, and if possible, to make him (the enemy) pull back to the coast certain formations about to be committed. This was the primary object of the operation.....The secondary object was the destruction of the enemy forces and material on the island of Brac.

The Simonds orders to 43 Commando put all this the other way round. 'OBJECT: 1. To destroy the enemy garrison of BRAC ISLAND. 2. It was hoped that this would cause the enemy to move strong formations from the mainland interior to the coast, thus relieving pressure on Marshal Tito's HQ.' In practice this switch probably had no effect on the course of the battle; had the operation lasted longer than it did, some reconciliation of aims might have become necessary.

During the night 1/2 June landing craft of the Royal Navy and Partisan schooners brought to Brac the varied components of the raiding force, the Partisans who were to mask Supetar and Sumartin, the RSR mountain guns who were to support the latter, and the battery of eight 25-pounders of 111 Field Regiment whose priority task was to support 43 Commando's attack on the Nerezisce defended complex but which could also be turned on to targets elsewhere. Forty-five craft in all sailed from Vis harbour and Komiza between 8.30pm and 10pm. Most carried troops - 2500 Partisans, 900 British and about 100 Americans of the Operations Group. There were escorts of motor gun boats and motor launches. The armada travelled by night because most of its various routes would by day have been in full view of German positions on Solta, Brac, Hvar and from a number of places on the mainland. German observers, aside from alerting the Brac garrison to the sheer size - unprecedented - of what was heading its way, would also have alerted the Luftwaffe, still very much alive and formidable. There were major Luftwaffe bases at Mostar and Zagreb, both within easy range, and several satellite airfields elsewhere, also within range.

At half past midnight on the morning of Friday, 2 June, 43 Commando, augmented by 40 Commando's Heavy Weapons Troop of four 3-inch mortars and four Vickers belt-fed medium machine-guns, accompanied by the 40 Commando troop allocated as porters, plus a force of Partisans, pulled in to Blaca Cove on the south-west of Brac. The Commandos made the journey in a Landing Craft, Infantry, LCI 260, crewed by experienced and trusted friends. Their voyage had been unimpeded. 'The landing and re-embarkation arrangements for the Commando', reported 43 afterwards, 'were excellent. The beaching and handling of LCI 260 was again beyond reproach.' The absence of reproach was generated by more than admiration for the seamanship demonstrated by the LCI's captain. He had put the troops ashore dry-shod, a consideration highly valued by people faced with hard cross-country marching who did not want inevitable ardours to be amplified by wet feet, socks, boots and trousers. The landing was unopposed as well as dry. In a long snake of a single-file column, the marines marched off towards Nerezisce, about four miles to the north-east in a straight line, nearer to nine by narrow, winding, stony tracks that crossed a seemingly endless succession of ridges, valleys and gulleys.

In addition to the weight of their equipment and individual weapons - in the fighting troops these ranged from the heavier Brens and 2-inch mortars through rifles and Tommy guns to pistols - every man on this occasion was burdened with a 3-inch mortar bomb weighing ten pounds. There were no mules available. The ground was impassable even to so versatile a vehicle as a jeep. Everything had to be carried on the back, including the Vickers machine-guns and the 3-inch mortars of the two heavy weapons troops. The Vickers, broken down to their components of barrels and tripods, the mortars to baseplates, barrels and bipods, were, with one competitor in close unwonted rivalry, the heaviest loads of all. The competitor was the sum of the medical stores of the Regimental Aid Post, packed in ninety-pound loads on the backs of Captain Ralph Bazeley of the Royal Army Medical Corps, of his medical sergeant and of the two orderlies who made up his medical team. Between them they also had two heavy Airborne stretchers, of clumsy design, to manhandle wherever they went.

The landing at Bol of 111 Field Regiment's battery, also unopposed, took place at one o'clock in the morning, shortly after 43 Commando had left Blaca on its cross-country march. The eight 25-pounders, quickly put ashore from a Landing Craft Tank, were soon positioned on a little plain to the east of the village. The Partisans, who had accompanied the LCT in their schooners, pushed inland at speed, and before long were fighting Germans at a number of different places. One of these was the observation post on Vidova Gora. It held out with diminishing resistance until noon, when Partisans finally overran it and took prisoner the survivors of its garrison. The Gunner Forward Observation Officer, with his accompanying signaller, at once took it over and began to register the range and bearing of targets that seemed likely to be in need of treatment later.

Farther to the east the Partisans, backed by the 75mm mountain guns of the Raiding Support Regiment, were pressing the Germans satisfyingly back from Humac towards Sumartin. No 111 Field Regiment's gun positions at Bol came under sporadic and mostly ineffectual, shellfire as the morning wore on, from locations that were difficult to identify. On the north coast, the Partisans given the task of bottling up the German garrison of Supetar had reached the outskirts of the town, but were being heavily mortared by the defence and shot at by artillery from the mainland.

By 7.45am the leading troop of 43's five rifle troops, still on a mountain track but by now in daylight, was approaching from the west the German strongpoints on the hilltops behind Nereziscè. These stongpoints were on the summits of the metrically named adjacent peaks, Point 622 (the Commando's prime objective), Point 542 and Point 648, integral parts of an interlocked defensive system. Broadly speaking, and allowing for the mishaps inseparable from an operation of war carried out by night with little time for preparation and none for detailed reconnaissance, matters had so far gone well. There had been no losses on the sea-crossing. Every component of the ground force was more or less where it should have been, doing or ready to do what it was meant to do. Aircraft of the RAF flew overhead in an abundance previously unwitnessed in the islands, bombing Sumartin and Supetar and machine-gunning throughout Brac anything that they identified as hostile. A feeling developed within 43 during the day that the pilots were a touch too easy-going in their identification procedures. The marines were twice shot up by Spitfires.

When, at 7.30 on the morning of 2 June, 'E' Troop after an all-night march, was put in to a rather tentative attack upon a German entrenched position on Point 542, an encouraging artillery shoot from the 25-pounders at Bol was dropping upon that summit and upon Point 622. German soldiers were seen moving about freely on both these hills. 'A' Troop, led by Captain Jock Hudspith, ran into a minefield. The support available was judged by Simonds to be inadequate. Both attacks were called off.

Their attack was replaced, as the morning wore on, by Partisan attacks on the other, southern side of the feature. These were supported by continued accurate shelling by the 25-pounders in Bol and by mortar fire from the heavy weapons troops of 43 and 40 Commandos. The Partisan attacks did not succeed. By 1pm they had petered out. Observers, both those professionally involved in directing the shell and mortar fire and a large number of self-interested spectators, noticed a disquieting effect of the fall of shot. To some extent it kept German heads down. It did little physical damage to German defensive positions blasted into solid rock and as often as not roofed by tree trunks placed side by side.

During the early afternoon the Commando, resting in loosely dispersed troop positions on the hillsides and valleys, were extensively mortared and machine-gunned from Point 622 and were shelled by some distant guns. It was noisy, but largely harmless. At 3pm three troops set out for a forming-up position prior to an attempt on Point 543. Their route took them through Nerezisce. The route of a passing patrol of four Spitfires of the Royal Air Force took them over Nerezisce. The marines laid out their silk identification panels. The airmen were indifferent or uninstructed and they fell into acute and foully expressed disfavour when they roared down in a spirited attack upon those whom they had come to help. By good fortune only two marines were wounded during this episode, but it was an unhappy opening of the Commando's Brac casualty list.

The agreed plan for the Point 542 attack was that 'B', 'D' and 'E' Troops would come on to the objective from the north in concert with a similar Partisan assault from the south, the whole to be preceded by a half-hour concentration of shelling from the battery at Bol. The shelling was intense, accurate and precisely on time. The three troops of 43 left their start line on time. The Partisans did not conform. Their brigade commander sent his woman interpreter to Colonel Simonds's headquarters, fifteen minutes before the attack was due to begin and halfway through the supporting artillery programme, to say that his people would not, after all, be joining in. No 43 Commando went ahead alone. They soon reached the outer minefield wire, which they cut or blew gaps in with Bangalore torpedoes (lengths of metal piping packed with explosive and designed specifically for gapping wire entanglements). Mines were lifted and some progress was made in the face of a growing volume of Spandau and mortar fire, doubly strong because the Partisans were not there to attract their share of it.

At 4.45 pm German reinforcements were seen to be moving up from the south-east. They were a threat to the exposed flank of the three troops. At five o'clock Simonds decided to break off the fight, which was becoming pointless. The battery at Bol, which in all accounts by the foot-soldiers of the Brac operation is mentioned with unreserved admiration, shelled the German holdings heavily to cover the withdrawal of the three troops. The RAF, who in the interim had had time to restock with fuel and ammunition, shot them up once again as they marched through Nerezisce, thereby knocking a further dent in the well-being of inter-service relations. Simonds concentrated his entire command for the night of 2/3 June in an all-round defensive position. They had had little sleep and had put in a lot of hard marching during the previous thirty-six hours. Sentries, signallers and orderly officers aside, they slumbered deeply.

Few of the Partisans had much sleep on that night. Different groups of them put in individual attacks on every German position to the south of Nerezisce. German heavy artillery from the mainland shelled the area around Humac continuously. The fighting lasted throughout the hours of darkness. None of the Partisan assaults was successful.

One small but essential entity belonging to the Commando also did badly for sleep. Captain Ralph Bazeley and the staff of his Regimental Aid Post had inadvertently become separated from the main body of the commando during the night approach march. Shortly after dawn Bazeley briefly acquired a hospitable Partisan who refreshed the party from a goatskin container filled with watered wine. More permanently, Bazeley became the proprietor of two donkeys. The donkeys were loaded with the two awkward Airborne stretchers and with much of the weight of the medical stores. Homing on distant bangings and thumpings, Bazeley walked towards where battle seemed to be engaged. Corroborative visual indications that he was going the right way came from the sight of Spitfires shooting up what he assumed to be Germans, but which may well have been 43 Commando.

It was almost dusk when Bazeley led the way into Nerezisce. The donkeys at once disgraced themselves by breaking loose and bolting for a pond that was in the middle of the village. In this they stood hock-deep, slaking their thirsts and befouling the local water supply. There were no troops, Commando or Partisan, in the village, but friendly civilians showed Bazeley the track by which the Commando had left. The donkeys were enticed from the pond with difficulty. The party set off upon what it hoped, wrongly, was the last leg of its deferred journey. Night fell with Mediterranean haste. After an hour or two of tramping along in almost total darkness, illuminated from time to time by the gun flashes and flares of neighbouring Partisan attacks, Bazeley told his team to settle down, and went ahead on his own. In the middle of the night he found Commando Headquarters on a ridge. Bazeley was by then very tired and soon became very offended. Nobody, it seemed, had noticed his absence. He climbed into a handy sangar for a brief sleep.

A nearly full moon had arisen by the time he awoke. By the light of this he was shown a saddle, on the far side of a small valley. The saddle was occupied by Captain Gerry Schooley and 'B' Troop. Bazeley was instructed to instal his aid post next to 'B' Troop. He went back to collect the staff of his sick bay, pointed himself towards where he thought the saddle was, and soon discovered that in the intricate uplands of Brac one moonlit silhouette looks very like another. Once again he told his followers to settle down while he went ahead to get the route right. In the course of this search he was shot at by a Commando sentry, bumped into some Partisans who after a suspicious interrogation through their interpreter showed him where to go, was shot at again by the Commando sentry on his way back to collect the unit's medical resources, and finally reached 'B' Troop shortly before dawn.

Bazeley's welcome by 'B' Troop was less than whole-hearted. His donkeys were of different sexes, and fell in love as soon as they reached the end of their journey. They celebrated this event by a noisy consummation that disturbed those marines who were sleeping, and provoked austere comment from the wakeful ones about the military value of silence as an adjunct to concealment. Bazeley was too tired to pay serious attention to these complaints.

Developments in the battle elsewhere on Brac were beginning to suggest that the raid's object, as defined by No. 2 Special Service Brigade, of drawing some of the heat from the hunted Tito in Bosnia, was at least in part being achieved. German resources committed to the frustration of the Brac attacks were increasing. Intelligence reports suggested that 2000 German reinforcements were expected to arrive on the island during the night of 2/3 June. German batteries on the mainland had been in almost incessant action against the Partisans in front of Supetar, who had withdrawn a short distance but were still in a position to block any German attempt at a breakout from the town. In the eastern end of the island the Partisans and their RSR collaborators pressed strongly towards Sumartin.

As a response to the warning about the 2000 additional Germans, Brigadier Miles (now at Force 266 Advanced Headquarters on Vis) decided to send over three troops of 40 Commando, led by Colonel Pops Manners. Manners and his depleted unit embarked in an LCI at Vis harbour at 11.30 on the night of Friday, 2 June, put to sea at 1.30 in the morning, and were landed at Planica, near Bol, at 3.45am on the Saturday. They marched inland at four o'clock, travelled for two-and-a-half hours, and settled down in a lying-up area, where they passed the rest of the day. With 40 Commando came 300 extra Partisans. At eight o'clock in the morning two further 25-pounders were landed at Bol to strengthen Pat Turner's battery.

In the area of Nerezisce, the daylight hours of that Saturday were relatively peaceful, but there was much preparing, conferring and considering. The 43 Commando war diary records that from ten o'clock until noon Simonds was at Jack Churchill's tactical headquarters, sited some distance from that of 43 Commando, where he was told to mount a night attack that same night. He would be sent detailed orders later, after Churchill had completed a detailed reconnaissance. Simonds left for 43 Commando and Churchill set off on his reconnaissance, which lasted for five hours. Meanwhile the Partisans asked for support from the two heavy weapons troops for an afternoon attack that they planned on Point 622. This they later cancelled after the heavy weapons had given their supporting bombardment.

Jack Churchill's personal recollection, over forty years later, was that he himself walked to 43 Commando Headquarters and spoke to Simonds there. Wherever the meeting took place is of small consequence. Churchill had become increasingly impatient with what he saw as Simonds's reluctance to press his attacks home and urged him forcefully to 'assault this bloody hill and knock the Germans off it', at the latest on that same night. No mention seems to have been made during this discussion of the arrival on the island of 40 Commando or that it might be put in simultaneously against the hill. Churchill returned to Brigade Headquarters. His brigade major, Alf Blake, framed detailed orders and wirelessed them to Simonds. These again seem not to have referred to an involvement of 40 Commando.

Simonds received his orders at a quarter past five: 43 Commando were to take Point 622. The start time was given as 9 pm. The Partisans would put in simultaneous attacks on the adjacent peaks of Points 542 and 648. At 6.30 Simonds co-ordinated the details of his attack with those of the Partisan commander. Artillery support from Bol, already arranged, began to fall accurately, noisily and persistently on all three objectives from 8.30 onwards. The shoot was timed to end at nine o'clock.

'C' Troop, on the left of the attack, was commanded by Captain Bob Loudoun. They had been lying up on a small escarpment, on which they were mortared occasionally, without hurt. During the evening, a runner from Commando Headquarters brought the order that the troop was to move. Led by Loudoun, guided by the runner, they went in single file over the shoulder of a hill. Major Neil Munro, the second-in-command, was waiting in the valley on the far side. Munro walked along with Loudoun, told him that the troop was going into the attack and ordered him to spread them out into an extended line. This often-rehearsed manoeuvre took little time. While it was being executed Munro, still walking with Loudoun, pointed out the objective. It was about a thousand yards ahead, a skyline of rocks and low scrub silhouetted in the light of a full moon. The German positions, invisible, were somewhere on either side of the skyline, which sloped downwards from right to left as Loudoun looked at it. Munro said that it was a three-troop attack. Captain John Blake with 'D' Troop would be on Loudoun's right. Captain Gerry Schooley 'B' Troop would be on Blake's right. The attack would be shot in by a timed programme from the 25-pounders in Bol, and by the Commando's heavy weapons firing from behind the start line. The start time was at once.

'C' Troop set out towards the skyline, over broken country of scrub, rocks and stone walls. They kept their own formation, but early on lost touch with 'D' Troop on their right. Quite soon, a lot of German machine-gun tracer fire came in their direction, all aimed high. Shortly afterwards, they walked into a fairly persistent mortar stonk, some of which, Loudoun suspected, came from the Commando's own mortars falling short. There was a tremendous amount of noise but there were still no casualties. The noise was at a crescendo when Loudoun, in front, reached the German barbed wire, 'an extensive entanglement'. He could hear Germans talking and moving about beyond the wire but he was unable to see if there was a second line of wire at an interval behind the first, which would have suggested that the intervening space was mined.

Loudoun summoned Marine Charlie Nicholls, the Bangalore torpedo carrier, to breach the wire. Nicholls came up 'with great speed, delighted to get rid of the bloody thing', which he had been carrying around with him for days. It blew a gap, one-man wide. Loudoun ran for the gap, but he was beaten to it by two men, Nicholls and Corporal Royle. Both went down, almost at once, Nicholls badly wounded in the leg, Royle unconscious and dying. German small-arms fire was concentrated on the narrow gap. Loudoun turned Royle on to his back, decided that there was nothing that he could do for him and made a rapid assessment of the immediate prospects.

The alternatives that presented themselves were easily defined. The first was to lead his followers one by one through a yard-wide gap which was under close-range machine-gun fire and around which a lot of explosions were going off from what appeared to be electrically detonated mines. Those few who got through the gap would then probably, but not certainly, find themselves in a minefield with more wire at its rear and no more Bangalore torpedoes to cut it. The second option was to look for a more accessible part of the hill to attack. Loudoun picked the second alternative. His decision was warmly disputed by Marine Reg Skinner, the former Mljet well-dweller, who, close behind Loudoun, became very incensed. Loudoun shut Skinner up, and told the nearest Bren gunner, Marine Raven, to fire past the gap.

Marine Ernie Cox, Bob Loudoun's MOA, went to see if he could do anything for Corporal Royle. Royle recovered consciousness for long enough to say, 'Don't bother with me. I've bloody well had it. Look after the next bloke.' Cox moved to the next bloke. This was Raven, the Bren gunner, by now badly hit. Loudoun, who had earlier shouted 'Come on, "C" Troop!', ordered a withdrawal. From the German side of the wire somebody else also shouted 'Come on, "C" Troop!', a call that has puzzled Loudoun to the present day. Was it by somebody from the 40 Commando attack which he did not yet know had gone in? Was it by a German pulling Loudoun's leg? Or was it, as suggested by Marine Harry Thirkell, who also heard it, a German NCO calling to his soldiers *'Kommen Sie hier!'*?

Casualties began to mount as 'C' Troop made its way back down the hill. Marine Snowden, seriously wounded, was carried down on a stretcher improvised from a groundsheet by Sergeant Bill Ash, Reg Skinner and two other marines. Skinner found an aid post manned by Americans from the Operations Group, and asked for morphia for Snowden. The Americans had none to spare. Snowden died a little while later. Bob Loudoun was hit in the ankle either by a mortar-bomb fragment or by a piece of mine (he has never determined which) and was unable to stand. Sergeant 'Bunny' Green gave him a pickaback. Lieutenant Gregory, with a painful wound in his foot, was helped down by Lance-Corporal Norris Peak. When yet another mortar stonk came howling down, Peak lowered Gregory for safety to a shadowy patch of ground that turned out to be a thorn bush. Gregory thought little of this and told Peak so. Similar stories of the unwounded helping the wounded prevailed across the hillside.

Because of a shortage of numbers brought about by unreplaced casualties from earlier operations, 'C' Troop had before Brac been reorganised into three sub-sections instead of the standard two sections of two sub-sections each. As a consequence of this rearrangement, Loudoun's second subaltern, Lieutenant Jack Stevens, had been left with no one to command, and had been ordered by Loudoun to stay on the start line. Stevens an Irish neutral of an independent cast of mind, had disliked this order and quietly ignored it. He had tracked the advance from close behind, and he now joined Loudoun, who had been put down with his back to a stone wall. Loudoun asked no questions about mutinous behaviour. There had been signs of a German counter-attack down the hill. Stevens, the only troop officer still on his feet (indeed the only officer of all three assaulting troops still on his feet), was at once put in charge of a covering screen to hold off any German interference.

At about this time, two strange marines arrived at Loudoun's wall. He asked then if they were from 'D' Troop or from 'B' Troop. They said they were from neither, they belonged to 40 Commando. Loudoun was incredulous. It was news to him that 40 Commando were on Brac, let alone taking part in the assault. Sergeant Green resumed his lifting, and carried Loudoun along a path that led past Commando Headquarters. Loudoun reported to Simonds and added that he had just met two marines from 40 Commando. Simonds refused to believe him.

Corporal Peak, the escorter of Lieutenant Gregory, met a tall, fair NCO from 'B' Troop later identified as Corporal Shearer, who fetched a stretcher and two Partisan girls. Gregory was loaded on to the stretcher and carried to Dr Bazeley's Regimental Aid Post.

Meanwhile, Marine Jeffs - Loudoun's troop signaller - had been wounded, not too badly, by grenade fragments in his back and shoulder. Every time he tried to move from his cover somebody either took a shot at him or threw something at him. The sound of bagpipes, moving from right to left across his front behind the ridge, suggested to him that an improvement was imminent. His assumption was that the Highland Light Infantry, the only pipers of whom he knew, had come to put things right. His confidence increased when German fire in his vicinity quietened, and when the Very lights of a success signal soared into the air above the main German position. Jeffs stood up, and looked around the silent, moonlit ridge. He saw some movement, started towards it and was taken prisoner by four German soldiers.

'D' and 'B' Troops, to the right of 'C', found themselves in similar cases but with variations. Their approach was a climb over similar difficult, broken ground. There was Spandau tracer firing high, some through error, some in accordance with the standard German procedures for indicating the axis of advance of attackers so that they could be engaged by mortar and gunfire. Both troops suffered casualties on their way up from heavy mortaring, broke into the German forward positions, and with rapidly accumulating losses could make no further progress. There were small-arms and grenade exchanges amid the insistent din of the mortaring. Captain John Blake of 'D' Troop was killed. Both his subalterns were wounded. Over to the right, Captain Gerry Schooley of 'B' Troop used wire-cutters while being shot at to gap two successive barbed-wire entanglements and ordered the wounded Troop Sergeant-Major Hugh Fuller to collect all casualties who could move and take them down the hill. Schooley set himself up with a small party in some overrun German trenches. His two subalterns were wounded. So were four sergeants of the two troops. The number of experienced leaders still on their feet was diminishing fast.

The holders of this precarious lodgement were puzzled after a while by a persistent and unexpected sound that penetrated the overall level of noise. From their right and then growing louder as it moved steadily across their front behind the Germans they were facing, came the swirl of pipes.

The end of the involvement of the three troops of 43 Commando on the slopes of Point 622 is summarised in the unit's post-action report:

> 2215 hours  Enemy counter-attack in strength from left flank. Remnants of 'C' and 'D' Troops driven back to lower slopes of hill. 'E' Troop at bottom of hill heavily mortared.

2230 hours   Ammunition exhausted and casualties heavy. Commanding Officer decided to break off fight.

Word of this decision of Simonds either did not reach Gerry Schooley and his 'B' Troop party or if it did, was found by Schooley to be impossible to implement. He stayed where he was on the shoulder of the hill, defending the captured German trench position.

In the penultimate paragraph of his report Simonds listed his casualties: 'Captains JP Blake and RG Schooley missing. Reason to believe Captain Schooley killed assaulting the objective. 13 Other Ranks missing or killed. Captain Loudoun, Lieutenants Gregory, Nunns, Odendaal wounded. 47 Other Ranks wounded.'

No records survive of the precise starting strengths of the three troops who went in to this attack. Each was in theory sixty-five strong. Unreplaced casualties from previous operations, sickness and absences on courses and so on invariably meant that in the islands the full and theoretical totals were never met. At a reasonable guess the manpower committed by each troop was about forty-five, giving an overall total of 135, all ranks. In less than two hours, sixty-six of these were to be put permanently or temporarily out of the war, more of them temporarily than permanently.

Simonds's headquarters were set up in small coppice on a ridge to the west of Point 622, the peak which was the Commando objective. Captain Ralph Bazeley had initially sited his Regimental Aid Post beside Commando Headquarters but once the attack began the ridge came under fire from German Spandaus, firing tracer on fixed lines. It was clearly no place for treating wounded. Bazeley shifted to a small house with an attached stable, in a sheltered gully. The occupants, an old woman, her daughter and a small child, gave Bazeley an hospitable welcome and incorporated themselves into his medical team.

The first casualties to come in were treated individually by Bazeley. The numbers soon became so great that he had to delegate the swabbing, cleaning, bandaging and injecting to his medical sergeant and his orderlies, who in the more complex cases worked on advice and instructions from him. He performed no surgery. That had to be deferred until the patients could reach the properly equipped hospital on Vis. The aid-post work was a patching-up process. The patched-up who could walk made their own way down to the beach where an LCI awaited them. A shuttle of stretcher-bearers carried the more seriously hurt. The old woman took some down on a donkey. The leavers were replaced by a steady stream of new arrivals, Partisan as well as British, some carried in, some helped in, some walking or limping. The carriers and helpers were Commando stretcher-bearers and Partisan girls. These girls, mostly in their teens or early twenties, who searched the hillside for wounded while under mortar and machine-gun fire and some of whom were themselves killed or wounded, were much admired by 43.

Bazeley only discovered later that two other medical teams were working busily within a few hundred yards of his own, one from the American Operations Group, the other a temporary Partisan hospital established in Nerezisce. The flow of casualties to Bazeley diminished, and then stopped altogether. He saw his last patient off towards the beach and then turned his attentions to tidying up the house and the stable. He picked up used dressings, empty morphia syrettes, cigarette ends, sweet papers, and everything else that might indicate to German searchers the use to which the buildings had been put. He wanted no reprisals to fall upon the kindly old woman, her daughter and the child. They refused his offer of evacuation to Vis, and he said goodbye. He heard later that the house had been burned down. There were unconfirmed accounts of the shooting of the family.

The surprise appearance of the two 40 Commando marines at Bob Loudoun's position, the sound of bagpipes on the hilltop, and the sight of the Very light success signal slowly became explicable. There seems to have been a signals breakdown, not surprisingly with the sets then available and in that hilly country. Colonel Jack Churchill's intention of using three 40 Commando troops in an assault on the hill simultaneous with that of 43 had not been made known to Simonds. In the event the 40 Commando attack went in late. A guide had got lost. Eventually, Churchill leading and playing his pipes, the three troops overran the summit. On the way up they passed Gerry Schooley of 'B' Troop of 43, Captain Jimmy Wakeling, late of 2RM, now of 40, called greetings to his old friend. Schooley was killed shortly afterwards. A strong German counter-attack retook their lost positions. Colonel Jack Churchill was wounded and captured. Colonel Pops Manners of 40 was captured and died of wounds. In all 40 Commando lost nineteen killed and about forty wounded.

On Sunday, 4 June, both Commandos re-embarked on LCIs; 40 in the morning, 43 in the evening, and set course for the island base of Vis. The RAF regained some of its dented popularity shortly before embarkation. Two Spitfires shot down two Messerschmitts which tried to strafe the beaches. 111 Field Regiment and the Raiding Support Regiment came back in their various craft on the same day. Most of the Partisans remained on Brac. So did two troops of No 2 Commando, who lost twenty captured in an abortive attempt to rescue Colonel Jack Churchill. The survivors, after several days, also returned to Vis. They reported that the hilltop, when seen by them on the first day of their expedition, had been littered with large numbers of German dead.

On 13 June 1944, Force 266 produced an 'Appreciation of the Effects on the Enemy of Operation Flounced'. Its findings were that Brac had been reinforced from the mainland by 1900 Germans, 'clearly a direct result of the attack'. There had also been much German nervousness about the possibility that they might be further landings along the Dalmatian coast. Some formations had been moved to counter this threat. Others had been frozen where they were. To the extent that none of these troops could be made available to harass Tito in Bosnia, Tito's predicament had been eased. At the same time no Germans had been sent from Bosnia to strengthen the coast. The pressure on Tito had not been increased but neither had it diminished. It had stayed constant, at a level of intensity that hamstrung his ability to influence and control Partisan operations. He had lost touch with nearly all his subordinate headquarters.

In the first week of June, Tito asked to be flown out of mainland Yugoslavia, to a new base from which he could reimpose his grip upon events without the distraction of being hounded through the forests and mountains. A few days later he established his new headquarters in a cave on the side of Mount Hum, the highest peak on Vis.

# CHAPTER ELEVEN

# HVAR 2, BRAC 2, SOLTA

On Vis, the routine of training, planning and the despatch of reconnaissance parties by schooner and motor launch continued as before. The summer became progressively hotter. The rocks shimmered under a burning sun and reflected a brilliant light. Daytime wear for off-duty troops was a pair of shorts and a pair of P.T. shoes. Recovered Brac casualties slowly rejoined from hospital in Italy.

Drafts of replacements for severe casualties including one of ten new officers came from the United Kingdom. Among the ten were Lieutenants Preston Britz and Venter, seconded from the South African Union Defence Force who added a cheerfully exotic touch to the unit's life.

In early July, Captain Jock Hudspith, with Lieutenant Odendaal, ten men, and an exceptionally powerful wireless set provided by Special Operations Executive, landed on Hvar to look into some information provided by the Partisans. A German patrol with regular habits was reported to make a visit to the village of Bogomilje at intervals of six to ten days. Outside the village the patrol customarily split into two parties. One picqueted the high ground on either side of the road. The other went into the village in search of loot.

On 5 July the patrol duly put in an appearance and did exactly what the Partisans had said that it always did. This time it did it under the close observation of Hudspith and his party, well concealed. Hudspith wirelessed back to Vis that there was a ready-made ambush target on offer. Colonel Simonds came over five days later to look at the ground, and was followed on the next day by three weak troops of his Commando, totalling one hundred men. These landed soon after midnight and were installed in their respective ambush positions shortly before dawn. It was an unusual dawn for an Adriatic summer. Rain drummed down. Low cloud drifted about on the hills and in the valleys.

The mist and cloud brought about an unplanned start to the operation. The German patrol, thirty men, arrived on time, walked unseen through the murk past the observation post that was to report its approach, walked unseen right through the ambush and arrived in Bogomilje, where it at once captured a surprised and resentful Captain Ralph Bazeley, who had laid out the apparatus of his aid post in one of the village houses. Bazeley had been a prisoner for a quarter of an hour before a break in the cloud cover made it evident to the ambushers that the sequence had not developed as forecast.

Simonds put all three troops into a simultaneous attack on the village. They went in making a great deal of noise, later referred to disparagingly by Bazeley, at the receiving end, as 'banshee and bayonet methods'. The Germans fought back well, from inside the houses. Lieutenant Mark Nunns was wounded after silencing with a grenade a Spandau firing from a cottage window. Captain Desmond Clark was also wounded in another shoot-out with a Spandau. Sergeant French chased one German for a hundred yards before downing him with a Tommy gun. The affray lasted for fifteen minutes. At the end of it there were seventeen German prisoners, eight German dead, five unaccounted for, and a liberated medical staff giving their professional services to the wounded of both sides - in the British case Nunns, Clark and three lightly hurt marines.

The troops, crammed tightly into motor launches, bringing their prisoners with them, were back on Vis before midnight, feeling rather pleased with themselves. The success had been on a small scale. It was some compensation for Brac.

By September there developed a change in the pattern of island operations. The original harassment for the sake of harassment, which had shifted into harassment for the sake of hampering the German thinning-out of numbers, reached its final phase of intervention to disrupt what had by now become a German implementation of an intention to evacuate the islands altogether. The British aim was to prevent as many of them as was possible from getting away to fight elsewhere.

On 11 September, all the German garrisons of Brac had been withdrawn from their outlying positions and had been concentrated in two pockets around the ports of Supetar and Sumartin, clearly awaiting embarkation. Two brigades of Partisans, two batteries of 111 Field Regiment, a troop of RSR 75-mm mountain guns and 43 sailed from Vis to make the German departure unpleasant. The Supetar group withstood the interference and extricated themselves by night to Split. The south-eastern group were held in. The navy sank every boat that tried to leave Sumartin and the adjacent coves. The Germans fought with courage and determination. For more than a week they held out against repeated Partisan attacks, supported by all the British guns and by medium bomber and fighter-bomber strikes by the RAF. Two hundred Germans at last surrendered to the Partisans. 43, who had been given what turned out to be the unexacting role of securing and patrolling the mountains in the north-west of the island, had one casualty, an illustration of the inconsequential nature of ill-luck among the by-ways of war. Lieutenant John Odendaal, who had been wounded during the June assault on the hilltop above Nerezisce, went back to examine the old German positions to see what the battle must have looked like from the German end. He trod on a mine and lost a foot.

Solta came next and almost immediately. Since Colonel Jack Churchill's removal of the entire island garrison by No 2 Commando and intimidatory use of the loud-hailer in March, Solta had been reoccupied by two German companies of No 892 Grenadier Regiment. These had set about the preparation of their defences in a more professional manner than had their predecessors. Grohote and Rogac, the scene of the 2 Commando exploit, were now protected by a wired-in minefield, fifty feet wide. Behind the minefield were four strongpoints, each further surrounded by wire and mines, and each consisting of clusters of concrete pill-boxes linked by trenches. One of the strongpoints held positions for a hundred men, one for sixty and two for forty. Outside the minefield, a large area to the south-east had been sown at random with *Schuh* mines, little wooden boxes easy to conceal, incapable, because there was no metal in them, of being identified by mine detectors, and designed to blow off the foot of anyone who trod on them. A German prisoner interrogated after the operation said that there were 32,000 mines around the positions. The defenders had the usual complement of Spandaus and small-arms, two Italian howitzers, four 81-mm mortars and on call, the supporting services of German coastal batteries behind Split, on Drvenik island and at Ciovo, south of Trogir. Solta had formidable and tested defences. There had been two major Partisan attempts on them earlier in the summer. Both had been repulsed. The one in June, mounted by the 1st Dalmatian Brigade with air support by the RAF, had involved two days of bitter fighting.

No 43 Commando returned in their LCIs from Brac to Vis shortly before midnight on Saturday, 16 September. Lieutenant-Colonel Ian MacAlpine of the Black Watch, who had replaced Simonds as the Commanding Officer of 43,* was at once told that tactical reconnaissance flown by the RAF 'seemed to indicate' that shipping seen in Drvenik harbour had evacuated part, possibly all, of the Solta garrison. MacAlpine was ordered to take 43 to seize and hold the island, after first destroying what was left of the garrison, if anything. He would have the support of the mountain guns and heavy machine-guns of the RSR, three small teams of sappers to deal with mines, and a train of sixteen mules with handlers from the Royal Army Veterinary Corps.

MacAlpine was a wary and experienced soldier who had fought as a young man in the First World War and who had commanded No 6 Commando in Tunisia in the Second. He was not altogether convinced by the RAF reconnaissance report, which seemed to him to owe as much to an assumption as to observation underpinned by firm evidence. His doubts grew when he heard that a recently returned patrol of the Highland Light Infantry confirmed that there were at least some Germans left on Solta, although how many was unknown. One normally reliable source of intelligence was not on tap. The entire civilian population of Solta had been evacuated by the Partisans. There were no longer any resident Partisans on the island either. MacAlpine declined to commit his Commando to what might be anything from a walkover to an under-supported assault on heavily defended prepared positions, until he had more information. He sent one of his troops to find it.

An LCI took Captain Ian Gourlay and 'D' Troop across during the late evening of Sunday, 17 September. Gourlay, who had recently joined the unit as a replacement for John Blake, killed on Brac, started his investigations as soon as it was light. The village of Gornje Selo proved to be German-free and without booby-traps. The hills

---

* *MacAlpine was the only army officer to command a Royal Marine Commando during the Second World War.*

around Grohote were occupied by Germans of aggressive dispositions who shot up Gourlay and his five-man patrol with Spandaus, rifles and mortars. That night, 43 Commando and its helpers came over, in an LCI that towed two ramped landing craft loaded with the mules and heavy stores, accompanied by two of the small Landing Craft Personnel and escorted by motor launches. Gourlay had guides waiting for them on the beach. The troops climbed up the narrow track of a rocky gully and deployed in a beach-head perimeter among the high ground.

Patrols sent out in the morning, one of them accompanied by MacAlpine, saw Germans moving about in Grohote itself and in outpost positions on the adjoining hills. Colonel Meynell, the commander of the Vis garrison, arrived in the evening with further news provided by RAF reconnaissance. Twelve ships loaded with German troops had been seen sailing from Solta to the mainland. The RAF believed that there were none left on the island. MacAlpine, who had been looking at Germans a few hours before, was disinclined to share this belief. He put the matter to the test early on the next day. Different hills around Grohote were allocated to individual troops for seizure. If the hills were unoccupied, so much the better. If they were occupied, the occupants were to be thrown off and fire was to be drawn from the main position in Grohote, so that German positions could be located accurately and an assessment made of their strength.

The hills were occupied. The first on the list, Podvlake, was a not very strongly held observation post. 'C' Troop, led by Captain Bob Loudoun, advanced in a long extended line through the rocks and scrub under machine-gun and mortar fire. The observation post got out, leaving something of a mess of spent cartridge cases and half-eaten food, and taking with them a clear picture of the topography of the low hill that they had abandoned. Mortar fire came down on Loudoun's troop almost at once. Loudoun disposed his two sections in an all-round defensive position. Digging in the stony ground here, as elsewhere in Dalmatia, was out of the question. The marines built sangars.

An hour after 'C' Troop, had established themselves on Podvlake, 'D' Troop Captain Ian Gourlay, and 'E' Troop, Captain Ralph Parkinson-Cumine, set out for their hills, two neighbouring bumps on Mala Staza, to the west of Podvlake. Both troops were mortared and shelled during their approach across the valley, were machine-gunned as they shot their way up the hill and were shelled heavily by guns from the mainland once they had taken their objectives. They too built sangars. Over on the right, Captain Jock Hudspith and 'A' Troop had reached Zukova. It was where they had been aiming for but was found to be in the middle of an unmarked minefield.

MacAlpine sent Lieutenant Jack Bolton with the 3-inch mortar section of the Heavy Weapons Troop to join Loudoun on Podvlake. Bolton mortared Grohote. The guns in Grohote, and in Split, Drvenik and Ciovo, shelled all the Commando's positions intermittently for the rest of the day and night. A 210-mm coastal defence gun in an emplacement behind Split was the biggest, noisiest and most distant. About the best that could be said for it was that it telegraphed its punches. There was an interval of fifty seconds between the bright flashing of its discharge in front of the mountains and the arrival on the Solta positions, with a sound like a railway train entering a tunnel, of projectiles that detonated mightily and made spectacular redistributions of rock and soil. MacAlpine, reflecting upon the proposition which he later summarised in his report, that 'it is manifest that valuable as may be the deductions made from (RAF) tactical reconnaissance, reconnaissances on the ground alone can establish the actual facts', signalled to Vis to ask for artillery and air support.

The next day was one of more shelling from the mainland, mortaring from Grohote, and further probing patrols. Bolton's 3-inch mortars firing from Podvlake and RSR 4.2-inch mortars firing from the beach quietened things down in Grohote. The manhandling of the RSR's heavy Browning machine-guns across broken country was a slow and wearisome business but they too were in action on Podvlake by the late afternoon, shooting up the German headquarters building in Grohote. Of the patrols, Parkinson-Cumine's, on the left, found one hill and two villages to be empty, but were heavily fired at by Spandaus in the main position. Of two patrols from 'A' Troop on the right, one was caught among the *Schuh* mines. A marine and a sapper each had one of his feet blown off, and despite a series of rescue attempts could not be brought back for another forty-eight hours.

The *bura* now intervened to complicate matters further. Violent, gusting winds, driving before them torrents of rain, drenched everybody. Gourlay's and Parkinson-Cumine's troops on the left underwent an additional deprivation. Mule trains carrying boxes of Compo rations intended for the two troops had earlier been forced back by concentrated shelling. Compo rations would get few marks in a Good Food Guide, but self-heating tins of soup, or mutton and vegetable stew warmed on Tommy cookers like modern fire-lighters, were more sustaining than the corned-beef sandwiches of haversack rations which, in most cases, had been finished in the first few hours. The two troops went hungry for two days. A naval LCP, with Captain George Frost, the Commando's administrative officer aboard, finally brought supplies through the storm. The LCP had nearly foundered several times during its voyage along the coast.

The storm also frustrated attempts to land the guns that MacAlpine had asked for. A battery of 25-pounders, embarked in an LCT with a squadron of the RAF Regiment, made the crossing in a high sea. The LCT's captain was unable to pick out through the spray and rain the recognition signal in the cove that he was heading for, missed it, nearly put into the German harbour by mistake and returned through the wild night to Vis. After that, Commander Morgan Giles suspended until the weather abated any further attempts to reach Solta by flat-bottomed landing craft, which were hard to handle in a heavy sea. The weather also ruled out the air support that MacAlpine wanted. The Vis strip was water-logged. Aircraft were unable to take off. MacAlpine continued to request both artillery and air support.

The storm was not a deterrent to German shelling. Their coastal guns were registered on all targets, and they banged away steadily. The Commando and RSR mortars and machine-guns banged back into Grohote. Hudspith's troop on the right suffered more casualties from the pernicious *Schuh* mines. One of the patrols sent out to rescue the two men who had lost feet earlier at last got through to them and pulled them back to cover but were unable to get them back to the main body of the troop. Rescuers and rescued were caught by machine-gun fire from two German posts in the main position. To cover their extrication the 3-inch mortars put down smoke, the Vickers machine-guns engaged all nearby German positions, and a further rescue team of marines, sappers and Corporal Smith, the 'A' Troop medical orderly, who had been wounded on the previous day, inched forward searching for mines and defusing them as they went. Lieutenant Richards, of the Royal Engineer detachment who had accompanied the Commando on the operation, finally cleared a gap, and the earlier wounded were brought back. Three more had to be brought back with them: another sapper, another marine and Richards himself, all of whom had feet blown off. 'Great courage shown by Lt. Richards RE', reads MacAlpine's report.

The German shelling, the shooting by the heavy weapons of both sides and the only slightly diminished storm continued for the rest of the day and for the early part of the night. In the small hours of 23 September a series of flashes and heavy explosions came from the direction of Rogac cove. To many of the besiegers these seemed to be a further instalment of the thunder and lightning of the storm. The troops nearest to Rogac reported a different version. RN gunboats, they said, had come close inshore, opened fire and hit two German ammunition dumps.

At 6 am Major Neil Munro took Major Pat Turner of 111 Field Regiment to watch a 3-inch mortar shoot into Grohote. The purpose of the shoot was to indicate German targets to Turner for future attentions by his guns. There was a puzzling absence of response from the garrison. At 8.30 an 'A' Troop patrol reported that it had reached the forward German wire, had fired into the harbour and had provoked no reply. MacAlpine at once ordered an advance into the town. It was a slow progress, much delayed by the need for the sappers to neutralise a profusion of booby traps and mines. Parkinson-Cumine and 'E' Troop were at last through to Rogac harbour by the early afternoon. Five German soldiers gave themselves up. The bodies of many more were floating in the water.

At 11.15 on the night of 22 September two motor torpedo boats, Nos 655 and 633, left Komiza harbour and set course for Solta. No 655 was commanded by Lieutenant MacLaughlen of the Royal Canadian Naval Volunteer Reserve; No 633 by Lieutenant Rendall, also of the RCNVR. The Senior Officer of the MTB flotilla, Lieutenant Burke, another Canadian, was aboard 655. Burke had emergency instructions from Commander Morgan Giles. The two boats were to stop the evacuation of the German garrison of Solta from Rogac cove, planned for that night. (No records survive to indicate the source of this information, which was not known by MacAlpine and 43 Commando. The most likely origin seems to have been a wireless intercept of German naval traffic.)

The two MTBs were off Rogac shortly after 1.30 am. They immediately sighted three I-lighters, which had just left the beach, heading for the mouth of the bay. The MTBs ran in and attacked with their guns at 200 yards' range. All three lighters were hit by the guns of both boats. The lighters replied with sporadic 20-mm fire. This soon ceased. In a second run across the bay the MTBs closed the range to fifty yards and scored further hits. One lighter blew up with two violent explosions, showering the decks of the MTBs with debris. Burke then ordered 633 to stand off, and 655 went in to the bay alone to finish off the other two lighters. It was not needed. The craft had already gone down. No 655 illuminated the shoreline by firing at the rocks with incendiary Oerlikon ammunition, which bounced upwards and gave a serviceable light but nothing was seen. A limited amount of machine-gun and light mortar fire came from the shore. All missed. During the next hour or so, both MTBs made further searches of the bay, one with the help of star shell, but still no further boats could be seen.

They lay off the bay until 3.30 am, and then turned for Komiza and home before they could be caught in daylight within the range of the German coastal batteries.

Some Germans did get away from Solta. Two Poles, who survived the sinking of the lighters, and who had hidden in a slit-trench until they could surrender to the British, said that a party of about eighteen other survivors had signalled across to Split for help and had been taken off by E-boats soon after dawn. An earlier lift by lighter might also have been evacuated safely. Between 100 and 120 were killed in the explosions or drowned in Rogac cove.

MacAlpine, with a group of his own and Gunner officers, made a detailed inspection of the German defences. The consensus was that they were some of the strongest seen by anyone present. In MacAlpine's opinion they could not have been overrun without heavy air and artillery support on a scale not available in the Balkans. His message of thanks to the Royal Navy, in which he referred to 'a perfect combined operation', was more than a conventional piece of good manners.

There was one last casualty after the Germans had gone. Hudspith's minefield wounded, after being attended to by Dr Ralph Bazeley, were carried by Hudspith, Bazeley and six marines to a nearby beach, where an LCP was waiting. The wounded were loaded aboard. The doctor and the 'A' Troop party went back overland towards their positions. It was by now dark. They walked into another scattering of unmarked *Schuh* mines. A marine stepped on one, had his foot severed, and died later. The party waited until daylight and then cleared their way out.

Solta was the last of the major British operations in the Dalmatian islands. It lasted for a week, and cost 43 Commando two killed and sixteen wounded. The sapper detachment had three wounded. Afterwards there were a few more reconnaissance patrols, some more provisional planning, and an abortive attempt by Lieutenant Preston, backed by 'B' Troop of 43, to talk the German garrison on Uljan island into surrendering. It all came to nothing. The Partisans were soon the sole owners of all the islands. A nine-month episode of spasmodically violent Yugoslav history, with a relatively small number of British and a still smaller number of Americans contributing to the making of much of it, went out without any more bangs and with no whimpers. The war simply moved on.

# PART FOUR

## THE LAND OF THE SOUTH SLAVS II: MONTENEGRO

# CHAPTER TWELVE

# FINNEYFORCE AT RISAN

In the autumn of 1944 the Germans began to pull out of the southern Balkans. Their withdrawal was constrained geographically by the narrow, winding Balkan roads that in southern Yugoslavia provided only three possible routes through Montenegro. The westernmost was along the coast through Kotor and Risan; the middle one ran through Danilovgrad and Niksic; and one farther inland ran through Kolasin.

By October the German Army Group E, gathering in its garrisons as it progressed, was clear of most of Greece and Albania. When its advanced guard, found from the German XXI Mountain Corps, were emerging into Montenegro, Tito asked for British artillery support to help the Partisans to harry the German withdrawal. The newly formed and by many, distrusted British headquarters for the supervision of Balkan operations, Land Forces Adriatic, responded promptly. The dispersed batteries of 111 Field Regiment reassembled in the neighbourhood of Bari. No 43 Commando was brought back from Vis, also to near Bari. A field unit of the Royal Engineers was acquired. And 'Floydforce', whose task was 'in general to give the greatest possible artillery support to the Yugoslav National Army of Liberation', sailed from Bari for Dubrovnik on 27 October. Its commander was Brigadier J P O'Brien-Twohig, a flamboyantly moustachioed Irishman who had distinguished himself as a battalion commander in Tunisia, Sicily and Italy. The commandos had been given what was for them the uncustomary job of local protection of the artillery's gun-positions.

Politics, always present if not in the past over-intrusive with the Partisans, was soon found in Montenegro to be taking precedence over the requirements of joint participation in a fight against a common enemy. Partisan priorities were in the course of radical readjustment. Getting rid of the invader was still important. He must be harassed and damaged while he went, which was why the guns of Floydforce had been asked for. Meanwhile everything must be done to ensure that once he was gone there would be total Communist control of the country. In the eyes of Marxist ideologues, Floydforce was militarily welcome and politically suspect. Technically it was highly qualified in the business of delivering shellfire accurately onto German columns, but it was manned by representatives of an imperialist, capitalist power that was a potential threat to the revolution.

There was thus a certain weird ambivalence about many of the operational proceedings of the next three months. The mistrusted agents of the capitalist system, whose uncomplicated collective ambition was to get the job done as quickly as possible and to go home to demobilisation, were occasionally annoyed and often puzzled. They would have been more puzzled, and rather flattered, had they known that their small contribution to the ending of the war had attracted critical attention of the highest level in the Kremlin. The landing at Dubrovnik of a modest-sized force from four LCTs and three LCIs was described in a news agency report as a British invasion of Yugoslavia. Tito was in Moscow at the time for discussion with Stalin. In the course of these, Molotov produced the news report. Tito was asked for an explanation. He said that it was no invasion. It was an artillery force sent at his request. If the British tried an invasion, he would fight them. It was perhaps as well that this unusual interpretation of the responsibilities of one ally to another was not known to Floydforce at the time. The guests might have felt out of place.

The seven landing craft carrying the force tied up in Gruz harbour, on the north side of Dubrovnik, in the mid-morning of 28 October. The Commando disembarked, marched to a large shed with a concrete floor in a nearby timber yard and settled in, making philosophical assessments of the degree to which the unattractiveness of the concrete as a mattress was outbalanced by the evident fact the roof kept out the rain. The gunners attended to the unloading of the guns, the quads that towed them, the ammunition limbers, the supply trucks, the jeeps and all the other expensive paraphernalia that stimulated envy among the marines, who carried almost the entire inventory of their possessions on their backs. Brigadier O'Brien-Twohig summoned a conference of his commanders at five o'clock in the afternoon. The first part of Floydforce to take part in a form of warfare that blended some familiar elements with some entirely new modifications set out from Dubrovnik at seven o'clock on the following morning. This was Finneyforce. It consisted of 211 Field Battery, and 'C' Troop of 43 Commando. The Battery Commander, Major Pat Turner, was in overall command. 'C' Troop was led by Captain Bob Loudoun.

Finneyforce was to support the Primorska Group of the Partisans, who were trying to block the German breakout along the coastal route through Kotor and Risan. The Germans had been held temporarily at Risan, a small coastal town on a narrow alluvial plain at the head of the northernmost inlet of the Gulf of Kotor. Turner and Loudoun went ahead in a jeep to consult with the Partisan commander and to prepare their dispositions before their followers arrived. The followers trundled along well behind, slowed by heavy vehicles, by the eight guns and by mountain roads in understandably indifferent condition, the widths of which were in many places only a few inches wider than the wheel-bases of the bigger vehicles. There was also an abundance of precipitous, rocky drops, several hundred feet deep, usually where the road was narrowest. For the touristically inclined, the landscape, the few small towns and villages, and their inhabitants were something new. Vis and the other islands had had their social and domestic simplicities but there had been an ancient Venetian elegance about the little towns. Limestone rock had been plentiful but so had vineyards, olive groves and vegetable patches. There were none of those in these wild, bleak and lovely mountains.

By late afternoon the force had reached its leaders, Turner and Loudoun, who had been hospitably received by the Partisan Brigade Commander. He had joined them in their jeep, taken them to a vantage point from which it was possible to point out most of his own positions and some of the Germans', and showed on the map where those not in view were sited. The map was spread out on the bonnet of the jeep. Bob Loudoun suggested tactfully that there seemed to be an error in the placing of one of the German posts. If it was where the Partisans said it was, it was about 200 yards away and they were standing in full view of it. The Partisan confirmed cheerfully that that was indeed the case. A German Spandau gunner chose that moment to confirm it further by letting loose a sustained burst at the three of them. He missed. They withdrew prudently, with competitive dignity. Those were the first shots of the first battle to have been fought by the only British body of formed troops to have soldiered alongside a Communist army on the European mainland during the Second World War.

The gun position chosen by Pat Turner was on a small, rock-bespattered upland plain behind the tiny hamlet of Podhan. The guns were in action at first light on 30 October, the morning after arrival. Their targets were Risan itself, down on the coast at the foot of a 1600-foot escarpment with an estimated German strength in it of between 200 and 400 together with two guns, an old Austrian barracks at Ledenice two thirds of the way up the escarpment and occupied by about 200 more Germans; a defensive position, 'Midway Bunkers'; and a string of five old Imperial Austrian forts, sited in the previous century to protect the inland approaches to the fleet anchorage of the Gulf of Kotor. The forts were on commanding features, had stone walls six feet thick, steel doors and windows, and steel-lined weapon slits. The Partisans had made repeated, bloodily repulsed attempts on the forts. They had also made a series of similarly gallant and unsuccessful assaults on the two main strongpoints in Risan town - the sawmill and the hospital. The latter was a large, modern three-storied white building with a red roof upon which a red cross on a white background had been conspicuously painted. Like the sawmill, it had been fortified and garrisoned by German troops.

In one major essential, topography was kind to the gunners. High on the escarpment, approachable by a track out of view of the Germans and protected by a scattering of Partisan posts, was a compact rock shelf littered with huge boulders from which, when the weather was amenable, there could be seen in detail the entire layout of Risan, 1600 feet below and laterally less than a mile away. The panorama extended to most of the Gulf of Kotor, the only true fjord in southern Europe, an expanse of twinkling turquoise water enclosed by white limestone hills, 3000 abrupt feet high, that in some places rose vertically from the shore and in others were separated from the sea by narrow stretches of rocky flat land, seldom more than a few hundred yards wide. Along the eastern side of the Gulf, threaded around the base of the cliffs, and following the intricate line of a multiplicity of inlets, was the road from Kotor and the south, the road now in use by the German XXI Mountain Corps. From the high rock shelf most of it was visible. The stretches of it that were not, those hidden by some obtruding promontory, were in a military sense known about, because vehicles that disappeared into them could be counted, and the same number could be confidently expected to come into view again further along the road. The Gunner observation post, established in the eyrie of the rock shelf, permanently guarded by a sub-section of marines, had all the qualities of an invisible, moored balloon. Almost every overt German movement by day could be seen through binoculars, reported by wireless to the battery two miles to the rear at Podhan, and interrupted by accurately delivered shellfire of an intensity commensurate with the size of the target. In between shoots, the Forward Observation Officer and his marine protection party had one of the loveliest views in the world to admire.

Warfare, joined in so briskly on the morning after Finneyforce's arrival, came to a stop with equal briskness on the morning after that. It began to rain. It stayed raining in a relentless, drenching downpour that flooded the upland plain, washed out the stone sangars put up as defensive positions by the marines, immobilised vehicles, obliterated all view of Risan and the Kotor road from the observation post, and by virtue of a noisy, flashing background of thunder and lightning, made wireless communication impossible. Sodden blaspheming gunners and marines paddled dourly about in their dripping gas capes and saturated berets, the marines commenting freely upon a much-reiterated statement by their leader, Bob Loudoun. 'It would cost you hundreds of pounds', went the wording of this morale-boosting message, 'to come here in peacetime'.

Torrential rain, although never again of the intensity of the initial experience, was to be a recurrent curse upon the operation. Militarily it led to uncertainties about what advantage the Germans had taken of its cover to move up more troops. Domestically, its effects were unevenly distributed. The nature of the gunners' trade required that every one of them should travel in a vehicle. These were crowded but there was adequate room for spare personal kit, sleeping-bags, cooking equipment and the like. ('Some of the buggers sleep between *sheets*,' reported a marine incredulously.) The marines lived more austerely.

The weather was better on the day following the deluge. The Observation Officer in the high OP brought down shellfire on every German position in sight and registered the main ones. From then on, for three weeks, the fight to stop the Germans at the Risan block was almost ceaseless.

So far, the Germans had made a relatively unimpeded progress towards home. On their way through Greece and Albania they had had little difficulty in brushing aside attempted interference by lightly armed and politically divided guerrilla bands who were glad to see the last of them and whose harassment had been not much more than token. The Montenegrin Partisans had been a much tougher proposition. They fought with unmatchable courage. But they were under-equipped in knowledge, experience and material to stop a German army that, although it was heavily reliant upon horse-drawn transport and mule trains, had with it armour, artillery and plenty of trucks and was manned by seasoned troops firmly determined to fight their way home. Their unexpected confrontation with scientifically directed modern artillery dented German determination and confidence. They tried to negotiate a surrender, exclusively to the British. Written messages were exchanged between their German Commander and Turner, but the peacemaking came to an abrupt end when a German spokesman under cover of a white flag presented himself to the Partisan forward positions and was not seen again. The Partisans said that he had "committed suicide".

Pat Turner's plan was to keep German movement in Risan and along the coast road tightly under control, while at the same time giving priority to the destruction of the upland forts and the barracks at Ledenice. The reduction of the flank guard provided by the forts would clearly hamper seriously any German attempt to move farther forward. A second, equally urgent, need was to keep down the growing number of Partisan casualties incurred daily in gallant, doomed assaults on the forts. The courage shown in these repetitive attacks was superb. The tactics used were those of medieval siege warfare. Variously trying scaling ladders, the ignition against the walls of bundles of brushwood soaked with petrol, a battering-ram improvised from a tree trunk mounted on a farm-cart and pushed by a foot party, the Partisans advanced over open ground, armed only with their heterogeneous collection of small arms and grenades, and tried fiercely to close on regular infantry firing Spandaus and Schmeissers through steel-lined weapon slits in six-feet-thick stone walls. The consequences were inevitable. All attacks failed, with an appallingly high percentage of casualties among the attacking force.

The battle now became an affair of two linked but distinct fronts, with the guns centrally placed to join in on either side as required. Some inspired and unorthodox gunnery, the calculated use of a mixture of high explosive and solid shot armour-piercing shells, demolished the first two forts by 9 November. The survivors withdrew to the old barracks in Ledinice.

All eight of the 25-pounders, now supplemented by a troop of 75-mm guns of the Raiding Support Regiment and the 3-inch mortars of 43 Commando, who had just arrived, soon had matters other than the broaching of forts to attend to. For the past three days Partisans of the 2nd Dalmatian Brigade had been holding up the Germans on the coastal road near Kotor town. The Germans finally broke through and added another 200 men and two guns to their forward troops in Risan. It was so far a small accretion of minor immediate significance. If it were to be followed up in strength it could become serious. Parties of marines from 'C' Troop were sent off to prepare demolitions on two rock faces overlooking the winding road which the Germans would have to use if they broke out from the town. Gun cotton was packed where it would do the most good. Detonators were inserted into primers. Cordtex was laid from the detonators back to ancient-looking plungers, T-bars on cubical wooden boxes, of the type familiar to watchers of 1930's Hollywood movies.* Defensive positions were sited to cover the blow. There were rehearsals of an ambitious projected sequence of notional events, conducted with scepticism, which included the bringing down of the cliffs, a tidy little road ambush and the disengagement of the ambushers at the appropriate moment in a 15-hundredweight truck, capable if grossly overloaded of carrying about a quarter of them.

While these precautionary preparations for the disengagement of Finneyforce were

---

*Some weeks after these precautions were taken, and when they were no longer necessary, Bob Loudoun took a party back to recover the explosives. The cordtex -cutting explosive encased in what looked rather like insulated wire and capable of severing a tree - was in popular local use. Peasants had abstracted it. They found it convenient for lashing loads to donkeys.*

under way, the guns were busily making them unnecessary. The newcomers to Risan were either unwarned about or failed to pay attention to warnings of, the fact that they were conspicuous targets for observed artillery fire, put down with lethal efficiency. They had had things too much their own way for too long. They wandered about the streets, sight-seeing. They placed their guns artlessly. In a protracted and devastating shoot the 25-pounders and the 75s destroyed two German guns, forced the abandonment of the gun position of a third, and brought all overt movement in the town and its approaches to a halt. Local acoustic peculiarities amplified the din. The bang of the guns' discharges, the sibilant whistlings, developing into howlings, of shells in flight, the crashes of their explosions on impact, thundered in the enclosed amphitheatre of the Gulf, and echoed and re-echoed back and forth between the limestone crags and precipices of the looming mountains. Meanwhile Pat Turner shifted his attentions once more to the forts.

It was not an exclusive attention. Any movement in Risan still attracted a prompt flurry of whining, crashing shells. The strongpoints in the sawmill and the hospital were regular targets. A request to Balkan Air Force to put in an airstrike on these was met by an apology. The BAF had a long string of prior commitments elsewhere. Risan would have to take its turn. Turner signalled back a sort of banker's standing order: an airstrike as soon as possible on any morning between ten and eleven o'clock would be helpful.

In consultation with Bob Loudoun he also gave consideration to the problem of how to give further discouragement to users of the Kotor road by night. Although random shelling had forced German vehicles bringing up supplies and reinforcements to Risan to drive without lights, there was no reason to believe that the night traffic was not still substantial. It was decided that Loudoun should blow a hole in the road. After a careful study through binoculars from the high OP of possible options, he selected a likely looking culvert near Perast, about two miles on the Kotor side of Risan. With 300 pounds of ammonal packed into sandbags and prepared for immediate detonation by the inclusion in each bag of a string of guncotton primers knotted together by cordtex, the load carried on donkeys, Loudoun, three marines, a Partisan guide and the donkey handlers set out from Podhan at dawn for a hard march through the mountains. The guide was good. He led them to the south-east, close to but out of sight of, the German Ledenice defences, and round to the hamlet of Velenici, 2000 feet above the culvert.

They reached Velenici in the late afternoon. The Partisans had promised to provide a carrying party to help take the thirty bags of explosive down the steep, and in some places pathless, hillside. Loudoun had assumed that these porters would be Partisans. In fact, the Partisan guide had simply told the village headman of Velenici to provide a team. Since everyone of both sexes and of military age (as interpreted in Montengro in 1944, everyone between about eleven and the early seventies) was already away fighting, Loudoun moved down the slope in the gathering darkness like the Pied Piper, surrounded by chattering children and a lacing of stout-hearted but equally noisy old-timers. These led the demolition party faultlessly to where they wanted to go, dumped their loads and disappeared up the hill into the night. A marine and two Partisans went a hundred yards up the road on the Risan side and laid a necklace of light anti-vehicle mines across it. A small group of Partisans did the same on the Kotor side. Loudoun and other Partisans stacked the bags in the culvert, got very cold in icy water and had just finished the attachment of the cordtex leads to the detonators when there was an interruption, in two instalments.

Part One was the Risan roadblock team, sprinting. Part Two was a German truck that had driven over the necklace of mines without setting them off. Loudoun had intended to check each member of the party away in the prescribed manner before detonating the charges. There was no time for these niceties. There was also nowhere to go except down the road towards Kotor. The local cliff was vertical. Loudoun pulled the pins and the demolishers headed south at speed, moving rather faster than the truck, which, lightless, was being driven with caution. Loudoun found a gap in the bank, saw his party up and scrambled after them. The truck trundled slowly by, its occupants apparently having noticed nothing unusual. The culvert blew up with a gratifying flash and bang. Loudoun's group was showered by flying bits of road. The lorry stopped, amid raised voices.

An over-long pause for self-satisfaction, followed by a still longer search for a couple of Partisans who were temporarily mislaid, delayed the departure for home. This was unfortunate, because the next item on the operational programme was an artillery shoot on to the blow, timed for half an hour after the bang. The timing was exact. The Loudoun party left through a shrieking, crashing, zinging delivery of shells by its own supporters. No one was hit. At dawn they looked down from the mountain at their handiwork: a nice big hole; a truck wrecked on the mine necklace; a foot patrol in single file approaching the hole from Perast. The same view, from a reciprocal bearing, was available to the high OP. Road repairs in daylight were made impossible by shelling. The damaged truck was pushed into the hole by night and bridged with planking. But from then on Risan was closed to heavy transport.

Blowing things up in a good cause is militarily infectious. After the successful bang at Perast, Turner and Loudoun between them picked off the map a likely looking bridge in southern Montenegro on the only motorable road between the coast and the second, inner, potential German escape route. Lieutenant Jack Stevens of 'C' Troop was provided with mules, explosives and a small escort. He put in a hard, several days long mountain march, reaching his target, and found that the Germans, for unfathomable reasons, had blown it already. There was, however, some unexpected Grand Opera type consolation for Stevens. Sweat-stained, begrimed, and crumpled he was swept by welcoming Partisans on to the balcony of the old Royal Palace at Cetinje where, alongside a Partisan Corps Commander, he took the salute at a mass parade.

The third of the five forts was breached by the alternating solid-shot and high-explosive technique on 11 November. There was some inaccurate interference from the German guns in Ledenice, which were promptly wrecked by a massive concentration of over a hundred rounds from the other 25-pounders. The last two forts fell on the 17th. The survivors from these defences fell back on the old Austrian barracks at Ledenice, now isolated by Partisans from the Risan garrison. Unlike the forts, the Ledenice barracks had not been designed primarily for defence. They housed living accommodation and administrative offices. They were on a little upland plateau, overlooked by neighbouring high ground, now, with their protecting forts gone, in Partisan possession. During the late morning of the 17th, the eight 25-pounders, the two 75s, two 3-inch mortars of the Heavy Weapons Troop of 43 Commando and about 600 surrounding Partisans armed with a miscellany of rifles and captured Spandaus, poured a destructive, deafening and spectacular fire into a disintegrating collection of elderly buildings grouped together in a space about half the size of a soccer pitch.

The Germans held out until twenty minutes past one in the afternoon. They then showed a white flag, after which confusion ensued. Turner quieted his guns and the mortars. Partisan small-arms fire slowly dwindled and then stopped altogether. The Partisans understandably assumed that the white flag was a sign of surrender. They walked into the ruined barracks and helped themselves to German weapons, watches, rings and similar portable and useful items of loot. Pat Turner and Bob Loudoun, also under the impression that the white flag signified surrender, walked over together and met a very angry, very brave and very unrealistic German commander. This was an outrage, he complained, staring at the Partisans who were improving the size of their personal collections. All that he had wanted from the white flag was a truce during which his wounded could be evacuated. He had three proposals to make to put matters right immediately. His wounded should be taken to safety. Weapons and personal property sequestrated by the Partisans should be given back at once. The Partisans should return to their original starting points ('Get that rabble out of my position'), Turner and Loudoun should go back to theirs, and at an agreed signal the battle should recommence.

Turner pointed out succinctly the impossibility of enforcing these conditions, even had he wanted to, which he did not. The intended truce had already become a *de facto* surrender. The German commander at last reluctantly accepted it as such. The true depth of his gallantry in wanting to resume the fight was appreciated when his casualties were counted. In the shambles of his mountain barracks, on a grey November day, there were forty-three dead, seventy-odd wounded of whom six died later, and 197 unhurt. He had had a further seventeen killed during the shelling of the forts. The unwounded prisoners were marched away by the Partisans. The wounded were taken in British transport for treatment at the Gunners' Regimental Aid Post. Captain Bernard Kieft of the Royal Army Medical Corps, helped by captured German medical orderlies and by gunner and marine volunteers, worked throughout the night in tending the patients.

A working party of marines, reflecting gloomily that the job was properly one for the uninjured prisoners who had been marched off by the Partisans, buried the German dead in a mass grave. On a captured German cross, Turner's battery craftsmen inscribed in German: 'In memory of forty-three German soldiers who fell in battle.' Turner planted the cross himself, stood back and saluted the grave. A 'C' Troop guard of honour presented arms. These formal decencies completed, Pat Turner returned to the supervision of his guns, still booming steadily away into Risan.

During the night of 19/20 November, a German column either tried to retake Ledenice or possibly, in un-Germanic confusion about what had happened to it, tried to reinforce it. The column's composition - it included a mule train and horse-drawn carts - suggested the second. It was routed by Partisans. On the following morning the road was littered with dead German soldiers, dead mules and horses and wrecked ammunition wagons.

The next day was the busiest yet. There were strong indications that the Germans were building up for a determined attempt at a breakthrough. During the night, the sound of much movement of vehicles had come from the Kotor road. Further movement, all into Risan, continued throughout the day, heavily harassed by gunfire. German artillery from the south and the east repeatedly shelled the escarpment. Two 25-pounders were moved to counter this fire. The shooting continued for the rest of the day, intermittently and irregularly reaching a series of crescendos. The marines of 'C' Troop set up a roadblock at the head of the zigzag road that climbed the escarpment. When dust fell all sentries were doubled. A full stand-to was called before first light on 21 November. At the same time all guns fired an intensive defensive fire programme on to all likely forming-up positions for a German assault, and on to the routes leading to them and from them.

When it became light enough to see clearly, the Forward Observation Officer looked through his binoculars from the high observation post into Risan and gazed at what at first sight seemed to be the finest target of his life. The streets and the waterfront were swarming with people. A more detailed inspection showed them to be Partisans and civilians. The Germans had abandoned their westernmost breakout route as too difficult and too expensive. They had withdrawn during the night, southwards through Kotor and beyond, to turn inland in the hope of getting out by one of the other two routes.

Pat Turner moved down into the town that he had done so much to disfigure. Lieutenant McConville and Sergeant Bill Ash's sub-section set out after him a half hour or so later. They paused a third of the way down to look at what had once been a pretty, Adriatic coastal town in an unusually beautiful setting. Now the houses were battered and crumbled, and the neat gardens were pitted with the marks where shells and mortar bombs had exploded. From a distance there seemed not to be an intact pane of glass in the place. They were appraising all this destruction silently, when from out to sea they heard the distant sound of engines, growing noisier. Aircraft with Royal Air Force roundels swept into view, circled round the Gulf, formed up into line ahead and dived in succession to put in rousing rocket attacks on the sawmill and the hospital, targets suggested to them by Pat Turner in the long-forgotten banker's order. He was now sitting in one of them, wishing that the RAF would go away. Later in the day Balkan Air Force signalled a solicitous apology. Turner replied that the RAF couldn't hit a pussy-cat.

Risan was a mess of strewn rubble, broken glass, dead horses and mules, burnt-out German vehicles and two destroyed guns. There were many new graves and one more to be dug, for a German second lieutenant who had somehow been left behind at the time of the withdrawal had had his head beaten in by Partisans. Partisans clambered about the buildings, some of which were totally wrecked, all of them scarred by hits from shell and mortar fragments. The wards and corridors of the hospital were ankle-deep in rubbish, shattered glass, brickdust and piles of cartridge cases at abandoned fire positions. The Germans had left behind large stocks of small-arms ammunition and uniforms. Partisans helped themselves. Then they were fallen in, a ragged, ardent mixture of young and old, men and women, boys and girls, humping their miscellaneous armoury of captured Spandaus and Schmeissers and rifles over their shoulders, hung about with grenades. They left indomitably at the jog-trot which they favoured, heading towards Kotor along the road beside the lovely Gulf.

Finneyforce was not invited to join in the Partisan follow-up after Risan. Instead the force withdrew to Bileca to refurbish itself and to stay in readiness for intervention wherever else it might be required. In the three weeks between 30 October and 21 November its guns had fired a total of 12,000 rounds. It had done the job that it had been sent to do. One of the three German escape routes had been blocked, permanently. It is no denigration of Partisan courage and capacity to say that without the guns the Germans almost certainly would have broken through. The Partisans were the finest guerrilla force of the Second World War. But guerrillas are neither trained nor equipped to stop, as opposed to harass, a military machine of the size and with the resources, of XXI Mountain Corps of the German Army Group E.

At Bileca, Pat Turner's battery craftsmen, mechanically versatile, rigged a complicated apparatus which provided hot water showers. When his battery had been suitably cleansed Turner offered the hospitality of the showers to Bob Loudoun for his troop of marines. Loudoun accepted with gratitude. The marines were hygienically in much worse condition than were the gunners. They had shaved daily, washed the grime from their faces and kept their weapons clean. They were otherwise deficient in personal daintiness. For three weeks they had sweated over hills, had been saturated by rain and had slept in their one set of clothes on the beaten-earth floors of peasant cottages and livestock sheds. Some had acquired that common passport of Partisan warfare, lice.

Loudoun was and still is, immensely proud of 'C' Troop of 43 Royal Marine Commando. He had raised, trained, cherished and led them in action from Anzio onwards. He would personally see to it that every one of them would wallow in the steam and soap and wash away the muck of weeks. He decided that before doing so he would allow himself a little personal luxury. He would have a private bath, all to himself. He ordered one of his subalterns to take the troop out on a training exercise, telling the man deceitfully that he himself was unable to accompany his followers because of urgent, unspecified military business. When they came back, dirtier and sweatier than ever, they would be met by a glowing, scrubbed Loudoun, who would tell them proudly of the marvellous surprise he had for them.

He gave the troop ten minutes to get well clear of Bileca, rolled his towel neatly under his arm and walked happily to the Gunner headquarters. The sentry saluted. Loudoun returned the salute.

'Where's the shower?' asked Loudoun eagerly.

'They've just gone out on a training exercise,' said the sentry.

## CHAPTER THIRTEEN

# FLOYDFORCE: NIKSIC, CETINJE, PODGORICA

Colonel Ian McAlpine, who was really too old for this sort of thing, had left 43 for health reasons shortly after the Solta fight. Major Neil Munro led the Commando to Dubrovnik in October. 43's new and last, Commanding Officer took over in unpromising circumstances in November in Montenegro. His new unit was committed to a task, the protection of Royal Artillery guns, for which it was not designed, and in which, it might be argued, its trained talents were under-used. It was ill-clad for a Balkan winter. Its tenuous supply from Italy was inadequate. The allies it supported were an increasingly devious, suspicious, unscrupulous and politically abrasive Communist Mafia. One of its troops, Bob Loudoun's 'C', was operating away from the unit's main body and was on the coast in a private little war of its own.

Lieutenant Colonel Ian Riches had been commissioned in 1927. He was a signals specialist and a qualified interpreter in French and Spanish. He had been adjutant at the Plymouth Division from 1936-1938, was at Dakar with the Royal Marine Brigade, and briefly became the second-in-command of 2RM. After graduating at the Army Staff College at Camberley, he rejoined the staff of the Royal Marine Division, and then went as Assistant Adjutant General of the Corps. His last appointment before taking over 43 was as General Staff Officer I to the Special Service Group. It was an impressive record.

The fight at Risan was essentially a straightforward affair, with a clear objective successfully achieved by a sensible use of available resources. The rest of Floydforce, the larger part of it, led a more complicated and more frustrating existence. There were several reasons for this. The first was the need to take seriously potential threats, notably a recurrent one from Mostar, that never materialised. Gun positions and observation posts were reconnoitred, Gunner batteries or individual troops were deployed to cover a range of eventualities from a variety of attempted German incursions from the north, to the fall-back of the entire force to concentrate in the defence of Dubrovnik. The guns could only travel by road. The Montenegrin road system of the time was sparse. The number of usable roads was sparser still, because of blown bridges, some demolished by the Partisans, some by the Germans. Observation-post parties in search of suitable viewpoints from which to control shoots marched for punishing miles over mountain tracks on a Balkan massif upon which the winter was beginning to set in in earnest. They and their Commando escorts, carried heavy loads, shared sometimes with reluctant and underfed mules.

Commando demolition parties also put in some extensive mountain marching, most of it fruitless. In the Niksic area, Captain Ralph Parkinson-Cumine did an arduous march to see about blowing the bridge at Bioce. Germans, to whom the bridge's preservation was as essential as its destruction was desirable to their opponents, were guarding it in force. Parkinson-Cumine marched home again. The bridge was too hard a nut to be cracked by the unsupported troop attack for which he had been reconnoitring.

There was, in sum, much wearisome, profitless manoeuvring.

A second and major cause of frustration was political. There are few surviving old-timers from Floydforce who do not to this day retain an immense admiration and respect for Partisan courage and endurance. There are equally fervent recollections of tough, cheerful, hospitable peasants, who had endured three-and-a-half years of blood-soaked privation, who had had successive layers of ruin placed upon their already impoverished land, and who were still happily prepared to share what little they had left with strangers from overseas who had come to help them. But the chill wind of uncooperative suspicion, its point of origin the very top of the Partisan Command, was blowing chillier and more strongly. The symptoms showed themselves both in actual operations and in assorted incivilities in the Dubrovnik base. Operations were cancelled without notice or delayed for referral to Belgrade, where Tito was now based, for a ruling on whether they should be allowed to proceed. Patently false information was supplied in some cases to divert Floydforce from areas where, for convoluted long-term revolutionary reasons, they were unwanted. In Dubrovnik there were curfews for British troops, wine bars were placed out of bounds, civilians were forbidden to speak to foreign troops. In January British troops were allowed into the town on three days a week only. They had to submit to the inspection of their papers by Partisan military police. There was a demand, which was accepted, that British provost patrols should cease to appear in the town.

It was all a long way from the old, easy, camaraderie of the islands. It was a long way, too, from what might reasonably be expected by a force doing its best to implement its charter 'to give the greatest possible artillery support to the Yugoslav National Army of Liberation', and doing it in conditions of harsh discomfort that was often prolonged into physical hardship. On the British side the matter was taken up at the very highest level, the Prime Minister. On 3 December Winston Churchill sent a personal message to Tito through the Maclean Mission:

You seem to be treating us in an increasingly invidious fashion. It may be that you have fears that your ambitions about occupying Italian territories of the north Adriatic lead you to view with suspicion and dislike every military operation on your coast we make against the Germans. I have already assured you that all territorial questions will be reserved for the Peace Conference. And they will be judged irrespective of wartime occupation. And certainly such issues ought not to hamper military operations now.

There was no abatement of the suspicion and dislike. It continued to hamper military operations.

A major operation that went ahead only partially hampered was the block on the central German breakout route, on the road from the Albanian border through Podgorica, Danilovgrad and Niksic. It had been clear from the outset that this would be one of the routes tried, and that if the stopper were to be screwed down effectively at Risan, the Niksic road would attract an enhanced traffic. The road south from Niksic ran through a deep, rocky valley, bounded on either side by precipitous mountains that were scenically magnificent but useless for 25-pounder gun positions. An advanced position in the grounds of a monastery was judged to be suitable for mountain guns. A detachment of the Raiding Support Regiment with four 75-mm guns and a troop of 43 Commando for local protection took it over. The central element in the block was the bridge at Niksic. It was about 150 yards long, stone-built and supported by fifteen piers. Some of the piers had already been prepared for demolition by the Partisans. No. 579 Field Company of the Royal Engineers took over the job and took no chances. They put double charges on every pier.

By the 22nd of November the Germans were still out of range of the Niksic guns. Two 25-pounders were sent across the river to join the RSR's 75s already there.

Pat Turner's battery, its job at Risan finished, came up to Niksic later in the same day. So did a troop of No 64 Heavy Anti-Aircraft Regiment. The Niksic artillery force was now formidably strong. The Partisans said that it was no longer needed. They had held the Germans at Danilovgrad. Niksic was no longer at risk. The Germans were now relying solely upon their innermost route, through Kolasin to Sarajevo. A battery of 25-pounders and the RSR's 75s, and most of 43, stayed in Niksic in a defensive role and 'occupied their time in training, football and bartering for chickens, turkeys, pigs, sheep and sheepskins with the locals in anticipation of Christmas and still colder weather.' The other guns, and parts of 43, dispersed variously to Dubrovnik, Bileca and Trebinje. British participation in the campaign came to a temporary halt.

One possible way in which the guns could interfere with the German withdrawal was for them to be taken down to the coast at Risan, along the road through the old Montenegrin capital of Cetinje, and on to the south-west approaches to Podgorica. From there the guns could shell the German flank. O'Brien-Twohig put this to the commander of the Partisan II Corps. He, as a soldier, was personally in favour. He was unable to commit himself until he could get authorisation from Belgrade. Belgrade took ten days to grant it. On 5 December a reconstituted Finneyforce, commanded by Major Cheesman, the second-in-command of 111 Field Regiment, and consisting of a battery of 25-pounders, a section of 75s, 'C' Troop of 43 Commando, a detachment of the Long Range Desert Group and a detachment of sappers with a Bailey bridge set out in convoy. To all but the organisers it was the most enjoyable excursion of the campaign - scenically beautiful, touristically interesting, touch of farce here and there and not a drop of blood shed, except possibly internally from the hidden ulcers of senior commanders. The troops and the junior officers loved it.

Three bridges on the coast road between Dubrovnik and Risan were still down, blown by Partisans before Floydforce had landed. The column followed the narrow, by now familiar, inland road, through Vilusi and Grahovo, past the old gun positions at Podhan from which the attempted German breakout through Risan had been stopped, down the zigzag road of the escarpment, through Risan, over Bob Loudoun's by now repaired blow near Perast and on to another unrepaired blow shortly beyond it. At this obstacle there was a halt and a long argument.

Sentries were posted as a matter of routine. The arguers argued. The temporarily unemployed majority gazed admiringly at their surroundings. Up on the high plateau, before the descent into Risan, the views had been beautiful but unremittingly bleak. Backdrops of snow-covered sharp mountains, sometimes gleaming in patchy sunshine, more often obscured by mist or showers of rain or hail or snow. An inconsistently changing sky, clouds being blown away, other clouds replacing them, pure, clean air, rocky outcrops variously grey, white, fawn, mauve, ochre, in the shifting light. Down here, at sea level, there was a different quality to the loveliness. The glinting, sapphire-blue waters of the Gulf of Kotor lapped gently against the shore. Enclosing, grey-white limestone mountains towered irregularly on every intricate side. There were enchanting glimpses across the water of little villages of white-walled houses with red-tiled roofs, of tiny chapels on domed hills, of olive groves, vineyards and vegetable gardens. The physical beauty aside, there was also the matter of physical warmth. It was a relative warmth. It was December. But December on the coast of an inlet of the Mediterranean was different from December in the Highlands of Montenegro.

The argument was about who should repair the blow: a bridge over a stream running high from winter rain and snow and flowing into the Gulf in a torrent. Bits of the bridge, demolished comprehensively by the retreating Germans, projected erratically from the surface of the stream, white water bubbling and gurgling about them. The sapper detachment had been sent on slightly ahead of the rest of the force to put up a Bailey bridge. The parts of this particular Bailey bridge were still stowed in their trucks. A Partisan engineer who for the previous week or so had been trying to put things right by more traditional methods, said repeatedly that he did not want them. He was a stone-bridge man himself.

This admirable perfectionism was offset by a clear weakness in his case. Every time that he assembled a promising-looking agglomeration of stones they were washed into the Gulf by sudden surges in the torrent. These setbacks had not disheartened him. They had made him more stubbornly determined to do the job, in his own way. His professional pride was deeply engaged. He was unmoved by all attempts at persuasion, cajolement and bullying. He was indifferent to the spectacle of the long column of guns and vehicles, immobilised in a snake that wound away out of sight behind a projecting cliff. He eventually conceded that he would give way if somebody would bring him a written authority from the Partisan II Corps Headquarters at Niksic. This might have taken days. A more subtle approach was tried. A small section of the Bailey was assembled. He cast a professional eye upon it. He seemed to take a developing interest in it. The interest appeared to flower into secret admiration. At 3.30pm he weakened. The sappers set to work.

The Bailey was completed and in working order by 2.30 in the morning. The column left at dawn, winding its way beside the alluring Gulf. There was a halt in the old Venetian town of Kotor, a place of great beauty, last visited by British troops in strength when it was captured during the Napoleonic wars in 1811 in a combined operation mounted by sailors and marines from the ships of Captain William Hoste. If anyone in the column had ever heard of this exploit, which is unlikely, they did not refer to it openly.

Major Cheesman motored on ahead to make arrangements in Cetinje with the headquarters of the Partisan Primorska Group, and was at once cut off from the rest of the force by a landslide behind him on the road around Lovcen Mountain. The column leaguered for a second happy night on the coast. The two 'C' Troop subalterns were extravagantly welcomed in a hotel in Budva. They luxuriated in hot baths, climbed into beds with sheets and feather mattresses, and an hour or so later climbed out again. The switch to elegant comfort was too abrupt and they found themselves unable to sleep. They dossed down on the floor in the style to which they had become accustomed, using their packs as pillows. They slumbered soundly.

On the next morning, 9 December, developments were reported from several directions. Cheesman in Cetinje, once the capital of the old Kingdom of Montenegro, had been warmly and enthusiastically welcomed by Major Dalkovic, the Partisan commander. They had discussed the details of the operation. Dalkovic gave Cheesman dinner and a comfortable room for the night in what had once been the British Legation. Colonel Jago, the Commanding Officer of 111 Field Regiment, set out from Dubrovnik with his Regimental Headquarters and additional signals equipment to command the force. On Lovcen Mountain a Partisan working party cleared a path through the landslide. The Finneyforce column wound up into the mountains again, back to the hail and snow, and into Cetinje, a fascinating place where Rudolph Rassendyll and Rupert of Hentzau would have been in their element. A troop of 25-pounders went straight through the town and deployed on the Centinje-Danilovgrad road. They had arrived just too late. The Partisans were reported to have taken Danilovgrad.

Colonel Jago's party arrived that evening. He called an officers' conference at Force Headquarters in the Grand Hotel. A 25-pounder troop was detailed off to take up a position within range of Podgorica on the Podgorica road. A second troop was to join it at first light. A signal from Floydforce Advanced Headquarters in Niksic came in to say that the Partisan Command had given specific approval for the guns to open up in the morning. The orders group completed, the conference adjourned for dinner in the hotel dining room, with Major Dalkovic as its guest of honour. Glasses were being charged with *rakija* prior to a toast to success on the morrow when a second signal from Floydforce was delivered to the head of the table. This one read: 'PREVIOUS SIGNAL CANCELLED. ALL FORWARD MOVEMENT STOPPED. CONCENTRATE ALL FORCES VILUSI 10 DEC.'

Jago called another officers' conference after dinner. Earlier arrangements were unscrambled. Fresh orders were given. At first light the vehicles and guns of the column took up their places once more, this time facing the direction from which they had recently arrived. It was a nice drive down to sea-level again, along the road beside the lovely Gulf, up once more, zigzag, across the Risan escarpment, through the hail and icy rain of the plateau, and back to the partially destroyed, dismal village at the road junction at Vilusi. It had been a round trip of 180 miles. To adapt the Loudoun manifesto about the cost of coming here in peacetime, the undertaking had cost the British taxpayer rather more than hundreds of pounds in wartime.

Jago reported to O'Brien-Twohig, who said that Partisan II Corps had told him that Podgorica was on the verge of falling and had demanded the withdrawal of the guns to counter a new threat from Mostar. Jago went to see the Commander of the Partisan 29th Division at Trebinje. The Divisional Commander said that there was no threat from Mostar. The Germans had pushed a few strong patrols a little way south, presumably to help cover elements of Army Group E pulling out through Sarajevo. Jago went to Niksic to see O'Brien-Twohig again and returned with new orders. The travelling fiasco of the abortive ride to Cetinje was militarily irredeemable, but there was one superficially respectable option through which it could be made plain with an urbane bloody-mindedness that the leadership of Floydforce was unamused. The Bailey bridge outside Perast had by now become an integral and accepted part of the communications network in Montenegro. Jago had orders to repossess the bridge.

Three days after the return from Cetinje a little column once more went down to the coast. It comprised a detachment of the Field Company of the sappers, Lieutenant McConville and Sergeant Bill Ash's sub-section of 'C' Troop, 43 Commando, and Captain Peter Carey, a Croatian-speaking officer from the British Military Mission. Its instructions were enshrined in an impressive document shot through with bureaucratic verbiage and decorated with a seal embossed with the Royal Cypher of the United Kingdom of Great Britain and Northern Ireland, an effect achieved by pressing into the wax a General Service greatcoat button. For a number of essential reasons, proclaimed this mendacious piece of paper, it was important that the Bailey bridge should be held in reserve. The party's negotiators held obdurately to their brief. The Odbor, the Communist Party Committee office in Kotor, seemed to have no brief but over the *rakija* became plaintive about the complexities ahead of them if the southern littoral of Montenegro were to be severed from the northern littoral of Montenegro. The Brits pointed out that the thing had only been installed in the first place after sustained opposition from the Partisans' stonework enthusiast, who would presumably be delighted at the chance to try his hand again. But that was a decision for the Partisan to take. The British decision had already been taken. The Bailey bridge was manifestly a British bridge, put up by British engineers. It was wanted elsewhere for use in operations in support of Partisan operations. British engineers would now take it away.

The Partisans spokesmen said that they would have to seek instructions from their headquarters. The bridge collectors reported developments by wireless to theirs. There was further discussion and more *rakija*, in the Odbor. Telephoned assent finally came from an undisclosed level in the Partisan hierarchy. The bridge was efficiently dismantled. When, after mutual courtesies, the column left on the following morning the Partisans had already improvised a substitute for the Bailey. The new way of getting from southern Montenegro to northern Montenegro was by rowing boat.

While this rather ponderous farce was being acted out on the coast, more serious affairs were in progress on Army Group E's escape route through Podgorica. The Army Group numbered in all seven divisions. From the time of their first movement northwards, they had been under incessant daylight, and some night-time, attack by aircraft of Balkan Air Force operating from bases in Southern Italy. The scale of their interdiction from the air was by Balkan standards immense. In about 3000 sorties Balkan Air Force had destroyed thirty-nine locomotives, twenty railway wagons, 129 motor trucks and twelve aircraft by cannon-fire and bombing. The effect of this material destruction, and its accompanying loss of German lives, had been compounded by the danger to them, sometimes the impossibility, of using the roads by day. German troops, transport and equipment were building up into a congested mass in the area of Podgorica. Their rear and flank guards had to stay in place to cover this slowly moving concentration. One of the flank guards unable to disengage was at Spuz, and its adjoining high ground, about midway between Danilovgrad and Podgorica.

The only road between the battery of 25-pounders and the Raiding Support Regiment's troop of 75s, at Niksic, and the German force at Spuz was breached by thirty-one separate demolitions, some made by Partisans to hinder a German advance from Spuz, some made by Germans to hinder a Partisan advance into Spuz. An earlier attempt to circumvent this handicap by flying a troop of the RSR with their mountain guns, and with a Commando troop as escort, by Dakota and Italian Savoias from Niksic airfield to Berane to block the road there had been frustrated by the weather. The force had been loaded and ready for take-off when sheeting, icy rain reduced visibility to near nothing. The downpour lasted unbroken for eighty hours. The force unloaded their aeroplanes, waited for better days, found none and on 11 December sent off over the mountains, this time with mules, by Colonel Riches. They were unhealthy mules but they carried the guns and the ammunition to where they were wanted. The guns went straight into action in support of 10th Montenegrin Brigade. The Commando troop put out reconnaissance patrols.

Riches had meanwhile set about the problem of the thirty-one breaches in the road from Niksic to Spuz. The Field Company of the Royal Engineers was called for, and bridged the more technically difficult gaps. Every otherwise uncommitted man from the Commando and from the various Gunner units, hundreds of Partisans and as many civilians as could be mustered fell in to fashion a negotiable, and partially precarious, track for the guns. The road was open to artillery traffic on 13 December. A battery of 25-pounders and a troop of RSR 75-mm mountain guns went through to Danilovgrad. Two days later they were joined by four 3.7 inch anti-aircraft guns, used to fire at ground targets, of No 180 Heavy Anti-Aircraft Battery of the Royal Artillery.

All guns put down observed and lethal fire upon the constricted German traffic-jam north of Podgorica.

Brigadier O'Brien-Twohig ordered up another 25-pounder battery on the 16th. Since this was now a Gunner operation in strength, Jago took over command from Riches, and from then onwards co-ordinated the artillery policy. Jago made liaison arrangements with the headquarters of the Boka Brigade, 10th Montenegrin Brigade and Primorska Group, all concerned in the assault upon Podgorica and upon the hills dominating it. The Partisan attacks were, as ever, mounted with a daunting courage, but they were products of individual brigade initiatives, not under a central control. Four hill peaks on a range to the north-west of the town were the prime objectives. They varied in height from 700 to 900 feet and were steep, rocky and contorted. Jago conducted his part of the battle from his headquarters in a half-wrecked building in Danilovgrad.

On 17 December, while the sappers toiled at the construction of a Bailey bridge as a substitute for the stone one destroyed at Danilovgrad, six 25-pounders were ferried across the river and took up positions within range of the Bioce road. The Bailey was ready by the next morning. The other guns crossed. The Partisans captured one of the four peaks, from which there was a clear view of a crowded mass of German transport. An OP was set up on this position and the guns conducted a three-hour shoot into the traffic-jam. One hundred and fifty 25-pound shells were fired in all. They caused much observed death and destruction, and put out of action three German guns which had made an ineffectual attempt to interrupt the use of the Bailey bridge. These German guns lasted for eight minutes from the time of their first opening up.

One amenity to survive the mayhem was the civilian telephone system. At midday the Partisans announced their presence in Podgorica by telephoning from the town exchange. During the afternoon 10th Montenegrin Brigade, with supporting fire from a troop of 25-pounders, made considerable ground on a second of the four dominating peaks, but were unable to take the summit. An assortment of OPs was by now well placed on suitable mountain-sides, and the guns were registered upon nodal points, bridges, defiles and similar bottlenecks. They fired throughout the night. By nine o'clock on the morning of the 19th they had discharged 3200 rounds in twenty-four hours. This total was more than equalled by the bombs and cannon-fire from the airstrikes of Balkan Air Force. Early in the morning Lieutenant Nick Demuth was sent into Podgorica with a reconnaissance patrol of 43 to investigate the situation in the town. The Germans had moved out, but not as far or as fast as Demuth had thought. His patrol was heavily shot up by a stray German rearguard, disengaged itself circumspectly, had language difficulties with a body of Albanian guerrillas who had joined in the fight and wanted to put Demuth's patrol under arrest, talked themselves out of that, and went back to report to Colonel Riches.

It soon became evident that a great deal had happened in the course of the night. The Partisans had successfully assaulted all three of the peaks still in German hands, and now held all the high ground. The Germans, leaving a trail of bodies and abandoned wreckage of transport behind them, had exploited the darkness energetically. They had pulled out to beyond the Rivers Zeta and Morava, blowing all the bridges behind them. A great mass of them, moving doggedly northwards, was congregated in the neighbourhood of Bioce. The guns were moved forward as far as possible to engage this concentration. There was further difficulty and further hard marching, in the search for mountain OPs, but a Gunner light aircraft, directed a series of accurate concentrations of shells on to the escape route.

By the 21st the battle was as good as over. The Germans were straggling onwards towards Kolasin, harassed as they went by Balkan Air Force and by Partisans. Partisan wireless communications, improvised and understandably erratic, could not keep in reliable contact with their forward troops. The guns could only engage a diminishing number of targets that could be visually identified as enemy. There was a growing risk that Partisan units might be shelled in error. During the afternoon the last authenticated Germans had moved beyond the range of all but the anti-aircraft 3.7s, and these found less and less to do. Cease Firing was ordered. In driving snow on the next morning the force dispersed, some of it to Trebinje, some to Niksic. A few reconnaissance parties left to cross the River Zeta to inspect the damage. They counted 400 destroyed trucks, one light tank and five 105-mm guns. In an intact and abandoned ammunition dump there were 700 automatic weapons and rifles, and a large amount of artillery ammunition of a variety of calibres up to 21 centimetre. All of this went to the Partisans.

In the eight days between 14 and 22 December, British guns deployed against Army Group E fired 14,481 rounds. 43 provided security for observation-post parties and gun positions, and carried out a succession of mountain reconnaissance patrols. The intensified shelling of the Bioce road on 22 December was the last British active intervention in the campaign. A month later, without firing another shot except in training exercises, Floydforce embarked at Dubrovnik on a shuttle of LCIs and LCGs (Landing Craft, Gun) to return to Bari, there to break up into its various components in preparation for the final phase of the Italian campaign.

The achievements of Floydforce was considerable, its casualties light. Its problems had been partly physical and partly political. The physical ones - wild, rough country, a scarcity of roads capable of taking artillery, the marines unprovided with adequate mountain clothing - were surmounted or disregarded and were rarely understood. Floydforce and the Partisans shared one major aim, the destruction of as many Germans and of as much German military material as could be contrived. The Floydforce senior commanders, O'Brien-Twohig, Jago and Riches were professional soldiers trained in, and imbued with the ideas of the British system by which the declaration of war and its subsequent diplomatic and political conduct were the responsibilities of a democratically elected government. The actual fighting was the duty of the soldiers, who, whatever were their personal views about the quality, or even the sanity, of the politicians, carried out their orders with a disciplined loyalty. It was hard for them, and for the officers and men commanded by them, to adjust mentally to a working co-operation with allies who did not share that approach, and who in addition to the common destructive aim had further political aims, in their eyes of equal or greater importance.

# PART FIVE

## ITALY II:
## THE LINE, COMACCHIO, ARGENTA

# CHAPTER FOURTEEN

# REFURBISHMENT AND PREPARATION

When the Commando embarked in L.C.I.s at dawn on 20 January at Gruz harbour, adjacent to Dubrovnik, there were few feelings of regret. There was irritation and disillusionment with Partisan crassness and rigidity, admiration for Partisan courage and for the stoicism and hospitality of ordinary impoverished Dalmatian and Montenegrin civilians, some satisfaction at having been present at an unusual episode in British military history. There was also a general looking forward to the fleshpots of Italy without much further thought about what lay beyond them. During the previous autumn there had been the brief stretch in Putignano between the departure from Vis and the departure for Dubrovnik. But that interlude apart, although there had been occasional brief periods of leave for some, outside social life had been consistently bleak. The smelly little hill village of Putignano once again became the unit's temporary home but immediate steps were taken to do at least something to remedy the Balkan deprivations of the past year. Everybody who could be spared was immediately sent on a week's leave. Those who had to stay took their turn when the rest came back.

War-time Italy was a mess but all messes are comparative, and the Italian mess was not in the same class as the Yugoslav one. There was an elaborately equipped 8th Army leave centre in Bari, with bars, baths, restaurants, a cinema, reading rooms, libraries and occasional stage shows. There were plenty of other bars in the city and no officious Partisan security police to keep British troops out of them. The Italians were cheerful, courteous, and prone to outbreaks of song. Above all there were women, who looked and dressed like women and were not festooned with fragmentation grenades and slung about with Sten guns and bandoliers of ammunition. Also these women wore rather elegant shoes, if they wore any shoes at all, and not ammunition boots. Politics were not an issue. Discipline was ever present, but it was a relaxed discipline, in which anyone could do much as he wished so long as he did not make a conspicuously noisy idiot of himself. It was a good, refreshing time that everyone made the most of.

It was followed by an outburst of largesse that brought great comfort to old Balkan country cousins, hitherto accustomed to making do with the reach-me-downs left over by mainstream forces involved in more stylish embroilments. Like deprived children unexpectedly invited to a lavishly endowed Christmas party, the marines wallowed happily in new possessions. Fresh battledress replaced the threadbare, decaying things that had doubled as working clothes and pyjamas in a Montenegro of damp marches by day and lice-infested accommodation by night. Comfortably broken-in ammunition boots, worn down almost to the uppers, were discarded in favour of footwear of a vaguely mountaineering cast known as "S.V. Boots". These had crenellated soles of hard rubber and no-one minded much what S.V. stood for. Sleeveless leather jerkins, by now scuffed and distorted in shape, similar to those worn by the soldiers of Henry V during the run-up to Agincourt, accompanied the old battledress and the ammunition boots to the bonfire (or possibly to the Italian black market). In place of the jerkins came the most practical garments yet to have reached the Commando: sturdy thigh-length camouflaged airborne smocks, loose-fitting, four usefully large pockets secured by press studs, a flap like a tail that was fastened under the crotch and prevented the jumping jacket from riding up.

There was some sentimental resistance to the abandonment of worn-out green berets, travelled tokens of bygone strife, bleached by sun and salt, leather headbands starting to rot. In their place came substitutes of pristine verdancy with an almost luminous nap. Webbing big packs, date of birth *circa* 1910, secured by webbing straps that bit into shoulders towards the end of a hard march went too. The Bergen rucksacks that replaced them were mounted on light tubular frames that distributed efficiently the weight to be carried.

Parallel to this gents outfitting programme came a closely ordered scrutiny of existing weapons and the introduction of some new ones. All rifles and Brens were re-zeroed, the armourers spending days over the readjustment of individual sights. Worn Bren gun barrels were replaced. Similar attentions were paid to the Tommy guns carried by the senior N.C.O.s, and to the intricacies of the 3" Mortars and the Vickers Medium Machine guns of the Heavy Weapon Troops. The unloved PIATs were examined and checked for inaccuracies. The new weapons included man-carried Lifebuoy flame throwers, capable of incinerating an opponent at a maximum range of about 25 yards, and therefore tactically ridiculous as well, to some, morally abhorrent.

This refurbishment was accompanied by the arrival of replacement drafts of both officers and marines, the latter mainly from by now redundant landing craft crews of the Mediterranean Fleet. Several of the new officers were from the army, a necessary innovation at a time when Corps manpower was stretched to its limits. They were received hospitably and soon made to feel at home.

The Commando moved to Minervino for a period of intensive training, designed primarily to bring up-to-date the practices and techniques of a body that for more than a year had been quarantined in a Balkan backwater. The evolving sophistication of 8th Army's arrangements had, for the most part, passed 43 by. There was an urgency to the updating. For the first and only time in its existence, No 2 Commando Brigade was to fight a battle with all four Commandos operating together as a unified entity. For the officers and Senior NCOs there were lectures by and discussions with specialists from all arms.

Problems were posed, questions were put, solutions were hammered out. How did infantry co-ordinate their activities with tanks? When and how did infantry call for artillery support? If you were holding a widely spread-out position and enemy guns fired at you it was sensible for people at the extremities to take compass bearings on the gun flashes and for cross-bearings to be plotted on a map so that your own gunners could have a go. If the allied air forces dominated the skies, and a proportion of them were trained to give close support to advancing infantry, how did you bring them in to play? When a tank commander, the elevation of whose turret was several feet above that of pedestrian soldiers, could identify a target which they could not see, how did he indicate it to him? (The answer of a Major in the North Irish Horse was that the tank would fire 100% incendiary ammunition at the target. Questioned about whether this procedure would violate the Geneva Convention, he explained that the North Irish Horse were half neutral anyway).

These practicalities were investigated and discussed against a familiar background. There were speed marches, patrol exercises, signals exercises, section attacks, troop attacks, co-ordinated Commando attacks involving all five Fighting Troops and the Heavy Weapons Troop, all using live ammunition.

At the end of it all 43 climbed into a railway train of cattle trucks for a memorably happy four day journey from the south of Italy to the north. The trucks were clean and spacious and there was plenty of room to spread blankets, sleeping bags, and equipment. The train's progress was slow. At wayside stations Italian women sold fruit, cheese, wine and, regrettably, in some cases themselves. A constant supply of boiling water was available from the engine, over the distraught protestations of the engine-driver, for the brewing up of tea and for shaving water. Stops were frequent. Those so inclined were able to stroll in the countryside, confident that they would catch up on their transport without much trouble if it set off before they returned. At last the train arrived at Ravenna.

The ancient ochre-coloured city of Ravenna, the old elegance by now largely offset by sweating grey cement facades and nondescript scruffy tall brick terraces, once the capital of the Byzantine empire, was now the fiefdom of V Corps of 8th Army. To the rustics from the Balkans the city and the flat countryside surrounding it provided an impressive revelation. Red-capped military policemen controlled and directed the traffic. One-Way routes were clearly marked with placarded symbols: SUN UP, SUN DOWN, MOON UP, MOON DOWN. Dumps of stores and ammunition were laid out under guard behind barbed wire in roadside vineyards, access tracks bulldozed to each. The way to Corps, Division, Brigade and unit headquarters was indicated by arrowed signposts, decorated with the subheraldic stencilled devices of each formation - Galleon in full sail, Black Cat, Kiwi, Battle-axe. There was a multitude of vehicle parks, maintenance workshops, field hospitals, transport pools, dispersed clusters of tanks and artillery, low-loaders to carry the tanks over roads towards battle.

Off-duty troops from the international fighting community of 8th Army wandered like tourists through the narrow streets of the city: British, New Zealand, Indian, Gurkha, Polish, and a few from the newly formed Jewish Brigade. Interspersed among the business-like administrative offices of the various formations were NAAFI canteens, a theatre requisitioned for troops' entertainment, chapels for separate religious denominations, V.D. prophylactic centres and a bank that had been converted to an Officers' Club.

The Commando settled in in civvy billets. The accommodation was crowded, the furniture non-existent, and any conscientious modern social welfare worker would have condemned its use as an indefensible exploitation of the vulnerable. 43 rather liked it. It was infinitely superior to anything experienced during the by-now seemingly distant stay on the other side of the Adriatic.

The Line, rendered static by winter weather since December, lay some eight miles to the northwest. On 4 March, four days after their arrival in Ravenna, 43 entered the next stage of its acclimatisation. They went north in a convoy of trucks. They took over, from a battalion of Gurkhas of 8th Indian Division, a sector of the Line just southeast of the small German-occupied town of Alfonsine.

The land surface of Emilia Romagna is unremittingly flat and featureless. The land is fertile and well-farmed. It is criss-crossed by a variety of waterways, rivers, streams and canals, the major ones flanked by high flood banks to contain heavy winter flooding. The Line was not a continuous line, like the one that stretched as an attenuated trench-system from the English Channel to the Swiss frontier between 1914 and 1918. This northern Italian version was rather a series of interdependent fortified lumps, defended stone farm building complexes, slit trenches dug on river flood banks, in woods, each position sited so as to be covered by supporting fire from its neighbour.

Its German counterpart was laid out in much the same pattern. Near Alfonsine the enemy posts were about five hundred yards away. Further north slit trenches were separated only by the width of the narrow, sluggish-flowing river Reno. Antagonists lived in holes dug through the earth of the high flood banks on either side. The intervening distance between the two sides widened towards the sea until the British, in a pine wood at the base of a spit of land that separated the Adriatic from the shallow Lake Comacchio, were nearly a mile away across an expanse of low sand dunes from the nearest opposition. The Reno bent north before it moved lethargically till it discharged itself into the sea about two thirds of the way up the eastern side of the spit, thus leaving a distinctive tongue of land north of the pine forest.

As was right and customary at the time, a high level of security prevailed. Only a small necessary number of senior officers on the brigade staff and in the headquarters of the four Commandos knew of the plan that was now in active preparation. Lake Comacchio, an apple-shaped, shallow, brackish, silted and in places reed-bestrewn body of water was roughly seven miles from north to south and another seven from east to west. The spit that separated it from the sea was inconsistently shaped but was roughly 2-3 miles wide. The northern end of the lake was joined to the sea by the Valetta Canal. Along the north bank of the canal lay the spread-out houses of the small town of Porto Garibaldi. The canal lay about seven miles to the north of the forward edge of the pine wood in which 43 Commando were temporarily positioned. For planning purposes the spit became the Spit. The tongue of land between the River Reno and the sea became the Tongue.

The Brigade's task was to open the 8th Army's spring offensive by clearing this rough rectangle of sand and scrub of all its German defences as far as the Valetta Canal; and if by that time the Germans were retreating in disorder, to cross the canal and exploit whatever came to hand. The initial concept was that No 2 Commando and No 9 Scottish

## REFURBISHMENT AND PREPARATION

Commando should cross Lake Comacchio at night in a variety of boats and amphibious vehicles and land on the western shore of the Spit. Once they were ashore, 43, from a base in the pine wood at the foot of the Spit would move forward, clear the tongue, cross the Reno and turn to the north. They would there join up with the two Army Commandos and complete the necessary clearances. In the meantime, No 40 Commando would put in a dummy attack further west along the Reno and ferry one troop across to start clearing the north bank without exposing themselves to unnecessary casualties.

V Corps would provide as much support as possible to ease these various movements. Unforeseen developments, and the discovery of unexpected information, generated a progressive series of refinements to the plan, but it still retained its fundamentals: a waterborne advance over the lake by the army commandos and a thrust on land up the Tongue and across the Reno to the Spit by 43 Commando. 43's planners, directed personally by Colonel Ian Riches, were Captain Don Esson and Lieutenant Jack Stevens. In collaboration with their opposite numbers at Brigade and in the other Commandos, they studied maps and aerial photographs, marked out, identified and charted enemy-occupied positions (each was given a biblical code-name), approach routes, collected and collated intelligence reports, calculated the weights and nature of the reserve stores of food, ammunition and so on that would be needed after the battle was engaged, marked in sites where these stores could be assembled, and made arrangements for their delivery as required.

The artillery plan, which provided for a total of 150 guns in support, was discussed and finalised with senior Gunner officers. Specialist armoured troop-carrying vehicles that could swim, given exotic names - Kangaroos, Fantails, Buffaloes and Weasels - were moved unostentatiously towards the brigade area, there to be used for intensive training before they were put to real use. A multiplicity of other detailed arrangements had to be made, and all the elements in the scheme co-ordinated one with another.

Whilst the planners planned, in creditably preserved secrecy, the troops, for the most part unaware of what lay ahead of them, got on with their own little part of the war in the sector of the line south of Alfonsine. It was in a sense a process of familiarisation with the conditions to be expected in forward positions, and had no immediate tactical relevance to the battle ahead. The clusters of defensive positions, fortified farmhouses and occasional trench systems, were manned, improved here and there, and defended around the clock by an arrangement of a small proportion of people on full time alert and the balance on a more relaxed immediate standby. There was sporadic shelling, and occasional unexpected, and apparently ill-directed, ferocious outbreaks of small arms fire.

By night the emphasis was on patrolling the gap between 43's positions and those of the Germans. Of these, the last three predominated: large stone farm houses, Casa Morini, Casa Riccibitti and Casa Tosca. The intervening ground was fairly heavily mined, partly by the Germans, partly by 43's Gurkhas predecessors, and partly by the Canadians who had preceded the Gurkhas. Further complications were posed by abandoned vineyards, both by the vines themselves and by the long horizontal wires upon which the vines were trained.

During its one week of occupation, from 4th to 11th March, 43 sent out a total of 7 ambush and reconnaissance patrols. Most were uneventful. The ambush patrols failed to trap anybody into their clutches. The reconnaissance patrols carefully logged in the information for which they were sent, and added such snippets as the sound of coughing, the sight of a glowing cigarette, and so on in or around the German positions, which were then accordingly mortared by the Heavy Weapons Troop. One patrol from 'B' Troop, led by Captain Douglas Cotton-Minchin (Cameronians) was very heavily engaged from the enemy positions but returned with only one casualty. At the end of the week the Commando was shifted to the right to a six thousand yard front which extended from the Adriatic coast inland. This, although few realised it at the time, was immediately relevant to the forthcoming fight. Familiarisation here was both with conditions in the line, and with the actual ground which was due to be fought over.

The seamost side, in the pine wood, was the responsibility of 'C' Troop (Captain Shorty Roberts), 'A' Troop (Captain Martin Preston), and one section of 'B' Troop. The mortars and the medium machine guns of 'F' Troop (Major Jock Hudspith) were in position sightly farther back in the wood. To the West the other half of 'B' Troop (Captain Douglas Cotton-Minchin), 'D' Troop (Captain Ian Gourlay), and 'E' Troop (Captain Ralph Parkinson-Cumine) were dug-in in the flood bank along the south side of the Reno and in defended houses nearby. The farther west the line went the closer it came to the enemy. On the Reno itself the German positions were only about 75 yards away from the British ones. Although all precautions were routinely taken against a German assault, either in earnest or from fighting patrols, none ever materialised.

There were long periods of calm under a benevolent Italian spring sky, punctuated by occasional bursts of automatic fire, single shots, and mortaring and shelling of unpredictable timing and intensity. German observation posts, at their best difficult to locate, more commonly impossible to locate, kept a close eye on all movement and it was necessary for everyone to shift themselves with circumspection. The day-time single shots came mainly from 'B' and 'E' Troop's snipers to the west who between them claimed eight certain kills during the first week. Towards dusk, the Germans, slaves to habit, put down fairly heavy concentrations of mortar and shell fire on the same places at the same times on succeeding nights; and were in turn engaged by British counter-battery fire. By night, patrols were active.

A German position of company strength was dug-in near the tip of the Tongue. The object of the Commando patrolling was to dominate the sands between it and the forward British position in the pine wood. A total of 19 patrols from 43 went out on every night between 11th March and 18th March. Because the Adriatic is tideless, and the spring weather was almost windless, by the end of the week the entire beach was criss-crossed by footprints left in the sand by various patrols, with here and there the shallow slits scooped out by marines in ambush positions. As was to be expected in an area in which the Germans seemed to have no positive patrolling policy at all, many of these patrols were relatively uneventful. Some were not.

On the night of 15/16th March Captain Douglas Cotton-Minchin led a patrol which was trying to intercept what was thought to be a German party laying mines forward of its position. Cotton-Minchin ordered his patrol to go to ground to cover him and went on ahead by himself. What happened next has never been satisfactorily explained. There was an outbreak of heavy firing. He did not return. The remainder of the patrol withdrew, and were heavily shot at on their way home, two men returning with bullet holes through their clothing.*

Lieutenant Bill Jenkins, of 'E' Troop, spent an acquisitive few minutes in the early morning mist when he penetrated an unoccupied German post, clearly under slovenly management, and helped himself to several Mausers, a Panzerfaust, (a German anti-tank rocket projector), and the sight of a 81mm mortar, all left unattended. His patrol's return with these souvenirs stimulated much happy speculation about what the disciplinary proceedings in the German company office the following morning must have looked, and sounded, like.

On 19 March the Commando left the Line and moved to bivouacs in a training area at Sassi, south of Ravenna. The short period in the Line had cost one officer missing and twelve other ranks wounded. At the same time a great deal had been learnt about day-to-day living in the line, about the layout of the ground to its immediate front, and about German habits and predictable reactions.

Colonel Ian Riches was a far-sighted and meticulous operational planner. His preparations took in what should happen, and what might happen if the plan should become distorted into something slightly different. He also catered for the need to keep some resources in hand in case what happened was entirely unexpected. As with his operational planning, so with his training doctrine. The Sassi training programme was concentrated and thorough. Its first priority was to accustom the marines to the new amphibious vehicles. The bulk of these "funnies" had been allocated to the two army commandos who were to go in over the lake; but because of the requirement to cross the Reno 43 were allocated four Fantails, and a troop of Kangaroos manned by the 4th Queens Own Hussars. There were also five assault boats and four collapsible rubber intruder dinghies. Fantails, or L.V.T.s, were lightly armoured tracked vehicles designed to cross flooded areas and to climb muddy banks. Kangaroos were armoured personnel carriers, A.P.C.s, converted Sherman tanks, the turrets and ammunition fittings of which had been removed to make them into large mobile taxis for foot soldiers. They were extensively waterproofed, part of this precaution being the addition to the exhausts of a high metal trunking, rather like the ventilation shaft on a ship. The tops of the shafts, which were possibly 6 or 7 feet high, were bent over so that the exhaust fumes could be discharged horizontally. There were also a few Weasels, small tracked carriers which were originally designed for towing sledges in the Arctic, now to be used for liaison and odd jobs in general over the sands of the Spit. The driving and maintenance of these vehicles was in the hands of their professional crews. What the marines had to learn was how to get in and out as quickly, and in as orderly a manner, as possible, and to squash themselves in

---

* *It was originally thought that Cotton-Minchin had been wounded and captured. The hope was that he would be recovered from some German hospital or prisoner-of-war camp once the war was over. But there was no subsequent trace of him. The Commonwealth war graves Commission have listed him as dead, but with no known grave. He is commemorated in a memorial plaque devoted to his regiment, the Cameronians, in the War Cemetery at Cassino.*

*It seems likely that he was either killed and buried on the spot by his immediate captors; or that he was the victim of an order, signed personally by Adolf Hitler, that all Commando prisoners were to be executed.*

as comfortably as they could in the small space available. Boarding and disembarkation were practised again and again until everyone knew what he had to do and how to do it.

'C' Troop were to make the original crossing over the Reno. They were given the canvas collapsible assault boats, heavy clumsy wooden-framed things with flat bottoms to play with. They rehearsed repeatedly in and about a handy canal. The boats were lashed to the sides of Kangaroos. They had to be unlashed, carried to the banks of the canal, launched and paddled across. On the way over a rope that was fastened to a stake hammered in on the near bank was paid out. Once across a further stake was thumped into the far bank, the rope was fastened to it and pulled taut. A ferry, or rather three ferries, were now in operation powered by people simply pulling on the ropes.

There was training in co-operation with Churchill tanks of the North Irish Horse, two troops of which had been supplied for the operations. There were repeated simulated attacks, using live ammunition on strong points.

40 Commando had taken over the section of the line earlier held by 43. Almost every night during the training interlude at Sassi, patrols from 43 were driven up to the line and went forward over the sands of the Tongue to ensure that there had been no last minute alteration of German dispositions, and generally to keep the area suitably dominated. One of these patrols, led by Lieutenant Stan Barnes (Royal Artillery) of 'A' Troop, managed to ambush a German patrol almost at the point at which it was leaving its own lines and was correspondingly more relaxed than it should have been. Barnes's party killed all six of the Germans and returned triumphantly with a rather macabre collection of blood-stained German weapons.

By the end of March training was as complete as training ever is. On the 27th Major Neil Munro, the second-in-command, moved up into 40 Commando's position in the pine wood with a small party to make the last minute preparations for the assault. Forming Up Positions for the various troops were carefully marked out on the ground with thick white canvas tape, easily seen by night.

On the evening of the 1st April the rest of the Commando followed and were concentrated in the wood by 6pm. A hot meal was provided and the troops then moved to their take off positions. At 7.30pm Colonel Riches held a final orders group with his Troop Commanders and all troops were ordered to stand by on 15 minutes notice from 10.30pm. Two standing patrols were put out by 'A' and 'B' Troops at 10.15 to take up positions 400 yards forward of the pine wood to prevent any possible, if unlikely, inquisitiveness by German patrols. Once these two patrols were in position the remainder of the Commando were formed up in their Kangaroos, L.V.T.s, Weasels, and on foot in order of march.

All was ready to go. The timing of the going was dependent upon the speed of the progress of No 2 and No 9 Commandos across Lake Comacchio, a lagoon that was more a partially-flooded swamp than a proper lake. If all went well, and it was accepted by Brigade that it probably wouldn't, the most optimistic estimate was that the two Army Commandos would land at midnight. 43 were poised to move as from then. But a sensibly flexible rider was attached to this provisional order. The lake crossers might, probably would, be several hours late. 43 were to stand fast until they were successfully ashore.

## CHAPTER FIFTEEN

# COMACCHIO: DAY ONE

However well trained in silent movement its executants are, the crossing of a broad, shallow sludge-ridden lake by about 600 men at night can only be noisy. Add the fact that a proportion would be moving in powered vehicles and craft and the travellers become noisier still. The best way to counteract any alarm felt in enemy breasts by the sound of protracted noise is to lull him in to the belief that it is an ordinary unexceptional phenomenon. For a week before the operation began 2 Commando Brigade orchestrated the generation of as much noise, some of it artificial, some of it practical, as possible.

Tanks and other tracked vehicles had clanked and rumbled up and down all the roads in the brigade area by day and by night. Further forward, near the Line, loud-hailers provided by psychological warfare specialists blared out endless extracts from Wagner, intermingled with strident propaganda, in a non-stop deafening stream. The 25-pounder guns of No 142 Field Regiment, Royal Artillery, carried out regular harassing shoots against targets all over the Spit. Low flying aircraft roared overhead and attacked opportunity targets. Sustained hullaballoo became the norm. It was under the cover of yet another repeat performance of all the elements in this familiar cacophony, that the two army commandos set out on their argosy.

Their journey was not a happy one. An essential component of their waterborne transport were the Fantails, the LVTs. Almost immediately after the start No 2 Commando reported that their leading LVTs were bogged down a few yards from the shore. Attempts to get the remaining ones floated from other points were all unsuccessful. At midnight the LVT Squadron Commander announced that they were all irrevocably bogged and would never make the crossing. Orders were then given for the transfer of all men in the LVTs to spare Storm Boats and Assault Boats, fast.

What happened next is summarised in the brigade report: "The preceding weeks of dry weather, which had lowered the level of water in the lake by a good six inches, the varying mud bottom with its patches of appalling quagmire, the failure of the LVTs, and the dragging, heaving, pushing of the craft through fifteen hundred yards of glutinous shallows had all contributed to an unbelievable confusion at the Start Line. 2 and 9 Commandos were inextricably mixed, some in Storm Boats, some in Assault Boats, all trying to find their leaders and their own sub-units. The scene was a nightmare mixture of "Venice by moonlight" and the end of the Henley Regatta transferred to a setting of mud, slime and a few inches of stinking water. It was getting very late and at this stage both Commanding Officers reported that the assault that night was impracticable and asked for a postponement. Brigadier Tod, upon whom alone the responsibility to decide rested, responded with a resolute NO.

A combination of inspired improvisation, bloody mindedness, adaptability, and brute strength, finally brought No 2 and No 9 to the western side of the Spit. (Years later, one 2 Commando Soldier claimed that he had walked the whole way.) Their piece-meal arrival was not in the planned sequence. Sub-units were haphazardly jumbled together. The first ashore of No 2 Commando were Commando Headquarters and the Heavy Weapons Troop accompanied by one section of a fighting troop. But they were there, they soon sorted themselves out and they set about making their presence felt. Once their leading elements were engaged, heavily supported by artillery fire, Brigadier Ronnie Tod unleashed 43 on the eastern, Tongue side of the Spit. In the pre-dawn mist at 5.00 am on the 2nd April, he gave the order. Dawn would be at 5.30.

Shortly before this order reached Colonel Ian Riches he had been becoming increasingly concerned about the predicament of the two troops that he had pushed forward during the night. If the operation did not develop and daylight supervened, both 'A' and 'B' Troops would be exposed to all sorts of trouble. He accordingly ordered them to pull back, and they were on their way when the long awaited signal to get started reached him. He at once turned them around again. A much reiterated military precept of the times was that order, followed by counter-order equalled disorder. There were no means available for Colonel Riches to explain his counter order to the two Troop Commanders and their followers. Trust and discipline prevented any sign of disorder. The two troops, cursing silently, went back to where they had started from.

Shortly before 5 o'clock on that Italian morning, stars shone brilliantly against a velvet sky, a sea mist was slowly developing, and the waters of the Adriatic were lapping gently against the eastern shore. Occasional distant bangs and rumblings came from westward, where 2 and 9 Commandos were making their initial lodgements. Into this superficially placid setting, came a sudden fierce intervention. The night sky to the rear was sundered by a continuous succession of flickering flashes, approaching sibilant whisperings in the sky developed into increasingly high decibel shrieks, and there was the mighty rolling, drumming sound of merged detonations as more than one hundred guns of the Royal Artillery engaged targets immediately ahead of 43 and elsewhere all over the Spit. For a very brief while the traffic in shell fire was all one way, the right way. German reaction was prompt. Their defensive preparations had been based upon the correct assumption that sooner or later this particular area would be attacked in force. Their artillery and mortars had long since been ranged on defensive fire tasks, concentrations of shot that could be brought down at short notice on areas likely to be crossed by attackers. The Germans at once joined in. An unexpected adjunct to their fire came from *Nebelwerfers*, some sort of rocket, which made eerie whooping noises and exploded with deafening cracks.

Into and through all this uproar moved 'A' and 'B' Troops, on a two troop front, 'A' on the right, 'B' on the left. Two hundred yards behind them came 'D' Troop, travelling in Kangaroos. The German fire was accurate and effective, and a short distance ahead of the wire that protected the first objective, code-named Joshua, the advance faltered temporarily and the troops went to ground. The Kangaroos of 'D' Troop bogged down in soft sand. The troop disembarked hastily.

At this point there was an unorthodox initiative, not recorded in any of the official reports, by Captain Shorty Roberts of 'C' Troop. 'C' Troop's designated role was to await the clearance of the top of the tongue, and then to move to the bank of the Reno and set up the ferry crossing. The troop's Kangaroos were thus festooned with the wooden frameworks and collapsed canvas skins of five Assault Boats, and the deflated rubber hulls of 2 ten-man RAF type rubber dinghies. Roberts was an engaging character, a Continuous Service officer with an infectious chuckle and the build of a rugby scrum half. He had spent almost the entire war at sea. He had joined 43 only about a month previously and he admitted to, or pretended to, a rather sketchy notion of the requirements of the war on land, ("I know absolutely fuck all about this shore-side fighting.")

During the Commando's brief training with armoured personnel carriers it had been emphasised that their functions were precisely what their name implied: they carried troops in relative comfort and safety to near the scene of the action. It was then the job of the troops to get out and deal with the enemy on foot.

Roberts, who either saw no reason to be hamstrung by these niceties, or who possibly entertained some brief fond recollections of the good old days of hunting the *Bismarck*, broke the temporary deadlock on the Tongue by putting in what amounted to a tank attack. His Kangaroos roared past 'D' Troop, past 'A' and 'B' Troops, and carried on until they flattened the German wire and arrived noisily, and throwing up clouds of sand, in the middle of Joshua. The German defenders, looking surprised, came resignedly out of their weapon pits with their hands raised. 'C' Troop jumped down from their Kangaroos to round up their prisoners. A fresh complication then became evident. The high waterproof exhaust vent in the leading Kangaroo, the one in which Roberts and Lieutenant McConville were travelling with Sergeant Bill Ash's sub section, had been screwed on the wrong way round by some incompetent fitter. The exhaust fumes, instead of disappearing safely into the atmosphere, had been discharged in to the bowl of the vehicle. Roberts and McConville, who had been hanging over the side, were only partially affected. Most of the troops inside had suffered substantial doses of carbon monoxide poisoning. The effect varied with the random distribution of the doses, but the overall pattern was that of widespread intoxication to be found at chucking-out time at a more than averagely rowdy public house.

The toxified victors, with mixed hilarity and slow-wittedness, disarmed their prisoners and formed them up into parties for dispatch to the rear under escort. There were a few German dead from the artillery shelling. There were more German wounded who lay or sat in a subdued line to be attended to by German medical orderlies. 'C' Troop then rather shakily mounted their vehicles, Roberts turned them south again, and they trundled back to the place in which they were to undertake their legitimate responsibilities for the river crossing.

Robert's coup at Joshua had not disposed of the entire strength of the German garrison on the Tongue. There were still plenty of outlying pockets of resistance, fighting grimly, who one by one were cleaned out by 'A', 'B' and 'D' Troops. The cleansing did not take long. A growing number of German prisoners, eventually totalling about eighty, were disarmed, marched back and delivered to the rear. Of the several 43 Commando casualties one of the dead was Lieutenant Stan Barnes of 'A' Troop, killed in the earlier shelling, not very far from the spot where five nights previously he had led the successful 'A' Troop patrol which had disposed of all six Germans in a German patrol.

It was now time for 'C' Troop to get their ferry into operation. The five Assault Boats, two of which had already been holed by shell fragments, and the two rubber dinghies were off loaded from the Kangaroos, assembled, or in the case of the dinghies, inflated and carried down to the river bank by parties already carefully rehearsed in how the job should be done. The ground beyond the far bank of the Reno was uncompromisingly flat for an expanse of about six hundred yards until it was intercepted by a transverse flood bank. The assembly and the launching of the boats, the thumping in of the stakes on both banks and the attachment and tautening of the joining ropes, was to some extent concealed by a thick cloud of smoke put down beyond the crossing point by the artillery, thickened up by smoke bombs from the 3" mortars of the Commando. For the first few minutes of the setting up of the crossing there was little enemy interference. That changed rapidly. 'C' Troop had established a shallow semi-circular beach head on the west bank. A small ferry party stayed on the river heaving the ropes to bring over the follow-up troops, 'B' and 'D'. A violent and prolonged concentration of enemy shell fire came down accurately on the crossing point. More and more of 'B' and 'D' Troops were ferried over and enlarged the beachhead.

It was then the turn of these two troops to put in a further attack over the flat land ahead up to the attenuated flood bank. The flood bank was the axis of a German company-strong locality, code-named Acts, which also housed an 88mm gun and an Italian anti-tank gun. 'B' and 'D' went in, behind a very heavy artillery concentration, at 10.42 hours. Inevitably there were more casualties, but the German position was over-run and a further eighty prisoners were taken. With the heat now lifted from them 'C' Troop had time to count its own casualties. Of the eight men who had manned the ferries, four were dead and one was very badly wounded. One of the dead was Marine Raven, the Bren gunner who had been seriously wounded at the gapping of the wire by Bob Loudoun and 'C' Troop the previous July in the Brac battle. Corporal Ted Saberton, one of the three ferry party survivors, put an outstanding performance throughout the crossing episode, and continued to do so for the rest of the operation.

43 had now entirely cleared the Tongue and had inserted a deep wedge into the centre of the German holdings in the southern part of the main Spit. Before turning north to join up with No 2 Commando and the rest of the lakeborne landers, it was necessary to do a great deal of tidying up among the cut-off Germans to the south. Whilst the 'B' and 'D' Troops attack upon Acts was still in progress, a sapper party moved up to the ferry site and supplemented the badly shot-about Assault boats of 'C' Troop by the installation of a genuine raft, with full pushing and pulling devices lodged on either side of the Reno. It was capable both of taking more troops quicker than the earlier improvisation, and could also carry reasonably heavy traffic.

'E' Troop carried in Fantails, escorted by two Churchill tanks of the North Irish Horse, had crossed the river higher up close to its mouth, immediately after the subjugation of Joshua. In theory all the vehicles should have swum across, turned south and cleared their way towards the 'C' Troop crossing point. What actually happened was that the leading Fantail, in which were Captain Ralph Parkinson-Cumine and Lieutenant Bill Jenkins with one sub-section manoeuvred round in a slow circle in the Reno, here at its mouth much wider. The driver had locked his controls, and seemed not to know how to unlock them. Intermittent bursts of Spandau fire came at the Fantail, its Browning machine guns shot in return, Parkinson-Cumine became angry, and Jenkins did his best not to laugh. The Fantail driver finally managed to beach his vehicle sideways-on on the far bank, thereby ending once and for all any prospect of his being able to demonstrate the Fantail's advertised capabilities of climbing it.

The troops jumped out and sank thigh deep into soft silt. The other Fantails made a more dignified crossing, but they too were unable to scale the river bank on the far side. The North Irish Horse Troop Commander decided that the water was too deep for his tanks to be able to wade it successfully, so they too had to stay out of things. 'E' Troop dragged themselves laboriously through the deep sucking mud, deployed, and advanced with neither the protection of the Fantails nor the tactical fire support of the tanks, across a flat, open, 600 yards wide plain. They were, however, provided with an altogether impressive alternative form of insurance. A moving curtain of high explosive shells, directed by the Gunner Forward Observation Officer with the troop, preceeded them until they were close to the objective. High explosive was then, at precisely the correct moment, replaced by smoke. 'E' Troop joined up with 'B' and 'D' Troops in the Acts battle, overran part of the positions from the flank, and turned towards its rear. From this vantage point they commanded the vulnerable rear entrances to the German strong points and called upon the Germans to surrender. They did, in droves. They had no other choice but for heroic suicide, an option which they showed no inclination to take.

Whilst the final disposal of the Acts position was being tended to, 'A' Troop, led by Captain Martin Preston, also crossed the river and was turned south to clear the entrenched German positions along the river bank and the few further inland. In addition to their small arms they used their PIAT to intimidate the more intransigent German machine gunners dug in on the flood bank. One projectile for each was usually enough. Machine gun crews surrendered without further ado. After seven hundred yards of successful progress, 'A' Troop ran into an unmarked mine field. Three marines were badly hurt on Schuh mines, and Lieutenant David Leatherbarrow lost an eye when a piece of the boot of a marine who had trodden on a mine, was blown into it. Immediately after 'A' Troop had crossed the river, 'F' Troop followed them and dug in their mortars and Vickers medium machine guns on the west bank of the Reno, ready to give whatever support was required wherever it was required.

At much the same time, with the final tidying up of the Acts objective completed, Colonel Riches consolidated 'D', 'B' and 'E' Troop into one force under the command of Captain Ian Gourlay, and directed them on to the only two major German localities still holding out in the south. The first, Hosea I, was held in company strength. The second,

Hosea II, which incorporated Casa Ronconi, the fortified farm complex that a few week earlier had much been the subject of much interested study from the far side of the river by 43's early patrols, was defended by a company and a half, which included one and a half platoons of a Machine Gun company. Within one hour of the success at Acts, Hosea I was reduced by an attack put in behind the by now customary, comforting, devastating, creeping, artillery barrage.

There were more wholesale surrenders, and a brief bizarre conversation between an English-speaking German Officer and Lieutenant Bill Jenkins. The German, interested in the mechanics of the thing, wanted to know what he had done wrong. Jenkins had neither the time nor the patience to give an Agony Aunt's advice on the best way to lay out defensive positions, and said so. The German's next reproachful question, "Why aren't you black?", a piece of ethnic confusion that presumably reflected the German's belief that he had been attacked by the brown men of 8th Indian Division, didn't get much of a reply either.

Hosea II was next. The garrison of Casa Ronconi put up brief resistance and then surrendered with a haul to the Commando of thirty prisoners. 'B', 'D' and 'E' Troops pushed on further south of the river bank and were preparing to assault the remaining strong points in Hosea II when there was a mass surrender of the enemy. A contribution to this collapse in German morale had come from 40 Commando. During the night, while 43 were poised waiting to go on the Tongue, 'A' Troop of 40 backed by two troops of Churchill tanks of the North Irish Horse, had quietly been ferried across the Reno in the southern-most sector of the operation. At 6.30am they had started to clear the north bank of the Reno. The tanks were early on held up by an impassable irrigation ditch. 'A' Troop of 40 were slowed by a widely sown minefield. They moved onwards steadily, but slowly, and to hurry thing along, 'E' Troop of 43 Commando were dispatched to clear from the rear the German positions code-named Mark, in front of No 40. 'E' Troop too ran into mine fields, but the track through them used by the Germans was well beaten down and clearly identifiable, and the troop got through without any harm. They then cleared out the occupants of all dug-in German positions, and as dusk fell linked up with 'A' Troop of 40 Commando. 40 accepted a not altogether welcome batch of fresh prisoners.

'E' Troop's next move was not all that welcome either. In common with everybody else they had had almost no sleep on the previous night. They had been fighting on and off from dawn until dusk, and, in the intervals between engagements, had been tramping through sand carrying heavy loads of weaponry and equipment. Immediately after the completion of the enterprise at the two Hoseas, 'B' and 'D' Troop had been ordered north in preparation for the join up on the Bellochio Canal with the lake crossers of No 2 Commando. 'E' Troops excursion to the south west had caused them to put in some extra mileage and some extra fighting. They felt that they deserved a rest. They did not get it.

They too were ordered north, and moved off wearily for a three and a half mile march over the sand and through the scrubby bushes. Three and a half miles does not sound much. To tired men, in those conditions, it was a long way. It was midnight before they finally reached the bridge at Peter, earlier captured by No 2 Commando, fed, put out

## COMACCHIO: DAY ONE

sentries, and slept deeply in the slit trenches previously dug by No 2 Commando. The position was stonked intermittently throughout the night by German guns. The noise awakened few.

The Bellochio Canal, a rather grandiloquent name for what was not much more than a partially dried up straight water course, ran in an easterly direction from Lake Comacchio to the mouth of the River Reno at a point not far short of the northern extremity of the Tongue. No 2 Commando's objectives had included the securing of the bridges over this canal notably one code named Peter. Both No 2 and No 9 Commando had met with mixed fortunes after the confusion of their sludge-ridden passage across the lake, but by 10.15am they had taken Peter. They were counter-attacked but held on without too much difficulty. 43 were to join up with them at Peter, but for most of the day the bulk of 43 were preoccupied with the neutralisation of the area to the south.

'C' Troop, however, still at the site of their river crossing, were free of commitments. In the course of the day they were directed on to the bridge Peter. Led by Captain Shorty Roberts, they set off across the sand, made good progress, and were confronted at a track junction by a dug-in German platoon position. As elsewhere throughout the battle, the Gunner forward Observation Officer accompanying the troop was lavishly efficient in his offer of artillery support. The position was drenched with shells, 'C' Troop followed up briskly and closely behind the barrage, and the position was taken without loss. Another 30 prisoners were added to the total approaching 400 already netted by 43 Commando. The clearance of this position opened the way through to Peter, although there were still some obstacles to be disposed of further to the west.

These were two entrenched localities known as Matthew I and Matthew II. In the original brigade plan they were to have been the responsibility of No 9 Commando. But No 9 Commando was still deeply involved in another biblical embroilment at a place known as Leviticus, and the job of clearing the Matthews was switched to 43. 'B' and 'D' Troops, returning northwards after their Hosea experiences, were committed to the attack. The Matthews were awkward targets, well defended by minefields, an intricate dyke system, and a strong sprinkling of Spandau positions. Care was taken in infiltrating 'B' and 'D' Troops to position from which they could assault and there were some casualties from mines, including Captain David Barnett the 'B' Troop Commander who had taken the troop over after the disappearance of Cotton-Minchin. The enemy surrendered when the the attack went in. By late that night 'B' and 'D' Troops had made their way to join 'C' Troop at Peter. 'E' Troop came in shortly afterwards. The four troop force, commanded by Major Neil Munro, was put into all round defensive positions and settled down for as much rest as possible during a night punctuated by sporadic enemy shelling and Spandau fire. Slightly farther back at the site of the river crossing, Colonel Riches was with his advance headquarters, with Major Jock Hudspith of the Heavy Weapons Troop, and with 'A' Troop who had made their way up from the south. They too were in defensive positions. The first day, successful, was over. Sentries and two patrols from 'C' Troop aside, the commando slumbered.

## CHAPTER SIXTEEN

# COMACCHIO: DAY TWO

At 7.00 O'clock on the following morning Colonel Riches attended an Orders Group convened by Brigadier Tod at his headquarters at Casa Simoni. The advance towards the Valetta Canal was to resume at 11am, with 43 Commando on the right and No 2 Commando on the left. No 2 Commando would have tank support. No 9 Commando would stay in reserve. Mines, wide irrigation ditches and general obstacles delayed the arrival of No 2 Commando's tanks and the advance was postponed until 2pm. The delay was not unwelcome to 43. At 8 o'clock in the morning the commando transport convoy had arrived at Peter in jeeps with replenishment weapons, ammunition, food and equipment. Hot meals were cooked, weapons cleaned, replacement ammunition distributed and packed into ammunition pouches, faces were shaved, and the extra three hours of loafing about in the spring sunshine were refreshing.

By 2pm 43 were formed up in a long single file, reminiscent of island days. 'C' Troop led, followed by 'E' Troop, 'D' Troop and Commando Tactical Headquarters. Behind Tac HQ came 'A' Troop, 'B' Troop and Main Headquarters. At the heel of the hunt were the Heavy Weapons of 'F' Troop who were to delay their start until jeeps and trailers caught up with them.

The ground ahead was the usual scrubby sand, the scrub here higher and thicker than in the southern part of the Spit although still dispersed in irregular clumps. Watches were synchronised carefully. Individual weapons were cocked and their carrying positions adjusted by each man to provide a suitable balance between comfort and speed of use. The ever reliable artillery concentration came down precisely on time and in the right place. As the advance began there was an enhanced alertness amongst everybody. The height of the clumps of scrub made for only irregular visibility, and farther ahead lay an extensive mine field. One element in the piece brought comfort to the 'C' Troop navigators at the head of the snake: the track that they were following was heavily studded with German footprints, all heading north. Where German feet could walk with impunity, so too could British feet.

To allow Brigade Headquarters to monitor the speed of the advance, two notional transverse report lines, James and Jeremiah, were plotted on maps. There was no point in lingering - indeed there was every point in pushing on as fast as possible to get through and beyond the minefields - and progress was fast. James was crossed just under 40 minutes after the start and Jeremiah by 2.55 pm. There had still been no opposition. The gunfire continued to crash down at intervals shortly ahead of the leading marines. A short distance north of Jeremiah the first mine field was reached. This was a pleasingly ordered affair. Unmarked mines are as big a threat to the side of the layers as they are to their opponents. This collection was marked off by agricultural looking triple strand barbed wire fences, attached to stout upright stakes, all measured accurately to the same height, all separated by identical intervals, and all dressed in straight lines to the right marker. At the point where the track met the leading edge of the wire, a gap of about 8 feet wide had been left, and the track continued through the minefield along a channel fenced off on either side in the same neat fashion as was the front edge. Behind these side fences were a succession of neatly stencilled placards, illustrated by Skulls and Crossbones and bearing the legend *Achtung Minen.*

The sand of the track itself showed no break in the reassuring volume of German foot prints, and 'C' Troop went straight in without too many misgivings about mines but with some reservations about what might happen if they were shot at seriously whilst still in this restricting lane-way. They were not shot up. They plugged on, fast, with the whole snake of the Commando following along behind. There was an exit opening, similar to the entry one, after several hundred yards. Thankfully they filed through it one by one, and continued along the track. There was now room to manoeuvre on either side of it should manoeuvre become necessary. There was a mild bend in the track, screened by unusually tall bushes, beyond which was clear land. The scrub had been cut. As soon became clear, from the evidence of the concrete bases of buildings, with colourful weeds growing around the edges and in cracks, all houses south of the Canal had been demolished to give the defenders in Porto Garibaldi clear field of fire. The Valetta Canal was not in immediate sight. Behind where it obviously was, was a line of joined houses, roofs of irregular heights, looking like the backdrop to an elaborate theatrical production. In front of the canal and the houses was a considerable number of German soldiers, milling about in apparent confusion.

'C' Troop set about exploiting the confusion and were at first successful. The leading section deployed into a loose line and made for the Germans, fast. Shorty Roberts, coming along behind, brought the second section along and ran towards the right flank. Some of the Germans fired. Some raised their hands in surrender. The marines pressed on through them, firing at those who had fired at them, ignoring those who wanted to give themselves up. In this melee the advancing line began to loose its cohesion. The canal bank was reached by a few. One ran over a shallow bridge across the canal. German Spandaus, firing at close range from the fortified houses, then opened up decisively. They were impartial about their targets, and fired long bursts indiscriminately at both the marines and at their hesitant comrades in front of them.

Marines and German surrenderers dived for what cover they could find. Slightly to the left, and to the rear, a marine Bren gunner took on the Spandaus. Corporal Tom Hunter, a quick-thinking Scotsman, who had been a model of cheerful, energetic effectiveness since the previous day's start of the battle, had immediately appreciated what was necessary to do to extricate his friends. He set himself up, completely exposed on a pile of rubble and fired methodical bursts at the muzzle-flashes of the Spandaus. He could not last. His intervention ended abruptly when he was shot through the head. For this ultimate sacrifical action, coupled with his outstanding contribution throughout the Comacchio battle, Tom Hunter was awarded postumously the only Royal Marine Victoria Cross of the Second World War. The distraction that he provided enabled numbers of marines to scramble to some sort of safe cover.

For the rest of the afternoon 'C' Troop was stuck. They lurked in folds in the ground, behind the debris of the demolished houses, and anywhere else that looked temporarily attractive. Any sign of movement attracted attention from the Spandaus. The Spandau operators, however, did not have it entirely their own way. The gunners shelled houses from time to time. After an hour or so, Hurricanes of the South African Air Force, carrying bombs, streaked in from the sea, had a good look, circled out to sea again and came in for a second time. They bombed the Porto Garibaldi houses with precision, after which the enthusiasm of the Spandau gunners diminished notably.

'E' Troop, led by Captain Ralph Parkinson-Cumine, had been immediately behind 'C' Troop in the advance along the track. Bushes masked their view ahead, but as soon as the sound of heavy Spandau fire showed that 'C' Troop were engaged, Parkinson-Cumine took his leading section to the right and moved up as fast as possible towards the sound of the shooting. The 'E' Troop section was at once engaged heavily. Sergeant George and Sergeant McKenna were both wounded, George badly (his leg was later amputated). Marine Maclean, at 28 one of the oldest men in the commando, and who had abandoned a career at a sheep farmer in Argentina to come home to volunteer, was killed. 'E' Troop's second section, led by Lieutenant Bill Jenkins, joined up with Parkinson-Cumine. As with 'C' Troop, they were pinned down by Spandau fire for the rest of the afternoon.

Shorty Roberts had been badly hit earlier on during 'C' Troop's attack, and was lying out in the open, unable to move. He did his best to look dead, but every time he stirred incautiously somebody fired another burst at him. Marine Reg Skinner, the Mljet well dwelling veteran, tried to pull him back but was unsuccessful. Skinner then crawled his way to 'E' Troop, and put a proposition to Lieutenant Bill Jenkins. Skinner was, in Jenkin's words, "absolutely insistent" that Roberts should be recovered straight away. (Those in 'C' Troop who knew what Skinner was like when he was being absolutely insistent, could imagine the flavour of the Skinner/Jenkins discussion). Jenkins improvised a white flag, fell in a stretcher party and, guided by Skinner, moved rather selfconciously out in to the open to collect Roberts. Rather surprisingly in the circumstances the Germans respected the white flag. Roberts, "still his usual unruffled self", was loaded on to the stretcher and brought back to safety.

Shortly after nightfall, Lieutenant McConville on the left with the survivors of 'C' Troop and Parkinson-Cumine on the right with 'E' Troop, made individual decisions to move back. The withdrawal was as silent as was possible. Hunter's body was left where it lay. A high proportion of 'C' Troop had been wounded but most of them could limp. The more serious cases were helped along by friends. One, Sergeant Reg Clinton, had been partially blinded and needed particular care. The depleted 'C' Troop party made its way back to the track exit from which they had emerged a few hours previously, moved cautiously down the track, and after about 200 yards were challenged.

Captain Bob Loudoun, the Adjutant, who had commanded 'C' Troop at Anzio, Ornito, in the Dalmatian islands and in Montenegro, had been becoming increasingly concerned about the fate of his old troop and had persuaded Colonel Riches to let him take out a relief party with stretchers and medical supplies. He now welcomed his former followers with warmth, and led them back down the track to Commando Headquarters. The Germans had been putting down random harassing artillery fire on likely nodal points, track junctions, bridges as so on, and a concentrated stonk caught the 'C' Troop party. There was only one casualty. The blinded Sergeant Reg Clinton was killed. Later, Bob Loudoun took out a patrol with a view to the recovery of Hunter's body. They heard German movement and talk in the vicinity, and Loudoun abandoned the project. It was distasteful to leave the Commando's dead unattended; to risk further lives in an attempt to bring in a body would be foolish sentimentality.

The strength and the determination shown by the defenders of Porto Garibaldi demonstrated that it could only be taken by a full scale set-piece attack. Brigadier Tod could see no sense in mounting one. His Brigade had done all that had been asked of it. A large and useful tract of land had been seized, and the forthcoming spring offensive of V Corps had had its prospects materially improved. 946 prisoners had been taken (43 Commando's share was 450); large numbers of the enemy had been killed or wounded; three enemy infantry battalions, two troops of artillery and a company of machine gunners had been removed from the board; and 20 artillery pieces, mortars and a number of rocket projectors had been captured. Brigadier Tod ordered 43 Commando to establish themselves on a line about 400 yards south of Garibaldi. Throughout the 4th April the Commando stayed in this line, was subjected to occasional shelling, and sent out some reconnaissance patrols. That night the Commando was relieved in the line by a battalion of the Coldstream Guards. By dawn 43 Commando were back in civvy billets in Ravenna, sleeping with roofs over their heads for the first time in more than a month.

They had lost one Officer and eight other ranks killed, and four Officers and thirty eight other ranks wounded.

A day or two later, Brigadier Tod passed on a message that he had been sent from General MrCreery, the 8th Army Commander, once the Corps Commander who had sent an elegant Thank You after Ornito. It congratulated the Brigadier and all ranks of his force "....on your most successful operation which has captured or destroyed the whole enemy garrison south of Porto Garibaldi. Your operation demanded careful and detailed planning and skill in execution. All ranks have shown a splendid enterprise, endurance and determination to surmount difficulties. Your success has helped the whole army plan. Well done indeed!". Whether this sort of fan mail from on high really gave much of a boost to the troops' morale is open to argument. It is less arguable that they would have been deeply vexed if they hadn't been sent it.

# CHAPTER SEVENTEEN

# ARGENTA

Any dispassionate analyst who looked at the military plight of the Germans in the spring of 1945 would rightly have judged that they had not long to go. German cities had been bombed to rubble by the allied air forces. In the East the Red Army was advancing through Poland into Prussia. In the West, American and British armies had crossed the Rhine. In the South, the long, hard, blood-stained slog for eighteen months up the length of Italy had brought warfare to the southern edge of the Lombardy plain. Far ahead, beyond the plain, were the Alps and the frontier with Austria, the southern marches of the metropolitan *Reich*. In winter weather the flatlands would have been unable to sustain the huge weight of tracked and wheeled vehicles that a modern army would use in an attack upon them. By the middle of April, 1945, the plain had dried out sufficiently for an attack to be feasible.

No 2 Commando Brigade's action at Comacchio had been the curtain raiser. V Corps now launched by far and away a much stronger and more sophisticated force of several divisions, Infantry and Armoured, supported by massive air cover in its final offensive of the war. Before these formations could really cut loose in the open country of the Lombardy plain, there was one bottle-neck to be negotiated. This was the Argenta Gap. The main highway to Ferrara and the north ran through the town of Argenta. The land surrounding the town for miles on either side of it is uniformly flat. Some of it was below sea level. To the east was Lake Comacchio and its adjacent marshes. To the west the Germans had flooded an area more than nine miles wide. Criss-crossing all this extensive wetness was a network of high flood banks projecting well above the water, and the causeways along which the major roads ran.

The capture of Argenta was V Corps first objective. German national prospects may have been without hope, but German soldiers on the ground showed no signs that they recognised this bitter fact. They fought as fiercely as they always had. The British 78th Division, backed by armour, attacked towards Argenta from the east and met a stout German resistance. 78th Division's final assault was timed for the night of 16/17 April. To the west of the town, 10th Indian Division were poised for a general drive northwest of Bologna.

V Corps decided that the breakthroughs of these two divisions would be assisted materially by a subsidiary assault along the flood banks to the northwest of Argenta, in an area where the river Reno bends sharply to the west. The job was allotted to No 2 and No 43 Commandos. Its nature was summed up in the official history: "2 Commando brigade...was given the ambitious task of fighting its way alone along the western bank of the Reno, under V Corps command to out-flank Argenta."

On 15 April, No 2 and No 43 left their billets in Ravenna and moved in trucks to the small town of Conselice, south of Argenta. On the night of 16 April they passed through the Irish Brigade of 78th Division and began the first phase of their advance. It was relatively uneventful. A few prisoners were taken, mostly lost souls who had mislaid themselves in the confusion of the past few days. After daybreak, local civilians applauded and proffered fruit, cheese and wine. Pretty girls blew kisses. Matters became mildly festive. It was clear that the Germans had withdrawn from this part of the sector, although how far they had gone was unknown.

There was a return to operational normality during the next night. Ahead lay two parallel canals which in turn ran parallel to the river Reno. All three waterways ran in straight lines for three and a half miles or so until they reached the westward bend in the river. Each was bordered by high grassed flood banks, about thirty yards wide at their base, tapering to a flat surface of about ten to fifteen feet wide, a total of four flood banks in all. At their southern end were sluice gates. Higher up, bridges carried a lateral road that led into Argenta itself. 43's peaceful forward movement of the previous day had brought them within close range of the sluice gates. No 2 Commando leap-frogged through 43's position, seized the sluice gates, and advanced along the flood banks towards their first objectives, the bridges over the canal and the Reno. The flood bank surfaces were devoid of any sort of cover. Concentrated Spandau fire opened suddenly on to 2 Commando from positions in houses built on top of the flood bank immediately behind the three bridges. No 2 Commando were for the moment checked.

By this time 78th Division were advancing slowly against strong opposition and had reached a position about two miles southeast of Argenta town. If the Commando brigade's commitment to help 78th Division forward was to be met it was essential that an attack against the bridges should be put in with whatever resources were immediately to hand. Tank support had been arranged, but the tanks were held up on the way and were unable to get fully forward until the afternoon. The guns of a Field Regiment of 8th Indian Division were on call and shortly after daybreak ranged on the bridges and the houses abutting them. There was an impressive air strike by the RAF, who dropped their bombs right on target, completely obliterated one house, scored direct hits on several others and then strafed the entire German locality. At 9.45am, immediately after the air attack was over, 2 Commando went in along the flood banks supported by the guns of the Field Regiment. There was no room for either manoeuvre or guile in this assault. The job could only be done by a series of rushes along the surface of each flood bank in turn, the rush shot in to its immediate target by support fire from the other two flood banks. It was elementary stuff but it worked. The Germans fought hard, but as each rush was pressed home they withdrew from one position after another. By 10.30am the area of the bridges had been cleared. Eight prisoners had been taken. The prisoners said that they were from a hundred strong *ad hoc* battle group, formed the previous day from remnants of 42nd Jaeger Division.

No 2 Commando pushed ahead for another five hundred yards along the dykes. They soon ran into heavy mortar and machine gun fire from a water pumping station and some houses. 2 Commando were temporarily stuck.

They were on the only dominating feature in miles of flat country. 78th Division were closing slowly from the east. It was evident to Brigadier Tod that the German reaction to the pressure in their midst of a precariously supplied vulnerable nuisance would be violent. The Brigadier called back No 2 Commando to the area of the bridges. There they dug in thoroughly.

In the first five hours after the capture of the bridges the enemy put in four counter attacks by up to two hundred men, each preceded by heavy concentrations of mortar and artillery fire. As with No 2 Commando's earlier assault, all these attacks were made straight down the bare surfaces of the flood banks. The attempts were broken up by No 2 Commando's small arms fire, and by some highly accurate shelling from the 8th Indian Division's artillery field regiment. Later, twenty German dead were counted north of the bridges. A proportionately larger number must have been wounded.

The constructive 2 Commando part of the enterprise had achieved a useful introduction to Ronnie Tod's remit, but if he were to meet it in full more work remained. It was to be done by 43 Commando. Tod decided to pass 43 through the No 2 Commando position by night to advance north and along the same bare and narrow access of the four flood banks. 43 were to be supported by 2 troops of tanks which had now arrived and their attack was to be preceded by a programme of artillery fire. The start time was fixed for 3.30am on 18 April. 43 were given three objectives: the power house and the houses from which No 2 Commando had earlier been engaged; a further group of houses about five hundred yards beyond the first objective; and the bend in the river Reno.

43 had had little luck with armoured support at Comacchio, and things went wrong with them from the start here at Argenta as well. There was only one constricted approach track accessible to tanks. The leading one drove over a mine, slewed round side-ways, and blocked the way for the rest of them. That was the end of the contribution from the tanks.

The start line was a transverse flood bank that linked the four longitudinal ones. 'D' Troop (Captain John Page (Royal Artillery)) and 'E' Troop (Captain Ralph Parkinson-Cumine) were on the left. 'A' Troop (Captain Martin Preston), were in the middle. 'B' Troop (Captain Mark Nunns) were on the right. All scrambled over the start line on time. 'D' and 'E' Troop gained about 400 yards along the flat ground west of the floodbank before they found themselves in among heavy artillery and mortar fire from their front, and close range Spandau fire from their front and from either flank. 'E' Troop were ahead with 'D' Troop following on behind. The initial bursts of Spandau fire were from so close that they passed over the marines' heads. Parkinson-Cumine, up with the 'E' Troop point section, saw no future in a head on direct assault. He put his troop in the care of Lieutenant Bill Jenkins, took two Marines, Woodger and Beale, with him, and climbed the inner floodbank with a view to finding out whether he could find a way around to outflank the forward German position. Jenkins at once heard further close-to Spandau bursts coming from the far side of the second flood bank. A few minutes later, Parkinson-Cumine and Woodger clambered back over the bank, and slithered down the side to Jenkins. Both were wounded, Woodger not too badly, Parkinson-Cumine by a burst across his chest that had punctured his right lung.

Parkinson-Cumine was strong, determined and athletic (he had captained the Ulster schools interprovincial Rugby side) but he was in no condition to go on. Jenkins stripped him of his equipment, examined his wounds and called for stretcher bearers. Before his departure Parkinson-Cumine asked that his equipment should accompany him on the stretcher. At the Regimental Aid Post he was found to be luckier than he had thought. The Spandau burst had shot away the metal shoulders through which ran the pin that secured the lever on a fragmentation grenade that he carried in a Bren Gun pouch attached to his webbing belt. The lever was now held in place only by the front of the pouch. An equally lucky medical orderly at the Aid Post discovered this freakish potential lethal embarrassment in time to prevent further mayhem among the increasing number of patients who where gathering for medical attention by Doctor Ralph Bazeley and his medical team. The orderly disposed of the pouch and the grenade with promptitude and delicacy.

Back on the sides of the left flood bank the Marines crouched low as the close-by Spandaus drilled away, and caused several more casualties. One of them was Captain John Page, the 'D' Troop Commander, whose leg and ankle was shattered by a burst. Lieutenant Bill Jenkins, just past his twentieth birthday, was now the front man of the left prong of the attack. He had inherited the leadership of both 'E' and 'D' Troops. He was not prepared to squander them in an expensive frontal surge. He followed the Parkinson-Cumine precedent, and scaled the flood bank to his right. It was still dark.

He was soon in the midst of a complicated early morning. Six yards ahead of him, on top of the embankment, was a wide iron-barred gate, about ten feet high, set in a tall fence that extended right across the flat land on either side as well. The gate was slightly ajar. Jenkins at first took this to be an over-obvious allurement and groped about systematically for trip wires that might detonate mines. He found none. He went carefully through the gate, stopped, listened and heard nothing. He edged himself forward for a further ten paces. There was still silence. He realised that he had now penetrated the German front defences. He had found what he wanted. He turned back to collect 'E' Troop and bring them along this interesting route.

He was approaching the gate on his return when there were shots from his near left. The first one induced a searing pain in his neck and flashing sparks in his eyes. As he swung round there was another shot and he felt a tremendous kick in his back. It lifted him off his feet and flung him face down on the ground. He was dazedly contemplating eternity, when it occurred to him that he was still thinking coherently. He tested his arms and legs. They worked. He took a No 36 fragmentation grenade from his pouch, pulled out the pin, and lobbed it down the bank. It exploded satisfyingly. He heard the swishing sound of a man running away through wet grass. Jenkins lay still for two minutes and then heard another man following the first. Jenkins gave the second man an encouraging burst from his Tommy gun, into the darkness below.

In the silence that followed he suddenly became aware of a rustling immediately beneath his ear. He was lying prone. He felt about with his hand and found that he was on the edge of a German slit trench. He quietly unbuttoned his pistol holster, took out his Colt .45, cocked it, and fired blind into the trench. A terrified man immediately shot up into the air like a Jack-in-the-Box, and pranced about in the dim light with his hands in the air shouting "Don't shoot. I'm an Austrian." Jenkins rose to his feet and told the Austrian courteously that he was OK for survival. He was now a prisoner. After a short interval two more figure disgorged themselves from an adjacent hole in the ground. They were a Spandau team who after satisfying themselves that Jenkins was merciful to their Austrian friend, also gave themselves up.

Corporal Walter Iredale, who had been wondering about what had happened to his temporary Troop Commander, and about what he could do to improve 'E' Troop's situation, appeared out of the murk and joined Jenkins at the iron gate. Jenkins thankfully handed over his three prisoners to Iredale, and told him to take them back and to return with a Section of 'E' Troop. They could then resume their move towards the pumping station along what seemed to be a sparsely defended by-pass. Iredale went away, leaving Jenkins once more on his own.

He wasn't alone for long. The light was improving and he saw, a short way to his left, about eighteen yards, a brick building. From behind this came a file of German soldiers, moving casually with slung weapons. Jenkins crouched and counted them. The ones in front paused, chattered among themselves, and waited for the rearmost ones to catch up. Jenkins counted seventeen. None of them looked in his direction.

As soon as he was satisfied that the full parade was fallen in, Jenkins rose to his feet in a menacing manner on the height of the embankment, pointed his Tommy Gun at this slovenly group of foes, roared *"Hande Hoch"*. Their reactions were sluggish. The thought began to cross Jenkins mind that if they didn't speed things up he would have to shoot the lot. At last they unslung their rifles and lowered them to the ground. Jenkins gestured graphically, with his Tommy Gun. They moved away from their weapons. Corporal Iredale put in a timely reappearance accompanied by a group of marines, and the prisoners were searched.

They had a surprisingly high level of leadership. There was a Major and a Company Sergeant Major. The prisoners went back under escort. Jenkins now had his troop signaller with him, and reported to Commando Headquarters. He was told to consolidate at the pumping station and not to move further forward to the cluster of houses behind them.

Immediately to the right of 'E' Troop, on the far side of their innermost flood bank, Captain Martin Preston and 'A' Troop had crossed the start line exactly on time. They were Spandaued as they negotiated the transverse flood bank, but nobody was hit. They moved forward, initially without incident, for about a quarter of a mile. There was then a noisy disturbance immediately to their right, beyond the flanking embankment. Lieutenant McConville, who was leading the forward section, halted the column and climbed up the bank to investigate. There was a lot of shouting, the ripping noise of

Spandaus firing, the more deliberate sounds of Schmeissers, and the sharp cracks of exploding grenades. No British weapons were being discharged. McConville concluded that two perplexed bands of Germans, deep in the fog of war as waged by night, were enthusiastically fighting one another, an entirely satisfactorily dilution of German resources. McConville slid back down the bank and 'A' Troop's advance resumed.

From immediately to the front came the muzzle-flash and crack of a German 88 firing at short range. It was so close that the bangs of the discharge and of the exploding shells were almost simultaneous. The first shell landed about one hundred yards ahead; the second about seventy five yards, the third about fifty yards. The gun crew was clearly adjusting its sights at mathematically calculated short intervals. The fourth shell showered the leading men in 'A' Troop with earth and pebbles. The marines went rapidly to ground. The fifth shell landed about three yards to the left of McConville. Fragments of it hit him, killed marine Hey slightly behind, and wounded two more Marines further back in the column. The wounded were sent to the rear and the advance continued. It was by now daylight.

To the right of 'A' Troop, insulated from them by the third floodbank, 'B' Troop had left the start line also precisely on time. Their early advance was also unimpeded by German opposition. In the developing dawn light they passed the crashings of the 88's onslaught on 'A' Troop, and were then held up by a fresh distraction. Their right boundary was the Reno, and from its far bank came streams of accurate small arms fire. The Troop Commando, Captain Mark Nunns, ignored all this and pushed ahead with his leading subsection. Nunns' party then found themselves on the edge of a German counter attack, mounted along the top of the embankment that separated it from 'A' Troop and directed at both 'A' and 'B' Troops. The counter-attackers were about one hundred strong. They were taken on by all the Bren guns and rifles of both troops. No 2 Commando, from their positions behind the start line, joined in by firing over the heads of the marines with their Bren guns, Vickers Machine guns, and three inch mortars. The counter-attack dissolved. Nunns single-mindedly strode on towards the objective that he had been given. The German counter-attack had split his troop, and the rear part of it was not with him.

To the west, where Lieutenant Bill Jenkins and 'E' and 'D' Troops had made the deepest penetration, there were further events. The pumping station in which Jenkins had taken up residence was faced to its north by a line of poplars. From slit trenches amongst these, four more Germans who if their minds had been in their work, could have done serious damage to Jenkins's people, emerged sheepishly and presented themselves for surrender. Their acceptance into the prisoner collection coincided with a wireless message to Jenkins from Major Neil Munro. Jenkins was to open the lock gates on the canal to his left, so that further troops could join him carried in storm boats. Jenkins was cynical about this proposition, but did what he was told. He was surprised to find at the lock gates an Italian attendant, a slave to routine, who apparently clocked in on time regardless of the impediments to his profession generated by one of the last battles of the Second World War. Jenkins made his wishes known by a mixture of rudimentary Italian and mime. The Italian obligingly opened the lock gates. No storm boats ever appeared.

The general flooding became worse.

Another person unaware of the shifting circumstances of the day was a tall German soldier who slowly climbed to his feet on top of the flood bank that ran to the east parallel to Jenkins's position. This character set about his morning loosening up exercises. He beat his arms about, stamped his feet. A 'D' Troop Bren Gunner wanted to shoot him. Jenkins, who was of a humane disposition, refused permission. He soon accepted that he had made a mistake. Ten minutes later the German opened up on the marines with a Spandau. The 'D' Troop Bren Gunner, now authorised to kill, took careful aim from the edge of the embankment. He was just about to squeeze the trigger when the Spandau gunner beat him to it. Two bullets went into his shoulder and he slid down into Jenkin's arms. A field dressing was applied to his wounds and he was able to walk back to the Aid Post. The German continued to rake the poplars. A chance ricochet hit Corporal Walter Iredale who was below ground in a slit trench. Iredale was sent back on a strecher.

Shortly after dawn, Brigadier Ronnie Tod gave considered thought to the situation in which 43 Commando was now placed. The diversion required of the Commando Brigade to help 78 Division's movement had been thoroughly effective. The Division had fought its way past the east of Argenta and was approaching the essential Highway 16, about a mile north of the town. 43 Commando were exposed in a narrow salient, with Germans on both flanks. There was little that 43 could now do to influence the outcome of the larger battle. Tod ordered a withdrawal to the bridges behind the start line. This decision was strenuously contested by Lieutenant Bill Jenkins, on the left, who argued in a wireless dialogue with Major Neil Munro that having got as far forward as he had, he saw no prospect of doing so again if the Germans re-occupied the position behind the iron fence. Munro shut him up. Jenkins marched his weary marines to the rear.

Elsewhere there was some wireless confusion, but the other troops soon came back too. An exception was Captain Mark Nunns who did not receive the message. Nunns, on the right, with one subsection of 'B' Troop, had kept on going forward after the abortive German counter-attack along the flood banks, and was a thousand yards deep into German territory. He had been wounded in the leg. His party returned at 11am, bringing with them as prisoners one German Officer and four German soldiers.

When Jenkins had safely installed his troop in their new positions, he examined his pack. The blow that had flattened him at the iron gate had come from a bullet that had driven through his portable belongings and had finally lodged itself in the 24-hour ration pack stuffed in his mess tin. Jenkins also took his painful neck to be examined by Doctor Ralph Bazeley. Bazeley clinically withdrew numbers of bits of the gate from Jenkins's neck. Lieutenant W.G. Jenkins was awarded the D.S.O., the youngest Royal Marine Officer in World War II to win this award.

With 43 now extricated, Brigadier Tod wanted to know where and in what strength was the residual opposition. Interrogated prisoners said that their *ad hoc* battle group had been considerably re-inforced during the night. 43 sent out three reconnaissance patrols. The first was shot up by Spandaus from the pumping station, late the property of Bill Jenkins and 'E' Troop. It thereby established the location of at least some unfriendly people, numbers unknown. The second crossed the River Reno south of the bridges, and explored the Reno's east bank. This patrol was fired at by Germans about one thousand yards ahead. The third patrol went into Argenta itself. There were no signs of the enemy in the town.

78 Division had meanwhile reached Highway 16 and were astride the road. V Corps unleashed 6th Armoured division through the Argenta gap, at first light on the following morning. To help the armour on its way the Commando Brigade was ordered to repeat its attack up the flood banks. For this purpose the brigade was furnished with three Wasps, flame throwers mounted in Bren Gun carriers. The assault was supported by an artillery Field Regiment of 25 pounders and a battery of the heavier, medium guns.

43 started off at 1.00am. Progress northward was steady. Most German slit trenches were found to be empty. A few, forlorn, abandoned Germans gave themselves up. Flame-throwing Wasp over-turned in a bomb crater, and the rescue of its crew generated more of a hold-up than the defending Germans had managed. 'E' Troop captured a mobile brothel, the ladies in attendance, sited in a farm house. By 3.15am 43 had reached the bend in the Reno. Patrols pushed forward for a further three thousand yards but found no trace of Germans.

There was further extensive patrolling on the following day. More dejected Germans gave themselves up without a fight. Another general advance met only jubilant Italian Partisans and festive villagers. All available jeeps were mustered in an attempt to catch up with the disappearing enemy. The jeep party from No 2 Commando covered about three miles before they were engaged by mortar and artillery fire. Casualties were nil. More prisoners gave themselves up.

The following day was one of further patrolling, no opposition met, and celebratory welcomes from Italian civilians. 10th Indian Division from the left linked up with 6th Armoured Division in front of the Commando Brigade's position. The fight of the two Commandos was over. So, although they did not know it at the time, was their war. That night they were back in billets in Ravenna. There were the accustomed exceptions. Six Other Ranks of 43 had been killed in the battle. Four Officers and nineteen Other Ranks were wounded.

On 2nd May, General Von Vietinghoff, commanding the German Army Group 'C', surrendered his forces in northern Italy and southern Austria unconditionally. General McCreery, the 8th Army Commander, completed his series of 'Well Done' message to 2 Commando Brigade. This one read:

"Now that final victory has been achieved I want to send you and all ranks of your brigade my very best congratulations on your splendid share in the battle. After your successful Spit operation your troops showed a magnificent fighting spirit combined with skill and enterprise in difficult operations which enabled V Corps to break out of the Argenta defile. This success was the decisive phase of the whole battle. Well done indeed."

43 saw no reason to disagree with the General.

# CHAPTER EIGHTEEN

# DIASPORA

The war was over. There was still much to do. The Commando's wounded, over sixty of them from their time in the line, from Comacchio and from Argenta, were scattered throughout Italy in hospitals in Bari, Naples and Rome. The Royal Army Medical Corps and Queen Alexandra's Imperial Military Nursing Service between them were superb in their standard of care, but their Troop Officers tracked down and visited unit casualties bearing messages of goodwill from friends. Other officers and NCOs, themselves wounded, waited until they were up and about and went the rounds of their own hospitals to call upon harder-hit comrades, to talk to them and to help with minor kindnesses, the writing of letters, local shopping and so on. Some of the not too badly hurt marines slowly rejoined. Others took longer. A few, those with amputations, or severe internal injuries, did not return at all.

Training, a daily feature of life throughout the war years, was temporarily given a miss. There was still an insistence on an excellence in turn out and saluting, but otherwise a general relaxation prevailed. A large leave party went to Florence for ten days or so. Less lengthy tourists took a look at Venice, Rome and other Italian delights. There was also a tedious corporate chore. The surrender of an entire German Army Group meant that an enormous number of prisoners had to be guarded and cared for. 43, like almost every other unit, were given a stint of prison wardening. Their particular charges were lodged in several acres of bare flat land surrounded by a barbed wire fence at Bellaria. There were no buildings for the prisoners but in the early Italian summer it didn't much matter. They dossed down in blankets on the ground at night, and by day wandered about within the cage in the sunshine, stripped to shorts and Afrika Korps type caps with long peaks. They were a deadpan, rather arrogant looking lot, but in an odd way were impressively dignified. Most were of powerful physique. They were supplied with food and water and looked after their own administration. They did it very well. They had no incentive to escape. There was nowhere for them to go and if any of them were rash enough to try they would soon have been butchered by vengeful Italians. Bored marines contemplated from outside the wire these representatives of the Master Race and thought wistfully of home.

There was one daily diversion, a formal German parade which was inspected by whoever happened to be 43's Duty Officer. The Germans were fallen-in in an admirably disciplined manner by their Senior NCOs. They stood rigidly to attention whilst their Sergeant Major, or whatever he was, marched to the Duty Officer, saluted, and reported the parade present. The Duty Officer then walked along the ranks of bronzed torsos, and until he got used to it, was disconcerted by German military habit unknown in the British Armed Forces. The Right Marker stared in to the inspecting Officer's eyes. The next man and the ones after him, did the same. Their heads slowly turned, one after the other as the officer made his way along the line until at the end of it he was fixed by the gazes of a hundred or so of his not long ago foes. Pausing briefly to wonder which of these bastards had tried to shoot him a few weeks previously he then repeated the pantomime in the second and third ranks. (A few years later, he possibly gave thought to the part that might have been played by a proportion of these corralled, defeated and stoical young men in the resurgence of post-war Germany).

These preoccupations did not last for long. 43 was told to pack its trappings, and was moved to a tented camp site outside Naples. Mount Vesuvius had recently erupted spectacularly and had added to the widespread environmental pollution of the Italian campaign. The camp was covered with a layer of dark grey volcanic dust that made its way into tents, clothing, boots, eyes, food and all exposed apertures. As discomforts went it was relatively tolerable, mitigated by the prospect of an early homeward journey in a troopship. In June the Commando, depleted, widely scarred, still recognisable by its bearing as the entity that had set out from the Clyde eighteen months earlier but now manned largely from successive waves of replacements, feeling rather pleased with itself but clannishly reticent about discussing its experiences with strangers, disembarked at Southampton. Everyone was immediately given two weeks leave.

They reassembled at Alton in Hampshire. Dispersion followed. Some went to occupation duties in the wreckage of post-war Germany. Those who had volunteered for further service against the Japanese in the Far East went first to a Holding Commando and then to No 45 or No 46 Commandos. The old hands, in it from the beginning, veterans of Iceland and Dakar, due for early demobilisation, stayed together for a short time in Hampshire. What was still anachronistically known as the War Diary recorded their daily activities. They fell in each morning for "farming duties". They helped to bring in the summer harvest: an aptly constructive and peaceable ending to a five year pilgrimage.

# POSTSCRIPT

In the post war re-organisation of the British armed services the Commando role, initiated by the army during the perilous summer of 1940, became the exclusive prerogative of the Royal Marines. There was a single Commando Brigade of three Commandos, numbered 40, 42 and 45. In the early 1960's, there was a brief period of Treasury expansiveness, and a fourth was added. 43 was reborn. Its second life was short and it saw no action in any of the contemporary post-colonial campaigns.

No-one from the original 43 served in the reconstituted one but some links with the past were preserved. Every year, on 2nd April, Comacchio Day was commemorated. Governmental retrenchment led to its disbandment in 1968.

From the early 1970's onwards international terrorism, for centuries a minor lethal nuisance, became a rapidly developing threat to western countries. Terrorists of varying political persuasion, financed by wealthy sympathisers or exploiters, were better trained, better armed and equipped with more sophisticated destructive devices than ever before. The advent of mass air travel gave them a new mobility across frontiers. They also had a fresh large range of objectives to chose from: passenger aircraft, high speed trains, ships, prominent politicians who were difficult to guard effectively right round the clock, nuclear installation and the like.

The production of North Sea Oil had burgeoned during the decade. A successful terrorist attack on one or more oil rigs was a possibility that had to be weighed. Every rig in the North Sea could not be given permanently manned defences. A specialist unit of the Royal Marines was formed to deal with the problem. The new organisation became operational in May 1980. It was named Comacchio Company, and the modern Corp's link with the wartime 43 was once more revived. The prime task of Comacchio Company was oil rig protection, but it also took on responsibility for the safeguarding of the more sensitive aspects of Royal Naval shore installations. In 1983 its commitments were expanded, its numbers enlarged, and Comacchio Company, became Comacchio Group.

In 1987 their oil rig protection responsibilities were shifted elsewhere. Since then their main task has been the safeguarding of the British Independent Nuclear Deterrent. They maintain an inherent versatility. In the 1990s, for example, they provided boarding parties during the naval blockade of Iraq which preceded the Gulf War; guarded a variety of sensitive allied sites in Saudi Arabia during the war itself; and later sent a troop to complement 3 Commando Brigade when the brigade was helping to protect the Kurds in northern Iraq. At the same time half a troop, including specialists in small boat work, went to Bangladesh to help in the devastation and flooding that followed the major cyclone in 1991.

Comacchio Group's link with 43 is preserved by its representation, customarily by its Commanding Officer, its Regimental Sergeant Major and some chosen Marines at 43's annual re-union.

# AWARDS

To Members of the 2nd, BATTALION ROYAL MARINES
and 43 COMMANDO ROYAL MARINES
(whilst serving with these two units)

## VICTORIA CROSS

| | |
|---|---|
| Corporal Thomas Peck Hunter | Italy |

## DISTINGUISHED SERVICE ORDER

| | |
|---|---|
| Lieutenant Colonel I.H.Riches (later Commandant General R.M.) | Italy |
| Lieutenant W.G.Jenkins | Italy |

## MILITARY CROSS

| | |
|---|---|
| Captain J.P. Blake | Italy |
| Captain J.C.D. Hudspith | Yugoslavia |
| Captain B.I.S. Gourlay (later Commandant General R.M.) | Yugoslavia |
| Rev. Ross Hook Chaplain RNVR | Italy |
| Captain R.N. Parkinson-Cumine | Yugoslavia |
| Captain D.S. Barnett | Italy |
| Captain M.L. Preston SAUDF | Italy |
| Captain M.R. Nunns | Italy |

## MILITARY MEDAL and BAR

| | |
|---|---|
| Sergeant R.D. French | Yugoslavia and Italy |

## MILITARY MEDAL

| | |
|---|---|
| Sergeant T.C. Gallon | Italy |
| Marine C. Nicholls | Yugoslavia |
| Sergeant K.R. Pickering | Italy |
| Lane Corporal E.C. Saberton | Italy |

Lance Corporal C.W. Smith RAMC　　　Yugoslavia
Marine J.R. Squire　　　　　　　　　　Italy

## MEMBER of the ORDER of the BRITISH EMPIRE

Captain (QM) W.M. Harris　　　　　　Italy
Major N.G.M. Munro　　　　　　　　Italy

## BRITISH EMPIRE MEDAL

Colour Sergeant A.J. Brown　　　　　Italy
Sergeant H. Connolly　　　　　　　　Yugoslavia
Lance Corporal K.S. Jones RAMC　　　Italy

## MENTION IN DISPATCHES - TWICE

Major N.G.M. Munro　　　　　　　　Italy and Mediterranean
Captain D.B. Clark　　　　　　　　　Italy and Yugoslavia

## MENTION IN DISPATCHES

Sergeant C.W. Ash　　　　　　　　　Italy
Captain D.S. Barnett　　　　　　　　Italy
Corporal A.J. Bennett　　　　　　　　Italy
Lieutenant J.B. Bolton　　　　　　　　Mediterranean
Marine W.N. Broomfield　　　　　　　Italy
Marine C. Cooper　　　　　　　　　Italy
Marine P. Darrall　　　　　　　　　　Italy
CSM A. Dunn　　　　　　　　　　　Italy
Captian G. Frost　　　　　　　　　　Mediterranean
Marine S. Gartside　　　　　　　　　Italy
Marine A.G. Green　　　　　　　　　Italy
Lance Corporal T.K. Horne　　　　　　Italy
Corporal W.H. Iredale　　　　　　　　Italy
Captain R.B. Loudoun　　　　　　　　Italy
　(later Major General R.M.)
CSM P.S. Maidwell　　　　　　　　　Italy
Lieutenant J.F. Morris　　　　　　　　Mediterranean
Corporal H. McCaughey　　　　　　　Italy

| | |
|---|---|
| Marine L.H. Pearson | Italy |
| Marine H.W. Peaurt | Italy |
| Marine S.G. Riggs | Italy |
| Captain R.G. Schooley | Italy |
| Sergeant T. Seymour | Italy |
| Marine E. Siddall | Mediterranean |
| Marine R.J. Skinner | Italy |
| Marine G. Taylor | Italy |
| Lieutenant T.A.S. Taylor | Italy |
| Corporal A. Tugwell | Italy |

All those listed above are Royal Marines
(Regular or Hostilities Only) unless shown otherwise.

## SOURCES

Text - The United Kingdom, Iceland, West Africa and Italy
Published Works
CHURCHILL, Major General T.B.L. - Commando Crusade (William Kimber)
CHURCHILL, Winston S. - The Second World War, Their Finest Hour (The Riverside Press, Cambridge, Massachusetts)
MARDER, Arthur - Operation Menace (Oxford University Press)
MOULTON, Major General J.L. - The Royal Marines (Leo Cooper, London)

**Unpublished Papers**

Papers held by The Public Record Office, Kew
Commando Operations in the Mediterranean, 1943 - 1945
The War Diary of 2nd Battalion Royal Marines
The War Diary of 43 Royal Marine Commando

**Privately Circulated Papers**

A history of the period of Active Service of 43 Royal Marine Commando in the Central Mediterranean Forces until the end of the war in Italy.

Written summary reminiscence by Messrs George Belbin, Roy James, W.G. Jenkins D.S.O., George Lander M.M., Brice Somers, E.G. Stokoe, George Stratford and Bishop J.D. Wakeling M.C.

**Recorded or Telephone Contributions from:**

Mr C.W. Ash, Dr R.W. Bazeley, Mr F. Carrington, Mr D.B. Clark, Major W.D. Gregory, Mr J.C.D. Hudspith, Mr W. Iredale, Major General R.B. Loudoun, Mr N Peak and Mr E.G. Stokoe

## SOURCES

Text - Yugoslavia
Published Works
AUTY, Phyllis and CLOGG, Richard (eds) - British Policy Towards Wartime Resistance in Yugoslavia and Greece (London, MacMillan)
BEEVOR, J.G. - SOE: Recollections and Reflections 1940 - 45 (London, The Bodley Head)

CLISSOLD, Stephen - Whirlwind (London, The Cresset Press)
DAVIE, Michael (ed) - The Diaries of Evelyn Waugh (London, Weidenfeld & Nicolson)
DEDIJER, Vladimir - Tito Speaks (London, Weidenfeld & Nicolson)
DJILAS, Milovan - Wartime (London, Martin Secker and Warburg)
FOOT, M.R.D. - SOE: The Special Operations Executive 1940-46 (London, B.B.C.)
LLOYD OWEN, David - Providence Their Guide (London, Harrap)
MacLEAN, Fitzroy - Eastern Approaches (London, Jonathan Cape)
SAUNDERS, Hilary St George - The Green Beret (London, Michael Joseph)
SAUNDERS, Hilary St George - Royal Air Force 1939 - 45 Vol 3: The Fight is Won (London, HMSO)

## Unpublished Papers

A history of the period of Active Service of 43 Royal Marine Commando in the Central Mediterranean Forces until the end of the war in Italy.

111 Field Regiment, Royal Artillery. Report on operations with Floydforce in Yugoslavia.

Papers held by the Public Record Office, Kew. War Diaries of:
No 2 Commando
No 40 Royal Marine Commando
No 43 Royal Marine Commando
The Raiding Support Regiment
2nd Battalion, The Highland Light Infantry
Action reports by the commanding officers of various M.T.B.'s and M.G.B.'s of the Royal Navy
Summaries of various operations by the Royal Air Force

## Recorded Interviews

Mr C.W. Ash, Dr R.W. Bazeley, Colonel J.M.T.F. Churchill, Major General T.B.L. Churchill, Mr E. Cox, Mr G. Frost, Mr H. Fuller, Mr J.C.D. Hudspith, Mr W. Iredale, Mr R. Jeffs, Major General R.B. Loudoun, Mr N. Peak, Mr R. Skinner, Mr J. Stevens, Mr H. Thirkall, Mr F. Vautrey, Bishop J.D. Wakeling and members of the London Branch of the Royal Navy Coastal Forces Association.

# INDEX

**A**
Abbott Lt. 49
Abruzzi 25
Achnacarry - C.T.C. 20, 22, 27
Acts See Comacchio Code Names
Adelphi Hotel L'pl 13
Admiral's Regt. VIII
Admiralty 14, 19, 47
Agincourt 98
Alban Hills 27
Albania 77, 80, 94
Alexander F/Marshall 37
Alexandria 11
Alfonsine 100, 101
Algeria 25
Algiers 25
Allied Forces H.Q. - Caserta 40, 57
Alps 116
Alton-Hants 125
Ambassador/Consul British-Iceland 78
American 3rd Div. 27
Antwerp 1, 2
Anzio 25, 26, 27, 28, 32, 115
APC See Funnies 103
Appennines 25
Argenta-Defile 123
Argenta-Gap 116, 123
Argenta-Town 116, 117, 118, 122, 123, 124
Argentina 114
Army Staff College - Camberley 87
Armoured Troop Carrier - See Funnies 101
Artic/Arctic Circle 5, 103
Ash Sgt. Bill 65, 85, 92, 107
Asst. Adjt. Gen. RM. 87
Atlantic, Battle of 4, 5, 9
Austria 4, 116

**B**
Balkan Air Force 82, 85, 93, 94, 95
Balkans 4, 35, 77
Bangladesh 126
Barbarossa 34
Bari 32, 55, 57, 77, 95, 97, 124
Barnes Lt. Stan RA. 104, 108
Barnett Capt. David 111
Bazeley Capt. Ralph RAMC. 60, 62, 63, 66, 67, 69, 70, 75, 119, 122
Beale Marine 118
Belbin Lt. George 4
Belgium 4, 9, 10
Belgrade 88, 89
Bellochio Canal 110, 111
Bellaria 124
Ben Nevis 29
Berane 93

Biggs-Davison 2/Lt. John 3, 16
Bileca (Montenegro) 86, 89
Bioce (Montenegro) 88, 94, 95
Bisley 2, 3, 9
Bismarck, Battleship 107
Blaca Cove (Brac) 58, 59, 60
Blake Major Alf B/Major 63
Blakeforce (MLJET) 52, 53
Blake Capt. John 30, 42, 49, 50, 52, 64, 66, 67, 71
Blandford Lt. Col. H.C.G. 19
Bloody Foreland 14
Boak Marine 29
Boer Commandos 21
Bogdan Capt. Partisans 43
Bogomilje (Brac) 69
Bol (BRAC) 57, 58, 60, 61, 63, 64
Bologna 116
Bolton Lt. Jack 72
Borovik (HVAR) 49
Bosnia 34, 50, 63, 68
Brac 48, 56-63, 65, 66, 68, 70, 71, 108
Brindisi 44
British Exp. Force 4, 10
British Military Mission (Tito) 36, 55, 92
British Naval Cemetery-Vis 38
British Naval Attache-Madrid 14
British Divisions
1st 27  46th 28-32
56th 28  78th 116, 117, 118, 122, 123
6th Armoured 123
Britz Lt. Preston 69
Brookwood Rly Station 4, 5, 10
Brotherhood Major R.S.H.-H.L.I. 58
Broz-Josip 35
Bruges 1
Budva 91
Buffs (The) 22
Bulgarians 34
Bura 39
Burke Lt. RCNVR 74, 75
Byzantine Empire 99

**C**
Casa Morini 101
Casa Riccibitti 101
Casa Roncini 110
Casa Simoni 112
Casa Tosca 101
Cairo 34
Cameron of Lochiel 20
Canadians 21, 101
Cape Verde Islands 17
Carey Capt. Peter 92
Casablanca 15

# INDEX

Casey 2nd Lt. Liam 3
Cassino 25, 26
Cerney-Partisan-Vis 56, 57
Cetinje (Montenegro) 83, 89, 91, 92
Channel Islands 21
Cheesman Major 89, 91
Chetniks 35, 36, 49
Chiefs of Staff 12, 15
Churchill Govt. 11
Churchill Lt. Col. Jack 37, 40, 55, 57, 58, 63, 68, 70
Churchill Major Randolph 37
Churchill Brigadier Tom 25, 26, 28, 29, 31, 32, 37, 40, 41, 42, 51, 52, 53, 55, 57, 58
Churchill Mr. Winston P.M. 10, 12, 13, 15, 21, 37, 88
Ciovo (Trogir) 71, 72
Clark Lt.-Capt. Desmond 30, 32, 46, 49, 50, 70
Clinton Sgt. Reg 114, 115
Clyde River 6, 9, 18, 25, 125
Coldstream Guards 22, 115
Cole Lt. RNVR 46
Comacchio Lake 100, 101, 104, 111, 114, 116, 118, 124
Comacchio-Code Names
Acts 108, 109, 110
Hosea I & II 109, 110, 111
James 112
Jeremiah 112, 113
Joshua 107, 109
Leviticus 111
Mark 110
Matthew I & II 111
Peter 110, 111, 112
Comacchio Company RM 126
Comacchio Group RM 126
Combined Operations HQ 55
Commando Basic Trg. Centre 20
Commandos 21
Commandos-Army 21
No.2 26, 37, 40, 41, 45, 51, 53, 56, 68, 70, 71, 100, 104, 105, 106, 108, 110, 111, 112, 117, 118, 121, 123
No. 3, 21, No. 4, 21 No. 6 71
No. 9 (Scottish) 26-29, 31, 100, 104, 105, 106, 111, 112
2nd Commando Brigade 27, 32, 37, 51, 98, 101, 104, 105, 112, 116, 117, 122, 123
Commandos-Royal Marines
No. 40 21, 26, 51, 58, 59, 63, 65, 66, 68, 101, 104, 110, 126
No. 41 21 No. 42 126 No. 45 125, 126 No. 46 125
3rd Commando Brigade 126
Conselice (Argenta) 117
Coromin Dolac (HVAR) 43
Cotton-Minchin Capt. Douglas 102, 111

Cowan R/Admiral Sir Walter 32, 40
Cox Marine Ernie 65
Croatia 34
Crowther Capt. RAMC 32
Cunningham Admiral John 13, 15
Cutler Major 5, 7
Czechoslovakia 4

**D**

Dakar VIII 12, 13, 15, 16, 19, 20, 87, 125
Dakar French 12
Dalkovic Major-Partisans 91
Dalmatia 34, 45, 72
Danes/Denmark 4, 5
Danilovgrad 77, 89, 91, 93, 94
Deakin Capt. Bill 35, 36
De Bery Major Gerry 4
Demuth Lt. Nick 94
SS Derbyshire 27
Devon 11
Dieppe 21
Diego Suarez 19
Dinaric Alps 48
Dover Straits 1
Drvar (Bosnia) 55, 59
Drvenik Islands 71, 72
Duala-French Cameroons 17
Dublin 2
Dubrovnik 77, 78, 87-91, 95, 97
Dunkirk 10, 12, 20

**E**

Egypt 11
Eighth Army 25, 36, 97-100
El Alamein 25
Emilia Romagna 100
Emissaries-De Gaulle 12
England CSM Jock 4
English Channel 12, 100
Esson Capt. Don 101
SS Ettrick 13
Euston Station 13

**F**

Ferrara 116
Finneyforce 78, 80, 81, 86, 89, 91
First Sea Lord 20
Firth of Clyde 5
Flanders 1
Fleet Air Arm 15
Flete Castle 11
Florence 124
Floydforce 77, 78, 87, 88, 90, 91, 92, 95
Force Commanders Op. Menace 15, 16
Force 266 55-58, 63, 68
Foreign Office 14
Fort George-Vis 38
Fort William-Vis 38

Fotali 56, 57
France 4, 9, 10, 11
SS Franconia 8
Freetown 14, 15, 17, 18
French Army/Navy 5, 11, 12, 14, 15, 32
French North Africa 11
Free French VIII 12, 13, 14
French Sgt. R.D. 70
French Marine 'Froggy' 4
Frost Lt.-Capt. George 42, 73
Fuller TSM Hugh 66
Fuller L/Comm T.G. RCN 45-47
Funnies 103
Buffaloes 101
Fantails 101, 103, 105, 109
Kangaroos 101, 103, 104, 106-108
Wasps 123
Weasels 101, 103, 104
Fynn Major Ted 41

### G
Gallipoli 1, 2, 5
Garibaldi - See Porto Garibaldi 115
Garigliano River 26, 28, 29
Gatehouse 2/Lt. Michael 3
de Gaulle General Charles 12, 13, 15-17
Geneva Conventions 40, 99
George Sgt. 114
Gerlach Walter and Frau 7
German Army Units
Gp. C 123 Gp. E 77, 86, 92, 93, 95
XXI Mountain Corps 77, 79, 86
892 Grenadier Regt. 70
42nd Jaeger Div 118
Germany-Nazi 2, 4
Gibraltar and Straits 15, 18, 25
Gornje Selo (Solta) 71
Goums 32
Gourlay Capt. Ian 71-73, 102, 109
Gourock 5
Grablje (Hvar) 49
Grahovo 90
Greece 77, 80
Green Sgt. Bunny 65, 66
Greenland 5
Gregory Lt. Douglas 30, 42, 43, 65-67
Grohote (Solta) 71-74
Gruz (Dubrovnik) 78, 97
Guerilla Ops-Balkans 38
Gulf War 126
Gurkhas 101
Gustav Line 25, 26, 32

### H
Hampshire (County) England 20, 125
Hampshire Regt. 5th 31
Hawksworth M/General 28, 29, 32
Henley Regatta 105

Henry V 98
Hey Marine 121
Highland Light Infantry 48, 51, 58, 66, 71
Holland 4, 9, 10
Horlock Lt. RNVR 45
Hosea - See Camacchio Code Names
Hoste Capt. William RN 38, 91
Hudson Capt. D.T. 35, 36
Hudspith Capt./Major Jock 29, 30, 43, 61, 69, 72, 73, 75, 102, 111
Hull 3
Humac (Brac) 58, 60, 62
Hungarians 34
Hunter Cpl. Tom V.C. VIII 113-115
Hunton Adj/Gen. T.L. 20
Hursley Park Camp 20
Hvar Island 41, 42, 44, 48, 49, 56, 59

### I
'I' Lighters 46
Iceland VIII 5, 6, 9, 125
Icelandic Houses of Parliament 6
Icelanders 6, 8
Indian Divisions
8th Div. 100, 110, 117, 118
10th Div. 116, 123
Innes 2/Lt. Gilbert 3
Iraq 126
Iredale Cpl. Walter 120, 122
Irish Brigade 78th Div. 117
Irish Free State 11
Irish Rep. Easter Rising 2
Irwin Maj/General 13, 15
Isle of Wight 20
Italy 11, 36, 77, 87, 97

### J
Jago Lt. Col. RA 91, 92, 94, 95
James See Comacchio Code Names
Jeffs Marine 66
Jenkins Lt. W.G. DSO 'Bill' 103, 109, 110, 114, 118-122
Jeremiah See Comacchio Code Names
Jewish Brigade 99
Jelsa (Hvar) 41-43, 56
Jelsa/Starigrad Area 44
Jocks 58
Joint Planning Committee 12
Joshua See Comacchio Code Names
Jugboat 48
Jugo 39
Juraj (Hvar) 43
Jutland, Battle of 5

### K
Kaldalnes 8
Kali (Uljan) 49
SS Karanja 13

## INDEX

SS Kenya 13-18
Kieft Capt. Bernard RAMC 84
Killin Rly Station 19
King George III VIII
King Peter of Yugoslavia 34
Kingsdown 3
Kolasin 77, 89, 95
Komiza (Vis) 37, 39, 45-47, 52, 59, 74, 75
Konigen Emma 10
Korcula Channel/Island 43, 45
Kosivina Cove-Murter Island 46
Kosovo 34
Kotor Gulf 35, 78, 79, 90
Kotor Town 77-83, 85, 86, 91, 92
Knight-Lacklan Lt. RNVR 47
Kremlin (Moscow) 78
Kurds 126

**L**

SS Lancastria 8
Land Forces Adriatic 77
Lander Cpl. George 7, 8
Landing Craft
LCI 260 43, 59  LCI 281/LCI 308 52
Leatherbarrow Lt. David 30, 109
Ledenice 79, 81, 83, 84
Lee Capt. E 53
Liverpool/Dockers 13-15, 25
Loch Fyne 19
Lombardy 116
Long Range Desert Group 89
Loudoun Capt. R.B. 'Bob' 30, 53, 54, 64-68, 72, 78-80, 82-84, 86, 87, 90, 92, 108, 115
Lovcen Mountain 91
Lukoran (Uljan) 49
Lumley Camp 17
L.V.T.S. See Funnies 103-105

**M**

MacAlpine Lt. Col. Ian 71-75, 87
Macedonia 34
MacLaughen Lt. RCNVR 74
MacLean Marine 114
MacLean Brigadier Fitzroy 36, 37
MacLean Mission 88
Madden Admiral 2
Madrid-Naval Attache 14
Makarska (Dalmatia) 58
Mala Staza (Solta) 72
Manners Lt. Col. J.C. 'Pops' 25, 63, 68
Mark See Comacchio Code Names
Marakeesh 37
Matthew See Comacchio Code Names
McCartney C/Sgt. 41, 42
McConville Lt. Michael 85, 92, 107, 114, 120, 121
McCreery Gen. 28, 32, 115, 123
McKenna Sgt. 114

Meynell Col. 72
Midway Bunkers (Ledenice) 79
Mihailovic Col. Draga 35, 36
Miles Brigadier Force 266 55-57, 63
Millerchip Sgt. 'Chippy' 17
Minervino 98
Mljet 45, 51-55
Mole-Zeebrugge 1
Molfetta 37
Molotov-Russian F/Minister 78
SS Monarch of Bermuda 25
Monte Cassino 25, 26
Monte Faito 28, 29, 31, 32
Monte Ornito 28-32, 115
Monte Tuga 28, 29
Montenegro 34, 35, 77, 82, 83, 87, 90, 92, 93, 98, 115
Morava River 94
Morgan Admiral 56, 57
Morgan Giles Lt./Comm 41, 44, 45, 53, 73, 74
Morocco 25, 37
Moscow (Russia) 78
Mostar/Luftwaffe Base 59, 87, 92
Mountbatten Admiral Lord Louis 20
Mount Hum (Hvar) 49, 68
Mount Hum (Vis) 39, 48
Mountstephens Lt. RNVR 45
Mount Vesuvius 125
Munro Major Neil 24, 41-43, 51-53, 64, 74, 87, 104, 111, 121, 122
Murter Island 46, 47

**N**

Naples 25, 28, 124, 125
Naples Bay 25, 27, 28
N.A.T.O. 9
Naval Staff Course 2
Neilforce (Mljet) 52, 53
Neouwra-German Destroyer 45
Nerezisce (Brac) 56, 58-63, 67, 70
Newfoundland 5
Nicholls Marine Charlie 64
Niksic (Montenegro) 34, 77, 88-90, 92, 93, 95
Nordic Countries 4
Normandy 20, 37
Norse Settler 5
North Admiral 15
North Irish Horse 99, 104, 109, 110
Norway/Norwegians 4, 5
Nunns Lt.-Capt. Mark 67, 70, 118, 121, 122

**O**

O'Brien-Twohig Brigadier J.P. 77, 78, 89, 92, 94, 95
Odbor 92, 93
Odendaal Lt. J.R. 42, 43, 67, 69, 70
Office of Strategic Services 37

Omis (Dalmatia) 58
Operation Flounced 57, 68
Operation Foothound 51, 54
Operation Menace 13, 15, 16
Oran-N/Africa 11, 14, 16
Ordnance Corps 48
Ornito - See Monte Ornito
Ostend 1
Outer Hebrides 18
SS Oxfordshire 17

**P**
Page Capt. John 118, 119
Parkinson-Cumine Capt. Ralph 72-74, 88, 102, 109, 114, 118, 119
Partisans VIII Dalmatian Islands-Parts Two and Three Mainland Yugoslavia-Part Four
Partisan Formations
1st Dalmation Brigade 42, 71
XXVI Division 57
Primorska Group 78, 91, 94
2nd Dalmation Brigade 81
Partisan II Corps 89, 90, 92
29th Division 92
10th Montenegrin Brigade 93, 94
Boka Brigade 94
Pavelic-Ante 34, 35
Peak L/Cpl. Norris 65, 66
Pearson Lt.Col. G.I. Force 266 56, 57
Peljesac Peninsula 44
Pembroke Docks 10
Perast (Kotor) 82, 83, 90, 92
Petain Marshal 11, 12, 16
Peter See Comacchio Code Names
Picton-Phillips Major and Son 3, 4
Planica (Brac) 63
Podgora 56
Podgorica (Montenegro) 89, 92-94
Podhan 79, 80, 90
Podmore Lt. Lawrence 3, 7
Podvlake (Solta) 72, 73
Poland 4, 116
Portishead R.N. Radio 35
Porto Garibaldi 100, 113-115
Preko (Uljan) 49
Prsnjak Islands 45
Preston Lt.-Capt. Martin 75, 102, 109, 118, 120
Previte Lt. M 8
Prussia 116
Public Records Office-Kew 55
Putignano (Italy) 97
Pym Major 6

**Q**
Queen Alexandra's Imperial Military Nursing Service 124
Queens The 48
Queens Own Hussars 4th 103

**R**
R.A.F. 36, 40, 42, 48, 55-58, 60-62, 68, 70-72, 85, 117
R.A.F. Regt. 73
R.A.M.C. 24, 124
R.A.V.C. 71
Raiding Support Regiment R.S.R. 37, 48, 51, 56, 58-60, 63, 68, 70, 71, 73, 81, 89, 93
Ramsgate Kent 22, 24
Rassendyll-Rudolph 91
Raven Marine 65, 108
Ravenna 99, 100, 115, 117, 123
Red Army 116
Rendall Lt. RCNVR 74
Reno River 100-104, 107-111, 117, 121-123
Reykjavik 5-8
Reykjavik Chief of Police 8
Rhine River 116
Rhineland 4
Richards Lt. R.E. 74
Riches Lt. Col. Ian 87, 93-95, 101, 103, 104, 106, 109, 111, 112, 115
Richlieu Battleship 16
Risan 77-83, 85-87, 89, 90
Roberts Lt. RN 41-43
Roberts Capt. 'Shorty' 102, 107, 111, 113, 114
Rock Gibraltar 18
Rogac (Solta) 71, 74
Rome 25, 26, 32, 124
Royal Artillery
64 Heavy A/A Regt. 89
111 Field Regt. 48, 58-60, 68, 70, 74, 77, 89, 91
142 Field Regt. 105
180 Heavy A/A Battery 93
211 Field Battery 78
Royal Engineers, 579 Field Co. 89, 93
Royal Marines VIII
Brigade WWI 1
Brigade WWII 2, 10, 12, 13, 15-17, 19-21, 87
2nd Bn RMLI 1, 2
Battalions
1st 2, 17
2nd 2, Part One
3rd 2, 17, 19
4th 1
5th 2, 17
Divisions Base/Admin.
Chatham 3
Deal 3, 19, 53
Eastney/Portsmouth 2, 3
Plymouth 3, 13, 87
R.M. Division WWII 19, 20, 87
Royal Navy VIII 11, 12, 36, 56, 59, 75
Force H 15

# INDEX

Grand Fleet 1
H.Q. Reykjavik 8
Coastal Forces 37, 45, 47
MTB/MGB 44
MTB 633 74, 75
MGB 646 47
MGB 647 45, 46
MTB 651 45, 46
MTB 655 74, 75
MGB 661 46, 47
Ships
HMS Ark Royal 14
HMS Berwick 57
HMS Fearless 7, 8
HMS Foxhound 8
HMS Glasgow 5-7
HMS Lion 2
HMS Renown 15
HMS Vindictive 1
Royle Cpl. 64, 65
Rupert of Hentzau 91
Ryde I.O.W. 20

## S
Saberton Cpl. Ted 108
St. Patrick's Cathedral N.Y. 57
Salerno 25, 28, 37
Sarajevo 89, 92
S.A.S.O. Senior Air Staff Officer 56
Sassi (Ravenna) 103, 104
Saudi Arabia 126
Scapa Flow 13, 19
Scedro Island 42, 43
Schooley Capt. R.G. Gerry 30, 49, 62, 64, 66-68
Scottish Highlands 20
Scots Guards 27
Selca-Brusje (Hvar) 49
Senegal-French W. Africa VIII 12
Serbia 34, 35
Sessa 28
Shearer Cpl. 66
Shetlands 19
Sicily 25, 77
Sierra Leone 14, 17
Simonds Lt.Col. R.W.B. 'Bonzo' 19, 21, 24, 28-30, 39, 41-44, 52, 58, 59, 61-64, 66-71
Skinner Marine Reg 54, 65, 114
Slovenia 34
Smith Cpl. RAMC 74
Snowden Marine 65
SS Sobieski 13
Solta Island 40, 41, 44, 48, 56, 59, 70-75, 87
Somers Brice Lt. 17
Somerville Admiral 15
Somme 1
Sovra Bay (Mljet) 51
South African Air Force 114

South Slavs 34, 35
Southampton 125
South Wales 20
Southern Ireland 11
Soviet Union 4, 34
Special Operations Executive-S.O.E. 34-36, 69
Special Service Battalion 21
2nd Special Service Brigade 25, 26, 57, 58, 63
Special Service Bde. H.Q. 58
Special Service Group 87
Spit (Comacchio) 100, 101, 103, 105, 106, 108, 112
Spit 58, 71, 72, 75
Spuz 93
Stalin 78
Stevens C/Sgt. 54
Stevens Lt. Jack 65, 83, 101
Stokoe Marine Ted 3
Sturges Col.-Maj/Gen. R. 5, 19
Sturgesforce 5, 19
Sumartin 57-60, 63, 70
Supertar 57-60, 63, 70
Sveta Vedelia (Hvar) 49
Swiss Frontier 100

## T
Tangier British Consul 14
Taranto 25, 56, 57
Third Reich 4
Thirkell Marine Henry 65
Tito Marshall VIII 26, 35, 55, 56, 59, 63, 68, 77, 78, 88
Tod Lt.Col.-Brigadier R. Ronnie 28, 29, 31, 106, 112, 115, 118, 122
Tongue (Lake Comacchio) 100-102, 107, 108, 111
Toulon 14
Treasury H.M. 14
Trebinje 89, 92, 95
Trogir (Ciovo) 71
Tunisia 25, 71, 77
Turner Major Pat 58, 63, 74, 78-86, 89
Tyndale-Biscoe Capt. 17

## U
Uljan Island 75
US Rangers 27, 28
US Special Operations Group 37, 40, 42, 51, 52, 59, 65, 67
Ustachi 35, 49
Unoccupied Zone-France 11

## V
Valetta Canal 100, 112, 113
Vaughan Lt.Col. Charles 22
V Corps 8th Army 99, 101, 115-117, 123
Velenici 82
Venice 105, 124

Venter Lt. 69
  Vichy France/French 11-13, 15, 16
  Cruisers 14
  Naval Squadron 15
Vico Equense 25, 32
Victoria Cross VIII 2, 114
Vidoya Gora (Brac) 58, 60
Vilusi 90-92
Vis Island 26, 32, 36-40, 48, 51,55, 56, 67-70, 73, 77, 78, 97
Town 37, 40-44, 47, 53, 54, 58, 59, 63, 71
Vojvodina 34
Von Vietinghoff General 123
Vrishir (Hvar) 49

**W**
Wakeling 2nd Lt-Capt. J.D. 3, 6, 8, 68
Walcheren 4
War Office 19
Washington (D of C) 37
West Africa 14, 19
Western Front 1
Whitehall 12, 16

Wilberforce Camp-Freetown 17
Williams Lt.Col. A.N. 'Nick' 2, 3, 5, 8, 9, 16, 19, 21
Woking Rly. Station 10
Woodger Marine 118, 119

**X**
X Corps 28, 32

**Y**
York and Albany Maritime Regt. 3
York and Lancaster Regt. 29
Yugoslavia 32, 34, 35, 48, 51, 55, 78
Yugoslav National Army of Liberation 77, 88
Yugoslav Navy Museum Split 45

**Z**
Zagreb (Luftwaffe Base) 59
Zarac (Hvar) 49
Zeebrugge 1, 2, 4
Zeta-River 94, 95
Zukova (Solta) 72

www.ingramcontent.com/pod-product-compliance
Lightning Source LLC
Chambersburg PA
CBHW081204170426
43197CB00018B/2921